D1643427

FIRST CRUSADER

BYZANTIUM'S HOLY WARS

GEOFFREY REGAN

palgrave
macmillan

For Diana and Keith

First published 2003 by PALGRAVE MACMILLAN™
175 Fifth Avenue, New York, N.Y. 10010 and
Houndmills, Basingstoke, Hampshire, England RG21
6XS. Companies and representatives throughout the
world.

PALGRAVE MACMILLAN is the global academic
imprint of the Palgrave Macmillan division of St. Martin's
Press, LLC and of Palgrave Macmillan Ltd. Macmillan® is
a registered trademark in the United States, United
Kingdom and other countries. Palgrave is a registered
trademark in the European Union and other countries.

ISBN 1-4039-6151-4

Library of Congress Cataloguing-in-Publication Data
available from the Library of Congress.

First published in 2001 by Sutton Publishing Limited.

First PALGRAVE MACMILLAN edition: April 2003.

10 9 8 7 6 5 4 3 2 1

Printed in the United States of America.

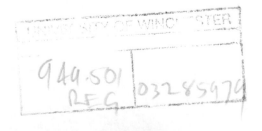

Contents

Acknowledgements

For their advice and help with this book my sincere thanks go to: Warwick Ball, former Director of Excavations, British School of Archaeology, Iraq; Professor Timothy Barnes, University of Toronto; Professor Martin Biddle, Hertford College, University of Oxford; Professor A.D.H. Bivar, formerly of the London School of Oriental and African Studies; Dr Glen Bowersock, Institute of Advanced Studies, Princeton; Professor Averil Cameron, Warden of Keble College, University of Oxford; Professor Michael Cook, Princeton University; Dr Patricia Crone, Institute for Advanced Studies, Princeton; Professor Fred Donner, University of Chicago; Dr Yasin Dutton, University of Edinburgh; Professor Reuven Firestone, Hebrew Union College, Jewish Institute of Religion, Los Angeles; Dr J. France, University of Swansea; James Gregory, University of Southampton; Professor John Haldon, University of Birmingham; Dr Paul Halsall; Professor Gerald Hawting, SOAS, University of London; Dr Georgina Herrmann, University College, University of London; Dr James Howard-Johnson, Corpus Christi College, University of Oxford; Dr Benjamin Isaac, Tel Aviv University; Professor Walter Kaegi, University of Chicago; Professor Etan Kohlberg, Hebrew University, Jerusalem; Professor Ella Landau-Tasseron, Hebrew University, Jerusalem; Dr David Nicolle, Institute of Medieval Studies, University of Nottingham; Dr Robert Ousterhout, University of Illinois at Urbana-Champaign; Dr J.P. Phillips, Royal Holloway College, University of London; Professor Jonathan Riley-Smith, University of Cambridge; Professor Michael Roaf, University of Munich; Professor Paul Speck, Byzantine Institute, Freie Universitat Berlin; Dr A.-M. Talbot, Director of Byzantine Studies at Dumbarton Oaks; Professor Warren Treadgold, University of Saint Louis; Dr Mary Whitby; Professor Michael Whitby, University of Warwick. I would also like to thank my editor Sarah Moore at Sutton Publishing.

Introduction

Since the days of the Emperor Constantine the stories of Christianity, of Jerusalem and the Holy Land, of the Holy Sepulchre and the True Cross have been inextricably linked with the East Roman or Byzantine Empire. From the triumph of Constantine over paganism at the battle of the Milvian Bridge in 312 to the 'dreadful day' when Byzantine power was destroyed by the Turks in the tragic battle of Manzikert in 1071, the defence of Christians and Christendom involved the Byzantines in holy wars for which the term 'crusade' has sometimes been used. Yet some western academics have guarded the term 'crusade' and denied it to the Byzantines as forcefully as Roman Christianity has tried to assert its supremacy over Greek Orthodoxy. Without seeking academic schism of the kind that split the Christian world in 1054 I have tried to suggest in this book that the blanket rejection of the concept of Byzantine holy war has been a mistake, notably in the case of the Emperor Heraclius's conflict with the Persians between 622 and 628.

In an important article Tia M. Kolbaba has summed up the subject of Byzantine 'holy war':

On the one hand, Byzantines did fight wars which they believed were divinely ordained and would be divinely rewarded. They sometimes defined their enemies in religious terms. They sometimes compared their leaders to prophets and themselves to the Chosen People of Israel. Most importantly, the ideology of the Byzantine Empire was based on a conviction that this empire was God's creation, the fulfilment of his will for earthly rule. This

Christian Roman Empire, with God's vicar anointed at its head, did God's work on earth. Its soldiers therefore fought for God when they fought to protect or to expand the empire. It seems illogical to dismiss all of this as not really holy war.

Yet this Byzantine species of holy war differs greatly from both Jihad and crusade.[1]

While accepting that Kolbaba is correct in seeing a distinct difference between the holy war of the Byzantines and that of the western crusaders or, indeed, of Muslim followers of the jihad, I cannot agree that this is true of the Persian wars of the reign of Heraclius, which were unique in Byzantine history. According to Kolbaba, the wars that the Byzantines fought against infidels did not contain evidence of the sort of religious enthusiasms (visions and millennial excitement, for example) that were so common in the western crusades after the eleventh century. Neither were Byzantine armies made up of volunteers who were entitled to make a conscious decision to risk their lives on crusade. For her, the crucial difference between eastern holy wars and those of the West was what she called the 'cultural weight' that was attached to warfare in western Europe but was not present in the Byzantine world, so that the chivalric activities of heroes like El Cid or Roland were unknown in the East or, if known, were undervalued and were not essential to Byzantine elites.[2]

While Kolbaba's thesis is correct in terms of the Byzantine 'crusades' of the tenth century, described in the pages that follow as 'Ersatz Crusades', it is wrong in the case of the Romano-Persian War of 622–8 for a number of reasons. With reference to the 620s, Kolbaba's allusion to a lack of 'religious enthusiasms', like visions and millennial excitement, is absolutely incorrect in terms of the Avar siege of Constantinople, during which the Theotokos (Mother of God) was seen fighting the enemy on a number of occasions. Warrior-saints were seen in other Byzantine battles of the period too. Michael Whitby refers to the Virgin as 'the supernatural protector of Constantinople [who] acted as the city's representative in the heavenly court . . . she procured a miraculous defeat of a Slav naval attack, Avar siege towers were destroyed through divine agency, and the Avar khagan claimed that he had seen a stately woman hurrying about on the wall'.³ These visions of the Virgin and others of the warrior-saints like St George and St Demetrius are typical of accounts of Byzantine warfare.

Kolbaba's reference to Byzantine armies not being 'all-volunteer' is, of course, quite correct. In war, Byzantines were soldiers with a religious purpose defined by their commander, who was often a general of profound religious inclinations himself – for example, Nicephorus Phocas or John Tzimisces. However, the Persian War was different: the commander, in this case the emperor himself, appealed to his soldiers as individuals rather than as units within an army. More importantly, during the winter of 624 Heraclius specifically directed his religious propaganda at Transcaucasian Christian volunteers from Lazica, Armenia and Georgia, who had no link with Byzantium other than through religion. Kolbaba claims that the true crusading force defines the enemy 'by his infidel status alone', something that she believes the Byzantines did not do. In fact, this is precisely the approach adopted by Heraclius, who either used biblical language to define the Sasanid Persians as the enemies of God or referred to them as pagan 'fire-worshippers'.

Kolbaba feels that Byzantine warfare 'lacks chivalric heroes such as Roland or the Cid'. I cannot agree with this. William of Tyre, for one, lists Heraclius as among the 'paladins' of crusading history. Furthermore, through the literary talents of George of Pisidia, Heraclius's military accomplishments became part of an almost biblical triumphalism that sees Heraclius compared to David, sometimes to Moses and Elijah and, through his six-year campaign, ultimately to God.⁴

Contrary to Kolbaba's assertion that Byzantines preferred discretion to valour, Heraclius did make a 'charge against all the odds' in the battle on the bridge against Shahrvaraz in 625 and in his single combats against Persian champions at the start of the battle of Nineveh, when one is reminded most strongly of Richard Coeur de Lion at the battle of Jaffa. In comparison with Heraclius, for whose 'chivalric heroism' we have much historical evidence, Roland and El Cid are merely literary creations. In the ancient world, only Alexander and Julius Caesar rank with Heraclius in military terms; only Constantine and Charlemagne as emperors. Heraclius was not only the 'First Crusader' he was the truest crusader, returning the relic thought to be the True Cross to Jerusalem and entering the city not with fire and sword like the crusaders of 1099 but as the simple penitent, carrying the relic in his hands.

Heraclius is one of the great tragic figures of history. Few men have drunk of such a poisonous mixture of triumph and disaster, of happiness and sorrow. No other soldier has faced disaster so widespread and profound, only to rise so high through his own personal efforts. In an age of faith, as the seventh century so obviously was, Heraclius lost and regained both the holiest of Christian sites, the Holy Sepulchre in Jerusalem, and the holiest of relics, the True Cross. After a titanic struggle, during which he led his army on campaign in Persia for six years, he achieved the overthrow of Rome's greatest enemy. He restored Roman flags and standards lost by a hundred armies and dozens of emperors in the wastes of Mesopotamia and the mountains of the Caucasus. He rebuilt not just an army but an entire military system, ensuring that what had been on the brink of disaster during the great Avar siege of 626 survived for another 800 years. Had he died at the height of his power in 630 his name would be listed among the greatest figures in history. Instead, the last decade of his life brought disasters to his personal life and to his work for the empire. He succumbed to the irresistible rise of Islam and with his health gone, his marriage challenged as incestuous and his mind debilitated by illness, he saw the work of a lifetime undone. In true tragic style, this great figure fell catastrophically from the height of his achievement and lived just long enough to feel every turn of the screw.

ONE

Epiphany

Gaunt from their ritual three-day fast, the haruspices in their conical hats and fringed mantles approached the temple steps to the sound of flutes. At their head walked a senior haruspex leading the sacrificial animal, while behind came others bearing vessels of sacred water and candles. The words 'Tula Eisna Sath' – 'Make the divine boundaries' – rang out and once these had been established, the water was offered as a libation to the gods. The haruspex leading the beast then appealed in a loud voice to Apollo, calling on the god to accept the sacrifice. His assistant cried out 'Flerchva ratum tur' – 'Carry out the sacrifice according to the law' – whereupon the chief official uncovered the sacrificial knife and by a swift, single movement cut the beast's throat with such precision that the animal scarcely made a sound, only toppling forward onto its knees amidst the pumping blood that poured out upon the flagstones. While the watching crowd murmured, sacred helpers stepped forward and began butchering the carcass. As they did so the chief haruspex was handed the animal's organs one by one so that he could examine them. First the animal's liver was brought forth, then the gall bladder, the heart and the lungs.[5]

As the blood-stained diviners pored over the organs the Augustus Diocletian and the Caesar Galerius, waited impatiently for the answer to the question which had been asked. They had witnessed hundreds of such occasions and felt no undue apprehension. Nobody present that day in Syria in 299 could have known that the future of Rome, the empire and the whole civilized world would be decided by these survivors of an Etruscan cult more ancient than Rome itself. Amidst the large crowd of onlookers that attended the

ceremony that morning there were a number of Christians, some
soldiers, some officials and rather fewer members of the general
public. To the Christian onlookers the process taking place was
merely one of the more pretentious aspects of the paganism they
rejected. How, they wondered, could the intestines of a brute beast
give any sign of a future already decided by the single, almighty God
they worshipped? Some made no attempt to hide the derision they
felt for the sacrifice before them. Some made signs of a Christian
nature to hold back the demons being summoned by the haruspices.
While the emperors continued to wait impatiently in the early
morning heat it became clear that the divination was not going well.

During the first two centuries of the Roman Empire the traditional
state religion, with its focus on ancient gods such as Jupiter, Juno
and Minerva, was in decline. The spread of Roman military and
political influence in the East opened the way for a variety of
Oriental cults to infiltrate the western lands of the empire. Rome had
traditionally been tolerant of private religious activities that involved
no political threat to the state or otherwise challenged law and order.
However, the onset of Christianity overturned Roman toleration and
led to periodic persecutions, conservative backlashes against the
'orientalization' of Rome. Cults from the East began to influence the
state religion and for a while, in the shape of Sol Invictus, it seemed
to move towards solar monotheism. The great winter festival of the
sun god, which was celebrated on 25 December, eventually found a
niche in the Christianity that developed under the Emperor
Constantine.

Two eastern cult religions – Christianity and Mithraism – won
the most support among the Roman masses and Christianity
flourished in the poorer areas of cities where its promise of personal
immortality had an immense emotional attraction for those living in
poverty. Roman critics of Christianity tended to associate it with
some of the more esoteric eastern cults, such as the worship of the
Syrian fish-goddess Atargatis, and this resulted in Christians being
accused of the most absurd aberrations. The Roman establishment
began to fear that Christianity offered a threat not only to the minds
of the people but, through its system of bishops, to the structure of
the empire itself. As the empire became larger and more diverse it
needed a much more complex and efficient organization.

By the late third century the Emperor Diocletian, an administrative genius, had concluded that the Roman Empire was ungovernable by one man alone. It was simply too large and too complex. As a result, in 286 he decided to share the burden by promoting one of his most trusted colleagues, Maximian, to the rank of Caesar so that he could rule the western provinces as co-emperor. While Diocletian ruled from Nicomedia in Bithynia, Maximian chose Milan as his capital and Rome, no longer well-placed to be the centre of such a vast empire, lost much of its administrative function though it still retained symbolic significance. Having reorganized the administration of the earthly empire, Diocletian chose to restructure heaven along the same lines. The dual sovereignty of himself and Maximian was now paralleled by the two gods who ruled the heavens. Diocletian, as Augustus, ruled under the aegis of Jupiter – or as he now was called Jupiter Optimus Maximus, the supreme god – while Maximian was the chosen one of Hercules, assistant to Jupiter among the gods. This linking of earthly and heavenly rulers prepared the way for Constantine's belief in himself as the chosen one of the Christian God.

Diocletian's administrative skills made him a hard taskmaster, creating work where there was none previously. In 286, running the empire had kept two emperors busy, but by 293 Diocletian believed there were enough administrative tasks to occupy four men. He created his tetrarchy, or rule by four – two Augustuses and two Caesars. Maximian was promoted to Augustus, with Constantius as his Caesar while Galerius was appointed Caesar to Diocletian. It was agreed that after twenty years the Augustuses should retire and hand over power to their Caesars. Constantius, the father of the future Emperor Constantine, ruled Britain and Gaul from Treves and adopted Sol Invictus as his guiding deity.

The empire that Diocletian created has been likened to a totalitarian state. It was based on a conservative reaction to social and cultural trends that threatened the traditional virtues which may have existed in the days of the early Republic but were hardly relevant in the multi-national state that Rome had become by the end of the third century. Diocletian seemed to expect Roman soldiers to be the same as the men who had fought for Rome in the Punic Wars. Where, he asked, were the men of Scipio Africanus?

Where were Julius Caesar's unconquerable legions? It was the eternal cry of the reactionary: tradition in the face of change. He feared that Greek and Oriental influences were diluting traditional Roman values of duty and service to the state and were encouraging pacifism and asceticism. Central to this process were the mystery religions from Syria and the East which were spreading throughout the empire. It was patriotic to worship the old gods; Christianity smacked of loyalty not to the state and the emperor but to something foreign and indefinable.

The spread of Christianity had been particularly rapid. What had originally been a movement of the lower orders began to win converts in the higher social levels in Italy and the western provinces. Even members of the senate and senior army officers became Christians. By the late third century over ten percent of the empire's population was Christian. Paganism now began to strike back at the growing threat of this 'state within a state'. As with most of history's great persecutions, the target group was first 'demonised' to justify its mistreatment. Christians were thus accused of every unnatural crime, from incest and sexual perversions to infanticide and cannibalism, as described by Minucius Felix writing in the third century:

They [Christians] recognize one another by secret signs and tokens; they love one another almost before they are acquainted. Everywhere a kind of religion of lust is also associated with them, and they call themselves promiscuously brothers and sisters, so that ordinary fornication, through the medium of a sacred name, becomes incest. And thus their vain and mad superstition glories in crimes. I hear that in some absurd conviction or other they consecrate and worship the head of an ass, the most repulsive of beasts – a religion worthy of the morals that begot it. Others say that they reverence the private parts of their director and high priest, and adore them as if belonging to a parent. Whether this is false I know not, but suspicion naturally attaches to secret and nocturnal rites. To say that a man put to death for a crime and the lethal wooden cross are objects of their veneration is to assign altars suitable for abandoned and impious men, the kind of worship they deserve. What is told of the initiation of neophytes is as detestable as it is notorious. An infant covered with spelt to deceive the unsuspecting is set before the one to be initiated in the rites. The neophyte is induced to strike what seems to be harmless blows on the surface of the spelt and this infant is killed by his random and unsuspecting blows. Its blood – Oh, shocking! – they greedily lap up; the limbs they eagerly distribute; and by this victim they league themselves, and by this complicity in crime they pledge themselves to mutual silence . . . Furthermore, they threaten the whole world and the universe itself and its stars with fire and work for its destruction . . . Not content with this insane notion, they add to and weave old wives' tales: they say that they are reborn after death from the cinders and ashes and with unaccountable confidence believe in one another's lies . . .[6]

By the middle of the third century persecution was widespread but sporadic and was generally carried out at local police level. Christians became an outlet for local thuggery and violence. When criticism of the government became too strong in a particular area then the local officials would direct public hostility on to the Christians. Yet the persecuted became stronger rather than weaker, more unified by shared suffering and more intransigent. Towards the end of the third century Christianity began to be viewed as an internal threat to the entire imperial order. A minor incident might be enough to fuel a struggle to the death between paganism and Christianity, an incident such as a failed divination.

As the haruspices continued to study the entrails of the sacrificial beast Diocletian shifted his weight from one foot to another and swatted the flies that began to swarm around the blood-soaked altar. It was very hot and the ceremony was proving very tedious. The master seemed to be taking an age to reach a conclusion. The animal's liver had been scrutinised and then set aside. Next the other organs had been checked one after another. Then the liver had been recalled. Diocletian was beginning to feel every one of his fifty years. Now the diviners were consulting together. The emperor could see the tension in the back of their necks and one of the younger ones was actually wringing his hands. Something disastrous was portended. Diocletian whispered to one of his guards; the soldier strode over to the haruspices and tugged the sleeve of the master. Whispers were exchanged and then the haruspex turned towards the emperor, his face a mask of anguished confusion. He approached Diocletian and Galerius uncertainly before throwing his arms in the air in despair. The divination had failed.

Diocletian called the master of the haruspices to come closer before asking, in a whisper, why the gods had refused him an answer. The man was adamant: the sacrifice and the subsequent divination had been obstructed by the ill will of some of the onlookers who had made signs that had blocked his work. Almost certainly it was the Christians who were to blame. Diocletian knew that there were Christians present in his household and that some of them had been with him in the crowd watching the sacrifice. He was furious. For many years he had tolerated Christianity but now its adherents were betraying him. There was no alternative but to root out the danger from the imperial household by insisting that every member willingly sacrifice to the traditional Roman gods. How much the subsequent mini-purge was the product of a knee-jerk reaction by Diocletian we cannot be certain. It seems more likely that the influence of the rabidly anti-Christian Caesar Galerius at his side was affecting the ageing emperor.[7] Tired, and eager to shift the burden of government onto younger shoulders, Diocletian began to feel that he had been too tolerant of the Christians. Even his own wife and daughter were Christian sympathizers, if not actual converts. Galerius, a star in the ascendant after his successful campaign in Persia, pressed Diocletian to issue a general proclamation against the Christians.

Diocletian may have been personally uneasy about a renewed persecution of the Christians but his hand was forced by the provocative actions some of them took. While Diocletian was in Antioch during 302 a Christian deacon named Romanus came into the city from Caesarea. Romanus was clearly seeking martyrdom: his subsequent moves were designed to provoke the Roman authorities. Appalled by the continuing popularity of pagan temples he took his protests to the emperor's court where the haruspices were busy with a divination. In a loud voice he denounced their activities and was promptly arrested by the emperor's guards. Rather than burning him forthwith – the normal punishment for the interruption of the sacrifice – Diocletian merely ordered that his tongue be cut out.[8]

Diocletian's rage at the Christians' presumption provided just the fertile ground that Galerius needed. When Diocletian returned to Nicomedia, Galerius persuaded him to consult his leading counsellors, military and civil. The outcome was never in doubt, as Galerius knew. The pagans called for an immediate persecution of the Christians while moderates and those who favoured the Christians kept silent in view of the storm they saw was about to break. Even now Diocletian was uneasy and only when Galerius persuaded him to consult the oracle of Apollo at Didyma was the matter settled. The wild rantings of the god's priestess were interpreted as referring to the Christians – 'the just on earth' – whose influence prevented true oracles from being given. For Diocletian this was the confirmation he needed. The festival of the Terminalia – 23 February 303 – was selected as the day on which the persecution would begin.

The hostility of many senior figures in the Roman world towards the Christians at this time reflected a genuine conservative reaction to what seemed to be a radical threat to Roman traditions. Pagan writers like Porphyry and Sossianus Hierocles considered Christianity to be a social and political threat to the empire, as well as a spiritual one. They felt that as more and more people abandoned their ancient gods in favour of the teachings of the Nazarenes the empire was increasingly in danger. Vitriolic as Porphyry was in his polemic *Against the Christians*, his effect was strongest in Italy and the western Roman lands. However, it was in the East that the real battleground lay between the new Christianity and the ancient religion of the Greco-Roman world. Here Sossianus Hierocles, who combined the roles of author and imperial governor of Bithynia, had a significant impact on Diocletian. Not only did Sossianus incite the populace with his rabidly anti-Christian tracts but, as one of the emperor's foremost advisers, he helped formulate imperial policy. Furthermore, once Diocletian was won over to persecution, it was Sossianus who saw to it that the anti-Christian legislation was carried out to its full extent in the emperor's capital, Nicomedia.

Once again the Christians played into the hands of their enemies. The day after the edict of persecution was made public, the praetorian prefect headed a large force of soldiers and officials who marched to the great Christian church in Nicomedia and razed it to the ground, burning bibles and plundering relics. They posted a copy of the imperial edict nearby. Yet again there were aspiring Christian martyrs on hand to make a bad situation worse. One such, known as Euetius, tore down the prefect's document and ripped it to pieces in full view of everyone. Euetius died a martyr's death, being tortured and burned alive the same day. Diocletian experienced the stubbornness of the Christians in the clearest possible terms: many Christian women eagerly accepted martyrdom, convinced that they would enjoy a happier time in the afterlife.[9]

The aim of Galerius and Diocletian in persecuting the Christians was a far cry from the insane cruelty of some earlier emperors. They and their advisers viewed Christians as products of eastern barbarism, akin to the Persians or the monotheistic Jews. Christianity was a threat to everything that Rome as a civilizing agent had come to stand for. Neither the emperors nor many of the pagan authors who influenced them were interested in the teachings of a crucified Galilean rabbi who had been rejected even by his own people. They had no wish to 'unlock the window of men's minds'. For them it was enough if Christians practised outward conformity and made token sacrifices to the ancient gods. Diocletian could not understand the drive towards martyrdom that inspired so many of the Christian fanatics and that, in turn, forced him towards judicial atrocities.

The effect of the edict of 303 was to place Christians outside the law. Assembly for worship was forbidden and Christian religious texts were confiscated and burned. All plaintiffs in Roman courts were required to sacrifice to the gods before their cases could be heard. This was intended to force wealthier Christians to abandon their faith for fear of having their worldly goods seized with no legal redress. In fact, the effects of the edict varied throughout the empire. In the western lands, where the Augustus Constantius held sway, the new laws were loosely applied and though churches were destroyed no Christians were executed. In Africa, the Caesar Maximian was far more severe and many Christians died in a holocaust of burning churches and texts. However, it was in the East that the most severe repression took place. Here Diocletian and Galerius forced all

Christians to offer sacrifices and libations to the gods and those who refused suffered martyrdom. Galerius purged the imperial household, apparently taking pleasure in overseeing the trials and executions in person. He ordered that 'no form of torture should be left untried'. The cruelty described by the Christian writer Lactantius evokes echoes of Nero. One imperial servant named Peter was apparently skinned and then roasted slowly over a fire in full view of both emperors. Diocletian's palace at Nicomedia became the centre of these gruesome persecutions and many Christians were tortured and killed there, including Bishop Anthimus, who was beheaded. Faced with imminent annihilation the Christians began to fight back and both Diocletian and Galerius were forced to take flight when the palace was burned down.

By this stage Diocletian was ill and exhausted, and Galerius had no difficulty in persuading his senior partner to abdicate. He bullied Maximian into doing likewise and the vacancies in the imperial college seemed certain to be filled by Maxentius and Constantine, son of Constantius. In 305, Constantine was a man in the prime of life and one of the outstanding military figures of his time. If elevation to the purple was to be based on merit then his success was certain. However, by this stage Galerius must have known of Constantine's sympathy towards the Christians. Constantius, although clearly a pagan, had failed to implement the edict of 303 in his lands and this may have earned him Galerius's hostility. Furthermore, Constantine himself had recently emerged as Diocletian's right-hand man in military affairs and this threatened Galerius's assumption of power. Thus when Diocletian bid farewell to his troops in a ceremony symbolically held alongside a statue of the emperor's favourite deity Jupiter, everyone present, with the exception of Galerius, expected him to remove his purple cloak and place it on the shoulders of Constantine. Instead, the weeping Diocletian summoned one of Galerius's nephews to become the new Caesar. Constantine, his face seemingly carved in granite, showed none of the tumultuous emotions that must have been close to the surface. The ceremony completed, he knew that Galerius would regard him as an enemy from now on and would not allow him to live for long. He therefore decided to flee to his father's lands in the West. The veracity of the story that he hamstrung horses to prevent a pursuit cannot be established. What is certain, however, is that here was a man of action who would prove a dangerous enemy to Galerius and his pagan supporters.

With just a few guards as companions Constantine rode westwards to avoid his pursuers and by good fortune found his father about to cross from Gaul into Britain to suppress a rebellion there. Father and son crossed the Channel together and travelled north to beyond Hadrian's Wall where they defeated the Picts and restored order to the province. However, on 25 July 306 at York the Augustus Constantius died surrounded by his children, pre-eminent among whom was Constantine. At the instigation of King Crocus of the Alamanni, who had accompanied Constantius on his campaign against the Picts, the British legions proclaimed Constantine emperor in succession to his father.

The elevation of Constantine to Augustus when he had recently been passed over by Galerius for the rank of Caesar was bound to offend the latter and Constantine did not feel ready to challenge the power of the Eastern Empire just yet. He adopted a more cautious approach. Acknowledging that Galerius was the senior figure within the imperial college Constantine sent him a laurelled image of himself and a document announcing that he had succeeded his father as Augustus in the West. Galerius, no doubt frustrated at the turn of events and unwilling to accept Constantine as his colleague, realized that he could do little for the moment except acquiesce. In fact, he sent a purple robe from the East to demonstrate that Constantine's elevation had been granted by him rather than the dead Constantius.[10] Galerius also declared that Constantine was to be merely Caesar while Severus, one of Galerius's cronies, was to be the new Augustus. Constantine accepted the insult for the moment, aware that time was on his side. He was playing for high stakes – nothing less than political control of the whole empire – and the title Caesar gave him the legitimacy he needed. Meanwhile, from his power base in the West he could watch as his imperial colleagues fought against each other and made his task easier. Within his own lands Constantine was determined to show that he was the master. He immediately restored the rights the Christians had lost under recent edicts and by this single action became the symbolic leader of Christians throughout the empire.

In the East and in the African lands, however, the persecutions continued for several terrible years. Bishop Eusebius was in Palestine during this time and his *Martyrs of Palestine* is one of the most vivid sources for the history of the period. He records the fiendish ingenuity of the tortures and executions inflicted on Christians there by successive governors, Urbanus and Firmilianus. One Christian called Agapius, for example, was condemned to be thrown to the beasts in the arena along with a murderer. Agapius was offered a reprieve if he would deny God, but he refused. The murderer was then pardoned and Agapius left to be savaged by bears. Against all expectations he survived but was then thrown into the sea with stones tied to his ankles. The virgin Theodosia was arrested at court for simply speaking to some Christians who were awaiting execution. When she refused to sacrifice to the old gods she was tortured and then thrown into the sea. In another incident the perversity of the governor is made clear: three young Christian men were castrated while some young Christian women of good family were delivered to notorious brothel-keepers. Sometimes mutilation by blinding or the cutting off of feet was substituted for the death penalty at the whim of the judges. Many hundreds of victims suffered in this way in Caesarea, including 130 Egyptian Christians in one day.

By 311 Galerius was dying of a painful cancer and was convinced that he had been struck down by the vengeance of the Christian God. Christian writers, like Lactantius, took particular pleasure in recording the horrible death of one of their most active opponents:

Suddenly an abscess appeared in his privy parts, then a deep-seated fistular ulcer; these could not be cured and ate their way into the very midst of his entrails. Hence there sprang an innumerable multitude of worms, and a deadly stench was given off, since the entire bulk of his members had, though gluttony, even before the disease, been changed into an excessive quantity of soft fat, which then became putrid and presented an intolerable and most fearful sight to those that came near it. As for the physicians, some of them were wholly unable to endure the exceeding and unearthly stench, and were butchered; others, who could not be of any assistance, since the whole mass had swollen and reached a point where there was no hope of recovery, were put to death without mercy.[11]

Galerius had continued persecutions in Rome's eastern territories but now he realized that he had failed and was suffering the consequences. He rescinded all anti-Christian legislation and called on Christians to pray for him. He died within a few months, leaving the Roman world split between his imperial colleagues. There followed a power struggle of bewildering complexity.

Constantine knew that the time for decisive action had come. Within weeks of the death of Galerius he set out to cross the Alps and invaded Italy, where the usurper Maxentius had seized control of Rome. Advancing with remarkable speed he swept his enemies out of northern Italy and moved southwards towards the capital at the head of a force of 40,000 legionaries. Maxentius had already demonstrated his hatred of Christianity in persecutions of such ferocity that they resembled those of the Emperor Nero and so Christians everywhere prayed for Constantine's success as if he were the Messiah.

The question of just how Christian Constantine was before his invasion of Italy in 312 has exercised historians for centuries. Whereas Diocletian and Galerius had claimed the patronage of the deities Jupiter and Hercules, Constantine's father Constantius had always invoked the particular support of Sol Invictus, the Unconquered Sun. It is likely that Constantine followed his father's example and there can be little doubt that there was confusion in his mind about the true differences between the Christian God and the sun god. It is hardly surprising that his so-called 'conversion' combined elements of both, an intertwining of the cross with the sun. Initially, Constantine did not feel the need to define his thoughts and this mixture of deities led him to introduce worship for Christians on sun days and the celebration of a divine birthday or Christmas at the winter solstice. Constantius, though a pagan through and through, had shown more toleration of Christians than his fellow emperors, Diocletian and Galerius, partly, one suspects, because he equated Christianity with sun worship and partly because his wife Helena was herself a Christian. His son Constantine must, therefore, have grown up in a more tolerant atmosphere than most aristocratic Roman pagans of the period.

This much is based on the hard evidence of observers and historians. What followed, however, has entered the history books through the minds of the faithful. Constantine's army approached the outskirts of Rome, and Maxentius responded by breaking down the bridges over the River Tiber to hamper his progress. Yet, as the Caesar of the West neared the site of the Milvian Bridge, where the decisive battle was to be fought, he experienced an epiphany, the effects of which have echoed down the ages. In later years, Constantine swore on oath that the following events occurred to him before the battle. Bishop Eusebius has left the most famous account of the vision:

A most marvellous sign appeared to him [Constantine] from heaven, the account of which it might have been difficult to receive with credit, had it been related by any other person. But since the victorious Emperor himself long afterwards declared it to the writer of this history when he was honoured with his acquaintance and society, and confirmed his statement by an oath, who could hesitate to accredit the relation, especially since the testimony of after-time has established its truth? He said that at about midday, when the sun was beginning to decline, he saw with his own eyes the trophy of a cross of light in the heavens, above the sun, and bearing the inscription Conquer by This (Hoc Vince). At this sight he himself was struck with amazement, and his whole army also.[12]

The same night, Constantine related, he had a dream in which Christ appeared to him and instructed him to make standards in the form of the Christian sign he was shown. When he awoke he sought out the Christian bishop of Cordoba, Hosius, who was travelling with the army. Hosius explained the dream to him and helped him to adapt the normal pagan standards of the Roman legions into the labarum, probably a Gallic word used to describe the standard that Constantine's armies used henceforth, combining Roman military symbols with Christian ones.

Constantine's 'vision' became the preserve of Renaissance artists rather than historians. We can never know the truth behind such an event nor even whether the idea originated with Constantine himself rather than some influential Christian adviser, like Hosius. Suffice it to say Constantine felt the need for some 'divine' protection in the forthcoming battle against Maxentius. Christian commentators were not slow to develop the idea and within four years of the battle Lactantius wrote a version of the story that is the one we have today.

The sign that Constantine added to the shields of his men was the upright cross with a loop at the top, a version of the Christian cross typical at the time. Eusebius, writing after the emperor's death, emphasized the uncertainty that Constantine felt at this decisive moment in his life. He knew that Maxentius was claiming the support of the old, pagan gods but remembered that his father Constantius had always relied on the 'one Supreme God', by whom he probably meant Sol Invictus. If he could be convinced, however, that this supreme god was none other than the god of the Christians then this would be enough for him to become a 'Christian'. Here the influence of Hosius during the march to the Milvian Bridge cannot be overlooked. According to Eusebius, the emperor, in the presence of the bishop himself, had sworn to the dream and vision story. Eusebius wrote that he had actually seen the first labarum made; it was covered in gold and jewels and had pictures of Constantine and his children attached to it. Significantly, however, the coins that were minted to celebrate the victory at the Milvian Bridge were clearly dedicated to Sol Invictus. They bore the inscription 'To the Sun, the Unconquerable Companion' ('Soli Invicto Comiti').

The modern historian finds such evidence difficult to credit. In an age of 'spin' one is constantly in danger of seeking a cynical, politically based interpretation of such events. The Christians in the emperor's army, like Hosius, had much to gain by establishing such a story as a factual event in the rise of a man who would shortly dominate much of the civilized world. It is surely significant, however, that there was no mention of this vision in the sky, even though it was apparently witnessed by many thousands of impressionable Roman soldiers, until it appeared in Eusebius's life of Constantine written shortly after the death of Constantine in 337, twenty-five years after the battle of the Milvian Bridge.

Constantine's 'conversion' to Christianity was not based on the teachings of a Galilean rabbi of the first century but on the power manifest in a single, omnipotent god, whether Sol Invictus or the

Christian God. By accepting the role of champion of this god
Constantine believed that he would benefit from divine aid in his
struggle against rivals who had the support of the ancient, traditional gods of the Greco-Roman pantheon. Victory at the Milvian
Bridge was a sure sign that he had the backing of a more powerful
deity than his enemies. Initially, the cross on the shields of his
soldiers was no more significant than the thunderbolt of Zeus or
Jupiter might have been on the shields of the followers of some
other leading Roman general. If that was the symbol of the sun god
or the Christian God then so be it. A man in Constantine's position
could accept none of the mildness of Jesus as the lamb of God; he
needed the support of a god of battles and the result at the Milvian
Bridge showed he had it. He was encouraged to believe this by
Christians who played down Christ's mildness and stressed that
Constantine was the chosen one of an all-powerful deity.

For one of the decisive battles in world history, the fight at the
Milvian Bridge on 29 October 312 was a relatively minor affair. The
leadership of Constantine and the high morale, one might even say
inspiration, of his soldiers made victory a foregone conclusion.
Maxentius had ordered his engineers to construct a line of boats
across the Tiber to replace the bridge which had earlier been broken
to prevent Constantine approaching the city. He then ordered his
troops out of the city and across the pontoon. Constantine,
meanwhile, in the excitement preceding the battle had openly
declared himself a Christian and had distributed Christian instead of
pagan labarums throughout his army. His Gallic and German troops
then tore into the enemy, bearing the sign of the cross on their
shields. The battle did not last long. Maxentius's army soon
panicked and attempted to get back over the pontoon and into the
city. In the chaos the bridge broke and many were drowned in the
river. Maxentius, either trying to rally his man or more likely
because all hope was gone, rode into the river in full armour and
was drowned as well.

The day after his victory Constantine entered Rome, not on a
donkey as Jesus had entered Jerusalem, but in an ornate chariot,
master of all he surveyed, the first Christian ruler in history. Instead
of going to the Capitol to sacrifice to Jupiter and give thanks for his
triumph, he infuriated many pagan Romans by signally rejecting the

mores of the past. The body of Maxentius was located and retrieved from the Tiber so that his head could be sent to North Africa to prove his death to any remaining followers there. Constantine then set about stamping his personality indelibly on the new regime. Maxentius had been building a huge basilica; Constantine simply acquired it and had it dedicated to himself. Inside, a statue of the new emperor was erected, ten times life-size and portraying him holding the labarum in his hand. The nature of the new regime was clear to all. Constantine was the Christian God's representative on earth. Nevertheless, Constantine never forgot that he was a Roman and the Porta Triumphalis, or Constantine Arch, was built by 315 to celebrate his victory over Maxentius.

Unchallenged in the West Constantine now arranged a meeting with his co-emperor Licinius, ruler of Rome's eastern provinces, in order to settle the religious policy of the empire. They met at Milan in February 313 and their alliance was sealed by Licinius's marriage to Constantine's sister, Constantia. The main outcome of this meeting was the so-called Edict of Milan. Licinius was himself a pagan but was prepared to compromise with Constantine, particularly as the anti-Christian policies of Galerius had already been revoked. As a result the official policy of the Roman state became neutral on the religious issue, with complete religious freedom being granted throughout the empire. This had been Constantine's policy in the western empire for some years, and in one form or another very much that of his father before him. In the eastern provinces, however, and in Africa, notably Egypt, successive pagan emperors had made martyrs of 3,000 Christians. This finally came to an end under Licinius. For a while the empire was at peace, politically and spiritually, while the co-emperors cooperated in most policies.

In the summer of 315 Constantine visited Rome to celebrate the tenth anniversary of his accession. Like three years earlier he did not sacrifice to Rome's traditional deities. Instead, he made a public statement of his own religious beliefs by arranging a meeting with Pope Silvester and ordering the construction of the city's first Christian churches. Significantly, the image of Sol Invictus no longer appeared on the coins that were minted in the empire. This did not mean that sun worship had been rejected; it indicated that a compromise had been reached by which Christianity had absorbed some aspects of the older belief. Sunday, *dies solis*, the first day of the week, was integrated into the Christian calendar along with 25 December, the birthday of Sol Invictus. It was a small price for Christianity – or indeed for Constantine – to pay to achieve a religious settlement for the whole empire.

Constantine, however, was not content to rule half an empire; his vision was for a return to the great days of Rome under Augustus with himself cast as the single, all-powerful emperor. In 317 he provoked Licinius into a brief war, gaining territory in the Balkans but not threatening his co-emperor's hold on the East. However, over the next seven years their policies diverged, notably on the religious issue. Licinius had never been more than a lukewarm supporter of the Christians and with so many living in his territory he began to fear that they would much prefer to be ruled by Constantine. Moreover, Licinius became impatient with the endless doctrinal disputes of the eastern Christians, notably the Egyptians, and the unrest that seemed to be caused by their bickering bishops. It is inaccurate to accuse Licinius of reintroducing a policy of persecution before 324 but it is clear that his patience with what he saw as a troublesome cult was growing thin. Moreover, the evidence of his own paganism increased as he entertained ever more extra-ordinary charlatans at his court. Soothsayers, sorcerers, augurs, prophets and every kind of heathen visionary was welcomed if they could promise an end to Christianity.[13]

Constantine's decisive struggle against his erstwhile colleague can be interpreted as a crusade in a political rather than a religious sense. Christians in the eastern lands prayed openly for Constantine to come to their aid but when he came it was not as a Messiah to rescue them but as a conqueror to unite the empire. Nevertheless, Constantine did not neglect to play the religious card. In 324 when he launched the decisive campaign against Licinius, his troops carried the labarum as they had done at the battle of the Milvian Bridge and the imperial standard was marked with the monogram of Christ. Tales of the miraculous powers of these Christian symbols spread through both armies and Constantine, as the chosen one of the 'Supreme Power', proved irresistible. As a *casus belli* Constantine claimed that he was acting as the defender of Christian interests in the eastern provinces and brought Licinius to battle at Adrianople.

Although his force was outnumbered two to one Constantine was
the better general. He led an army in which morale was high and the
apparently invincible Christian God was with him. Licinius fled the
field, abandoning his men, many of whom immediately took service
with Constantine. The Christian army pursued Licinius to Byzantium
where he was again defeated. Finally and decisively, Constantine's
son Crispus was victorious over Licinius's navy at Chrysopolis.
Licinius surrendered on a promise to spare his life, which was
negotiated by his wife Constantia. Sadly, Constantine did not keep
his word to his sister and ordered Licinius's execution only a few
months later. He then occupied the eastern provinces and united
them with the West. In the final battle Licinius's troops had been
equipped with the symbols and emblems of the old gods and the
clash of traditions and values was clear to all. It was as a Catholic,
'universal' Christian that Constantine brought unity back to Rome.

TWO

The Christian Empire

The first Christian emperor was a larger than life figure. Already approaching fifty years of age and with eighteen years of rule in the western lands behind him when he took control of the empire, he was a man of immense achievement and even more potential. The huge, sixty-foot statue he erected of himself typified the emperor's self-image – he was a direct challenger to the old pagan gods like Jupiter, whose statues had previously dominated the interiors of holy places like Sulla's Temple of Jupiter Capitolinus. As the chosen one of the greatest of gods, the Christian God, Constantine was displaying himself as equal or indeed superior to the gods of old.

The conversion of Constantine was not the sudden event portrayed by writers and artists. Even after his vision in 312 he did not immediately become a monotheist nor had he become a fully fledged Christian even by the time he united the empire in 324. From 312 his face ruled Rome, his stone face, the face of the last pagan emperor and the last Roman god. In the words of John Romer: 'Constantine's huge eyes stare straight out of his face, focused on eternity. The head is built like a piece of architecture; the hair locks together like the stones of a huge arch, the dome-shaped cranium above reflects the great round chin; the fleshy mouth is over large, weighty; the lids fit over the orbs of the eyes like brick vaults; the whole, a vast, immovable icon.'[14] But pagan Rome and Constantine's great statue were symbols of the past, a past Diocletian would have understood, and Augustus. It was part of the ancient world. And this world had not yet disappeared. With the vast majority of the empire's population still pagan Constantine knew that he needed to use carrots rather than sticks to ensure the triumph of Christianity. As emperor Constantine was still required to stand as pontifex maximus, essentially the high priest of the Roman religion and thereby direct rival of the Christian pope. Millions of pagans throughout the empire would still look to him as their head. Time and natural wastage rather than persecution or extermination would see the end of paganism.

Most of the Roman army remained pagan. Admittedly the legions that had come with him from Britain, Gaul and Germany to overthrow Maxentius had adopted the labarum as their standard and the cross as their shield insignia, but that did not make them Christians. These men had been loyal to Constantine and to his father before him. Should he order it, they would paint their shields with Jupiter's thunderbolt or the rising sun of Sol Invictus. At his age – fifty in 325 – how many more years did he have to command them? A new emperor might require obedience to the old gods unless Constantine could establish Christianity as the natural religion of the army and the ruling classes. He knew he must act quickly in bringing about a virtual revolution that would transform the old Roman Empire into the new Christian empire.

During his rise to power Constantine had learned much from the examples of his peers. The pagan emperors had not cultivated the affection of the people: Diocletian had been grim and distant; Galerius brutal and terrifying; Maxentius weak but cruel. Only Licinius had seen the importance of public opinion but even he had sought the solution to his problems in charlatans and pagan mumbo jumbo. It had been Constantius, his father, who had been his role model. Constantius had won the loyalty of his people not through fear but through generosity and good government. Constantine's conclusion was that the pagan gods had failed the men who worshipped them, while the Christian God had demonstrated his superiority by granting success to Constantius and now to himself, son of a worthy father. The way forward for Christianity was through improved public relations. The weakness of paganism must be made obvious and the strengths of Christianity undeniable. But pagans must not suffer persecution for by so doing, like the martyrs of Christianity, they would inspire others to follow their example.

Constantine was a pragmatist not a philosopher. If Christianity was to be the cement of his imperial power it was not enough for it to be a religion only of the afterlife, as many Christian thinkers believed it to be. He needed its strength in the earthly world and for that to be achieved he must give it a clear and obvious presence to compare with the temples of the Greco-Roman gods. Let bishops and theologians keep their philosophy to themselves. Ordinary Romans needed to see the very places where Christ walked and worked and died to save them all. Constantine began building shrines in Rome and other Italian cities to commemorate the martyrs of the faith. These Christian holy places were the building bricks of a propaganda exercise of astonishing thoroughness. Alongside the symbols of imperial power in Rome he constructed a mausoleum to St Peter – Jesus's rock, and Constantine's too – on which the new Roman Church would be built.

No one in the history of Rome came close to matching the building projects of Constantine other than Nero and most of his were merely a reflection of his personal megalomania. Constantine realized the political importance and the economic benefit of such an immense scheme of work. The money spent on churches, for example, not only helped the economy but rooted Christianity firmly in the eyes of the public, making it difficult to sweep away even if the pagans should return to power on his death. Huge donations from the emperor formed part of the funding of the new churches throughout the empire.

The structure of the churches built during the last decade of Constantine's reign carried a clear message. They were not like temples, mysterious and solitary, they were busy, public places, where the Lord met his people. Based on the basilica design, they were large and expansive, designed for religious ceremonies and as audience halls for local administration. They were simply constructed with timber roofs to keep costs to a minimum. As R. Krautheimer points out, 'The savings in cost would be spent more profitably in terms of political propaganda on precious decorations and furnishings.'[15] After all, Constantine was building hundreds of churches but only one Church.

Constantine soon came to realize that he was at war with history. For a thousand years Rome had been a pagan city and in simple terms the pagans had taken up all the best sites. The Christian parvenus could only exist on the margins and to challenge paganism in its own heartland was politically unwise. What was needed was a new Rome, even a new Jerusalem, which Constantine could make the centre of his Christian empire. And so the decision was taken to build a new capital on the site of the ancient Greek site of Byzan-tium, an entirely Christian city where the new symbol of the cross would be displayed on all the buildings. The city would be named after the emperor himself: Constantinople. Many conquerors in antiquity named cities in their own honour, not least the great Alexander, but Constantine ducked the accusation that he merely followed in the footsteps of greater men: he attributed the decision to God. The new emperor claimed the city was to be named less in his honour than that of God, who had 'sought out and judged fitting for his purpose my service . . . thrusting aside by some mightier power all the dangers that beset me, that the human race might be recalled to the worship of the august law'.[16] The new city, Constantinople, would thus be God's city and God would never suffer the presence of pagan temples like those in older imperial centres, including Rome, Antioch and Alexandria. Instead God's city would be filled with new Christian churches and the emperor's friend, Eusebius of Caesarea, was commissioned to produce fifty magnificently copied and bound editions of the Scriptures so that these churches could be equipped with the very best.[17]

From the beginning religion permeated the whole life of Constan-tinople and influenced the outlook of its citizens. The visible signs of religion met them at every street corner and sacred icons were cherished in every home. The coins of the realm were stamped with the True Cross; the games were opened with prayers; relics and icons were carried before the armies as they marched through the streets on their way to war. Constantine's capital became a city of churches, ranging from the vast and magnificent church of the Holy Apostles, a five-domed cruciform building which influenced the design of St Mark's in Venice, and where the ritual was chanted in the presence of the emperor with the most gorgeous ceremonial, right down to humble little shrines where the casual passer-by would enter to pay his devotion before a holy picture as he hurried home from his daily toil. There were many monasteries inhabited by monks from all parts of the empire. In addition, there were schools, hospices and infirmaries linked to monastic buildings, forming vast religious complexes handling all aspects of everyday life. Thousands of monks in their black dress worked in these quiet habitations and their influence on the life of the capital was profound.

The construction of Constantinople seemed to be a race against time. Rome may not have been built in a day but it seemed as if Constantinople was. Everything at least had to appear to be new and yet there were not enough skilled craftsmen in the empire to create a match for the marvels of antiquity in a few short years. As a result, the city became an exercise in 'mix and match' and a coat of paint was sometimes all that was needed to make the difference between pagan and Christian stonework. On 11 May 330 the city was formally inaugurated. It was more Roman – or even Greek – than Christian, even though Constantine would not have known it. Facing impossible deadlines the architects and builders had stripped the world of antiquity – and pagan antiquity at that – of many of its splendours so that buildings could appear transformed in the emperor's new Christian city.

Pilgrims later considered Constantine's new city a destination second only to the Holy Sepulchre at Jerusalem because what it lacked in original sanctity it made up for with tourist attractions and a museum-like collection of relics. They came from all over Europe to see the relics, some in the hope that they might offer cures for diseases, others attracted just by the fame or the holiness of the bones of saints or the splinters of wood from the True Cross itself.[18]

While the city that bore his name was under construction, Constantine took two further, decisive steps in establishing his Christian empire. In order to unite the divisions within the faith brought about by the Alexandrian priest Arius's views concerning the Trinity, he summoned bishops from throughout the empire to attend the city of Nicea in 325. As a recent convert to Christianity and as a politician and soldier rather than a theologian, Constantine tended to feel that disputes within the Church could be solved like most other disagreements – by compromise or by force. He believed that people of the same faith could not feel the bitterness of division for long without looking for a way of ending their feuding. Today, we may regard the emperor's views as impossibly naive but centuries of religious conflict have bred cynicism in us as we view the effects of bitter religious divisions within all the world's faiths, most of all Christianity.

At Nicea, Constantine tried to solve one of the earliest and certainly one of the greatest schisms in the Christian Church. The council met on 20 May 325 but it was apparent right away that it was not a meeting of members of a united church. Only six bishops came from west of Rome and the bishop of Rome, already referred to as pope, did not himself attend, sending two deacons in his place. By contrast, the eastern church was represented by between 250 and 300 Greek-speaking bishops. Constantine presided at the meetings and actually took part in the discussions – it was a brave or foolhardy theologian who drew attention to any weaknesses in the imperial arguments. Unlike anyone else at the council Constantine was concerned less with minutiae than with the achievement of unity. His church, as he saw it, must speak with one voice. At one stage he asked Eusebius to prepare a statement of faith that would bring the Orthodox supporters and the Arians together, but the former simply refused to accept anything to which the latter could agree. Having failed to achieve a compromise, Constantine the soldier resorted to force, pressurizing all the bishops, including Eusebius, to accept an amended statement of belief. He succeeded in persuading all but two bishops and Arius himself to sign the statement, after which Arius and his two supporters were excommunicated. Yet it still niggled in Constantine's mind that his church would somehow remain imperfect until he had won Arius over and two years later he extracted a confession of faith from the great heretic. As far as Constantine was concerned, the Church was now unified. Unfortunately, Christian bishops of the fourth century were men of absolute intransigence and in fact the great Arian debate was only just beginning. Nevertheless, the degree of unity achieved at Nicea enabled Constantine to present the council as a considerable achievement, which in some ways it was.

A second issue confronted at Nicea was the future of the Roman city of Aelia, which had been built on the ruins of Jerusalem. The Bishop of Aelia Capitolina, Makarius, suggested that the pagan temple dedicated to Jupiter or Tyche, which the Emperor Hadrian had built on the supposed site of the crucifixion of Jesus Christ, be demolished so that the Tomb of Christ could be revealed. Constantine realized the immense opportunity that was facing him. There could be no greater symbol of the triumph of Christianity and of himself as the first Christian emperor than the discovery of the tomb of Jesus. This would be something that ordinary people could understand. No longer would the faith be left only to the bishops and priests with their self-indulgent musings. If the Holy Sepulchre could be uncovered then everyone could visit the site that would become the centre of the 'new Jerusalem', itself replacing Rome as the centre of the world.[19]

For sixty years after its destruction by the Romans in AD 70 Jerusalem lay in ruins, a city of ghosts. Then the Emperor Hadrian decided to construct a new Roman city on the site. Colonia Aelia Capitolina, as the new city would be called, was intended to replace the holy city of the endlessly contentious Jews and their curious offshoot, the Christians, or Nazarenes as they were sometimes known. Hadrian issued a decree in AD 135, saying, 'It is forbidden to all circumcised persons to enter and to stay in the territory of Aelia Capitolina. Any person contravening this prohibition shall be put to death.'[20] Though aimed at the Jews in the aftermath of the Bar Cochba Revolt this clearly applied to all Semitic peoples and even to many of the Roman soldiers of the Tenth Legion, who had been recruited in Syria and Arabia. There must have been many exceptions to the rule.

Although historians have regarded the Christians who visited Jerusalem in the time of Constantine as the 'first pilgrims' this is probably not accurate. It is known that visitors from foreign lands did journey to Palestine, seeking the places where Jesus and his disciples had lived less than 100 or 200 years before. John Wilkinson refers to such Christians in the second century; they sought the birthplace of Jesus in Bethlehem and had specific knowledge that the Tomb of Christ, the Holy Sepulchre, was now to be found inside Jerusalem not outside, as the walls of the city had been moved. As Wilkinson points out, pilgrims in the vicinity of Aelia Capitolina in 130 may have met Christians who had personal knowledge of Jesus's disciples or even members of his family.[21]

Christians writing in the fourth century assumed that Hadrian deliberately sought to eradicate all evidence of their religion but it is doubtful that the matter of the crucifixion of a Galilean rabbi a century after his death was so much in the mind of a Roman emperor that he felt the need to eradicate it. Whatever Hadrian's reasons, the ancient quarry where the crucifixion took place and which housed the rock tomb where Jesus's body was taken and where Christians believed the resurrection took place was built over by Roman workmen in about the year 130. On top of the quarry a platform was constructed on which was raised a Roman temple, probably dedicated to Tyche.[22] Tyche was the Greek goddess of chance and is sometimes associated with the Roman deity Fortuna. She was also linked with the more beneficent Agathus Daimon, a good spirit and protector of families. Tyche is sometimes shown winged, with a crown and carrying a sceptre and cornucopia, though in other depictions she is blindfold and symbolizes uncertainty and risk. Martin Biddle has shown that Christian writers, notably Eusebius, who claimed the temple was dedicated to Jupiter or, even worse, to Aphrodite/Venus, were contributing to an anti-pagan campaign. Whereas Tyche was an 'acceptable Pagan figure', Aphrodite was absolutely unacceptable because she emphasized the carnality of human love. Eusebius was therefore suggesting that the Romans had deliberately attempted to pollute the site, which is unlikely.

Constantine was excited at Makarius's suggestion that the Tomb of Christ should be revealed and was only too happy for the excavations to take place. At this distance in time we cannot be certain about his motives or those of Makarius. Twenty-first-century cynics, weaned on the antics of totalitarian regimes, will suspect that the search for the Holy Sepulchre was just a means by which those in authority could bind the people to their power. Makarius wasted no time and the work began on two separate sites. We do not know on what information the bishop was acting in his choice of locations for the excavations. In the 300 years that had passed since the historical events of Jesus's life there had been many changes in that part of Aelia/Jerusalem. However, local sources – Jewish, Pagan and Christian – would certainly have been available to guide the archaeologists and builders. The task was truly a titanic one, nothing less than the shifting of thousands of tons of solid rock, as well as the demolition and carting away of a large Roman temple. One can only imagine the effects of the work on the local population, essentially pagan but no doubt swelled by Christian pilgrims flooding in to watch an event that could almost be regarded as a 'second resurrection'.

While the excavations continued, civil unrest was close to the surface. The Christian onlookers, filled with expectation but also fearing disappointment, began to goad the local pagans, insisting that debris from the temple site should be removed from Aelia/Jerusalem so that it no longer polluted what they were already beginning to consider their holy city. For two years the work continued. Makarius's faith must have been tried and tested many times. He knew that not only his own future but that of the Christian faith in the empire depended on the success of his project. Pagans in high places in the imperial administration would seek to exploit any failure by the Christians to validate their claims for the historical Jesus. The events of the reign of the Emperor Julian, a generation later, were to show how strong paganism still was and how ephemeral was Christianity's grip on the empire. For 300 years Christians had faced persecution; only for a mere handful had they been free to walk the streets untroubled. None of Makarius's followers wished to return to the bad old days. He must not fail.

Two years into the dig one of the greatest discoveries in human history was made as Eusebius, almost certainly an eyewitness, records:

And as one layer after another was laid bare, the place which was beneath the earth appeared; directly as this was done, contrary to all expectation, the venerable and hallowed monument of our Saviour's resurrection became visible, and the most holy cave received what was an emblem of his coming to life.[23]

The rock tomb was located beneath the main platform upon which the Roman temple had been built. This was hardly surprising in view of the antiquity of Jerusalem and the fact that it was as much a necropolis as a city of the living. Hundreds of rock tombs could be seen in the hills on which Jerusalem was built. Nevertheless, by common agreement this tomb was accepted as the one in which the crucified Christ had been placed after his execution. Cynicism had no place in the wave of emotion that followed the discovery. In fact, what the builders revealed would have been open to serious debate had the Christians not immediately identified it as the Holy Sepulchre. In view of the fact that our eyewitness, Bishop Eusebius, never recorded what it was about the rock tomb that identified it as the last resting place of the body of Christ,[24] we cannot know why everyone was so certain about its authenticity. We do know that sometimes graffiti was scratched onto the rock surrounding such tombs and it is possible that something of this kind survived the Roman building work to identify this cave. Christian catacombs often bore witness to the identities of the bodies within, though Jewish burial sites were generally not so revealing.

When the Emperor Hadrian ordered the construction of the temple, his builders covered over an ancient quarry. What had existed within the quarry in Jesus's time had remained untouched but had formed the foundations for the new temple. From this ancient quarry the Tomb of Christ had to be cut free like a nugget of gold found deep below ground. In order to separate the rock in the quarry from the stone used for the temple it is estimated Makarius's builders had to move a colossal amount of material, perhaps 16,500 cubic feet, with just the primitive tools of the time. During the digging the workmen discovered not just the Tomb of Christ but also the hill on which the crucifixion had taken place – Golgotha. This mound, for hill is rather an exaggeration, is now encased in the Golgotha chapel within the Holy Sepulchre Church.

Even Makarius and Eusebius, who did not agree on much, closed ranks on the 'great find', Eusebius commenting that the discovery was 'contrary to all expectation'. Constantine was beside himself with the pleasure of the moment, saying it 'surpassed all astonishment'. In an age of miracles, it was hardly surprising that so much simple faith on the part of ordinary believers should be rewarded with such a find. What is harder for the modern reader to accept is the alleged astonishment of those in authority that their political 'needs' would be fulfilled by an act of God rather than an act of man.

The excitement of the finds may have helped to ease the sufferings endured by Constantine at this time. The emperor, though acknowledging himself a Christian, did not undergo baptism until eleven years later when he knew his death was close. His decision has been rationalized by modern historians as a reflection of a desire to sweep away a lifetime's sins at the last moment. This may be true. However, another explanation is provided by the terrible events of 326 during which he displayed the weaknesses of an Othello and a Nero in a single moment. The precise details are unclear but there is some sense to be made of this tragic slice of family life. Constantine's eldest son, Crispus, was a married man with at least one child. He was an experienced commander who had won for his father the great naval battle that finally put an end to Licinius. Everything pointed to his succeeding to the imperial throne and proving a capable emperor. However, in 326 Constantine suddenly had

Crispus arrested and executed, after hearing evidence against his son and acting as judge in the case. From the confused details it would appear that Constantine's second wife, Fausta, accused Crispus of attempted rape and probably disloyalty to his father. When Constantine arrived in Rome a few weeks after the execution of Crispus, he was met by his mother Helena, who was dressed in mourning for her grandson. She told the emperor another version of events; it vindicated Crispus and accused Fausta of perjury. Fausta appears to have admitted her guilt and, under compulsion, agreed to commit suicide. She ordered the baths of the imperial palace to be heated far beyond normal temperatures and then suffocated herself.

Constantine was crushed by these events and realized that his Christian revolution was in danger. How could he, the chosen one of God, have made such a mistake? He had killed his beloved son, leaving himself with no successor above the age of ten. To have undergone baptism at this time would have been a farce. For a while he may have toyed with the idea of going to the Holy Land himself but the dangers of being away from the centre of power were too great. Instead, the eighty-year-old Helena agreed to undertake one of the great public relations exercises in history – a pilgrimage to the Holy Places, during which she would use the imperial purse to buy back the memory of those grim last few months. The grand progress of Helena around Palestine, probably escorted by Bishop Eusebius and certainly accompanied by all the panoply of imperial power, has moved from the realm of history into that of legend.

The dowager-empress Helena was in Palestine while the great discoveries were made at the excavations in Aelia Capitolina. Helena's personal piety need not be doubted and as an important part of the imperial machinery her very person had political significance, unspoken but widely understood. Just as Hadrian had Romanized Palestine with his pagan temples and public works some 200 years before, so Helena Christianized the province by building churches everywhere she went. Her pilgrimage culminated in the 'discovery' of the Holy Sepulchre and the True Cross.

While Helena was attracting both the attention of her contemporaries and the eye of history, Constantine was able to concentrate on establishing the political foundations of Christianity as a world religion.

He realized that his Christian empire needed deep roots if it were to succeed. Rome was still a pagan empire at heart and even an emperor could not change the situation by a stroke of the quill. As a result, a careful campaign was waged to stress continuity at the same time as change was taking place. If Christianity was to thrive in the lands of the Semitic peoples, it should be seen not as something that had destroyed the old beliefs but as a faith that had taken the best from the Jewish religion and incorporated this with the teachings of Jesus Christ. Thus Eusebius and his fellow bishops sought Old Testament justification for the new faith and for the part played in it by the Roman emperors. Constantine was hailed as a new Moses, arising to lead his people into the future and out of an 'Egyptian captivity' of paganism. Modern concepts like 'image consultants' come to mind as the emperor's panegyrists linked him with Abraham as the 'father' of his people, and sometimes with other biblical patriarchs.

In building his Christian empire Constantine was fortunate to have the help of Bishop Eusebius, though initially Eusebius was not an obvious choice for imperial adviser: he was not a believer in a reborn, physical Jerusalem and he was a supporter of Arius. Eusebius had became Bishop of Caesarea in Palestine in 313, only months after Constantine had been 'converted' and gained control of Rome. The vast expansion of Christianity had taken place in the lands of the gentiles, particularly in western Europe. In Palestine itself the Jews had resisted conversion to Christianity and only a small minority of the inhabitants of the old Jerusalem, the current Aelia Capitolina, were followers of Christ.

Eusebius rationalized this situation by stressing that Christianity as a faith belonged to no one place but had transcended the need for a location in any earthly sense of the term. For Eusebius the word 'Jerusalem' was now merely a name and not a place. It represented a celestial city not an earthly one. It was an idea not a reality. But such philosophizing did not make much sense to the average believer, or even to the emperor himself. Once ordinary Christians found they were no longer subjected to persecution they emerged from hiding and began to assert their victory over paganism. Like Constantine himself, these 'survivors' wanted to experience their religion as a living faith not an intellectual one that existed only in the minds of bishops and theologians. As a result, Eusebius was in a tiny minority who saw Jerusalem as only a celestial city. Most ordinary Christians – and the emperor and his mother Helena were to be numbered among these – would not be content until a religion of the senses existed, in which they could see what Jesus had seen, smell the trees on the Mount of Olives, hear the prayers at the holy sites, taste the waters of the River Jordan and set their feet in the footprints of the Lord. Before he could help in the construction of Constantine's Christian empire Eusebius had to compromise on the need for a physical religion related to a holy land and a holy city.

Constantine needed symbols and that is exactly what Makarius and Helena provided for him in the shape of the Holy Sepulchre and the True Cross. The next task was to make these relics the centre of a world famous site, to which all Christians could travel to experience the realities of their faith. And so Constantine ordered the construction of the Church of the Holy Sepulchre on the historical site of the Passion of Jesus Christ.

Modern reconstructions of Constantine's original Church of the Holy Sepulchre are inadequate in conveying the effect of this marvellous building. One of the first Christian buildings ever constructed, it had no rivals in its early days. Today nobody can imagine from a model how this miracle stood not just as a symbol of a faith but as a tangible link between heaven and earth. Pilgrims from western Europe did not journey from lands that boasted splendid cathedrals – such buildings were still many centuries in the future. Even Helena, who came from Rome, had only the lowly St Peter's, a shadow of its later Renaissance self, to draw on as a symbol of Christianity's physical presence. Europe in the fourth century had nothing except the glories of a pagan past to set against this pristine celebration of the living God.

Eusebius described the building as it developed. It was 'finished with carvings of panel work, and, like a great sea, covered the whole basilica with its endless swell, while the brilliant gold with which it was covered made the whole temple sparkle with rays of light'.[25] The complex of buildings begun by Constantine's architects Zenobius and Eustathius in 326 contained two holy sites, the Tomb of Christ and the site of the crucifixion, Golgotha or Calvary. The entry to the Church of the Holy Sepulchre was from the main colonnaded street of Christian Jerusalem, known as the Cardo. After ascending steps a pilgrim passed through a forecourt, or atrium, into a very large five-aisled basilica with a wooden roof. The basilica was some 200 feet in length. Beyond it the pilgrim reached a porticoed courtyard with the rock of Calvary in the south-west corner. At the western end of the complex was the holiest of holies, contained within a large rotunda known as the Anastasis, or Resurrection. Inside this magnificent building was the sepulchre itself, housed within a temple-shaped shrine called the aedicule. The rotunda had a golden dome and was open to the sky. The aedicule had been shaped from the bedrock which surrounded the Tomb of Christ and its exterior had been decorated to give the impression that it had been built as a temple.

Today virtually nothing remains of Constantine's great vision except the rock tomb itself. Pilgrims must be satisfied with a jumble of styles that serves only to emphasize the disunity rather than the unity of modern Christianity. Ironically, as the architect Robert Ousterhout has shown, the original design survived longer in the hearts and memories of the pilgrims and crusaders who came to Jerusalem to worship at this holiest of shrines than it did in the city itself. Some medieval pilgrims took back home with them not only the memory of the sepulchre's spirituality but its actual physical appearance. The inspiration of the site persuaded western Europeans to build reproduction holy sepulchres during the eleventh and twelfth centuries and it is these buildings – for example, S. Stefano in Bologna and the Holy Sepulchre in Cambridge – that give modern historians the best impression of how the original looked.[26]

The discovery of the Holy Sepulchre in 326 had convinced Eusebius of the value of tangible monuments and relics and henceforth he became the main instrument of Constantine's political campaign to create a new Jerusalem on earth. Part of the political message of the original Holy Sepulchre Church was contained in Eusebius's comparison between Constantine's new complex and the Jewish Temple destroyed in AD 70. In his biography of Constantine he wrote of 'New Jerusalem, facing the far-famed Jerusalem of old time.' Constantine – and Eusebius – saw Christianity replacing Judaism as the Christians took the place of the Jews as the 'chosen people' of God. The Ark of the Covenant had gone; the holy of holies was now the Tomb of Christ within the Anastasis. When the basilica of the Holy Sepulchre was dedicated in 336 Eusebius preached a sermon in which he specifically described the 'Martyrion of the Saviour' as the 'New Temple' of 'New Jerusalem'. He referred to relics that had previously been associated with the Jewish holy places but were now, apparently, part of the Christian sites. One example was 'an altar which has on it the blood of Zacharias', another was the 'horn of anointing' which was venerated alongside the wood from the True Cross and the ring of Solomon, all of which were displayed on Good Friday. In fact, it may be that even the aedicule of the tomb was borrowed from Jewish styles of the time of Jesus.[27]

The somewhat taciturn traveller known to history as the Bordeaux Pilgrim left us a brief account of what the holy site was like in 333 before Constantine's Church of the Holy Sepulchre was completed:

> On your left is the little hill of Golgotha where the Lord was crucified. About a stone's throw from it is the crypt where they laid his body, and from where he rose again on the third day. There at present, by order of the emperor Constantine, there has been built a 'basilica', that is, a church of wondrous beauty, which has beside it cisterns from which water is raised and beside them a baptistry where children are baptized.[28]

The role of the Emperor Constantine's mother in the future of Christianity was established by the discovery of the True Cross. Curiously, or perhaps not, this event was not mentioned by writers until the century after it happened. Eusebius, who would almost certainly have been an eyewitness to Helena's discovery, does not include it in his history of the Church, an incomprehensible omission if the event did take place during the dowager's visit to Jerusalem. For the record, the legend that grew up eventually overshadowed the discovery of the Holy Sepulchre itself. It is said that Helena located three crosses below ground and that the True Cross was identified by its ability to restore health to a sick woman of the city when lain upon her.

With the advantage of hindsight we can see that the mighty symbol of the cross better suited the circumstances of the fifth rather than the fourth century. Theologians like Eusebius believed in the spiritual realities that had been preached by Jesus. Salvation would come through contemplation of the divine, not an obsession with ancient remains which merely reflected the transitory nature of earthly pretensions. However, a new generation of Christian thinkers, who had not endured the persecution that Eusebius and his like had suffered under the Roman emperors, took a different view of the earthly Jesus and his martyrdom on the cross. The crucifixion and the resurrection became the central 'facts' of the life of the historical Jesus and, as a result, the wooden cross on which he died and on which his blood actually flowed became the central symbol of Christianity. Every Christian would be willing to sacrifice his or her own earthly life for it. The presence of such a symbol in battle, even if vastly reduced from its original size, was the signal to Christ's warriors that the Lord was with them in their fight and that the sacrifice that He had made might be required of them in His name.

The location of the True Cross by Helena, who was canonized after the discovery, was the most significant event in the birth of the new Jerusalem, yet the modern historian is left helpless in his search for evidence of its veracity. This tremendous event is probably as mythical as the accounts of the life of Jesus contained in the gospels. Modern cynicism makes us doubt the story of the discovery of the cross; it is altogether too convenient and the fifth-century theologian Sozomen, in his Church history, gives a suspiciously detailed account of the wondrous find. Whether St Helena discovered the cross or not is, of course, less relevant than the fact that the symbol of Christ's death was believed to have been found alongside the symbol of his resurrection. It was what Christians expected to find and where they expected to find it. It was representative rather than actual and bore witness to the faith of those who believed.

One fourth-century pilgrim, Egeria, has left us an interesting and useful account, written in 380, of how the True Cross was used in the Christian services on Good Friday.

The people are dismissed at the Cross even before the sun is up, and those who are more ardent go to Sion to pray at the pillar at which the Lord was scourged. They then go home for a short rest, but it was not long before everyone is assembled for the next service. The bishop's chair is placed on Golgotha behind the Cross, which stands there now. He takes his seat and a table is placed before him with a linen cloth on it. The deacons stand round, and there is brought to him a gold and silver box in which is the Holy Wood of the Cross. It is opened and the Wood of the Cross and the Title are taken out and placed on the table.

As long as the Holy Wood is on the table, the bishop sits with his hands resting on either side of it and holds it down, and the deacons round him keep watch over it. They guard it like this because the custom is that all the people, catechumens as well as the faithful, come up one by one to the table. They lean down over it, kiss the Wood and move on. And it is said that on one occasion one of them bit off a piece of the Holy Wood and stole it away, and for this reason the deacons stand round and keep watch in case anyone dares to do the same again.

Thus all the people go past one by one. They stoop down, touch the Holy Wood and the Inscription with their forehead and then their eyes, then kiss it, but no one dares put out his hand to touch it. When they have kissed the Cross they go to a deacon who stands holding the Ring of Solomon and, the Horn with which the kings were anointed. These they venerate by kissing them, and they start around about eight o'clock, with everyone going by, entering by one door and going out by the other, until midday . . .[29]

During the construction process Constantine sent clear instructions to Bishop Makarius that the complex of the Holy Sepulchre was to be decorated like no other church anywhere. Egeria, writing more than forty years after its completion, gives us a clear idea of just how wonderful the decoration was – ornate mosaics paid for by Constantine, as well as 'eucharistic vessels of silver and gold, and silver textiles with gold borders'. Egeria reveals how Constantine's church, within forty years of his death, had become the centre of the Christian world:

On the seventh day, the Lord's Day, there gather in the courtyard before cock-crow all the people, as many as the place will hold . . .

When the first cock has crowed, the bishop straightway enters and goes into the cave in the Anastasis, and the whole crowd streams into the Anastasis, which is already ablaze with many lamps. When they are inside, a psalm is said by one of the presbyters, and they all respond . . . After these prayers they take censers into the cave of the Anastasis so that the whole basilica is filled with the smell. Then the bishop, standing inside the screen, takes the Gospel and advances to the door, where he himself reads the account of the Lord's Resurrection. At the beginning of the reading the whole assembly groans and laments at all the grievous things that the Lord underwent for us . . . When the Gospel is finished, the bishop comes out and is taken with hymns to the Cross, where they all go with him. They say one psalm there and a prayer, then he blesses the faithful and the dismissal is given . . .

At daybreak, because it is the Lord's day, the people assemble in the Great Church built by Constantine on Golgotha behind the Cross. And they do what is everywhere the custom of the Lord's day. But they have this custom, that any presbyter who is seated there may preach, if he so wishes, and when they have finished, the bishop preaches. The reason why they have this preaching every Lord's day is to make sure that the people will continually be learning about the Scriptures and the love of God. Because of all this preaching it is a long time before they are dismissed from the church, which takes place not before ten or even eleven o'clock.[30]

By this stage, as we can see from Egeria's account, the True Cross was so much a part of the history of the new, Christian Jerusalem that, as a symbol, it exceeded in importance even the Holy Sepulchre itself. Furthermore, pieces of the original wood of the Cross had been sent or taken to the holiest and most worthy sites throughout the Christian empire and, indeed, the Christian world. We know that pieces were sent to Rome and to Constantinople as soon as it was rediscovered by Helena. From the fourth century the cross was clearly accepted by all Christians as the pre-eminent symbol of their faith, while the Holy Sepulchre in Jerusalem became the ultimate destination for all Christian pilgrims.

THREE

The New David

From the time of Constantine the Eastern Roman or Byzantine Empire regarded itself as the earthly representation of heaven itself, with the emperor the 'Chosen' of God and his people the 'Chosen People' in succession to the Jews who, by rejecting and murdering Christ, had lost God's favour. The emperor was both the 'Defender of Christianity' and the 'Champion of Orthodoxy'. All pictures of Byzantine emperors show them with a halo around the head, symbolizing both power and sanctity. An eleventh-century psalter in the Library of St Mark in Venice shows a miniature of the Emperor Basil II (963–1025) which conveys the Byzantines' image of their imperial rulers. The emperor is standing on a jewelled footstool. He is bearded and has a halo. In his right hand he holds a spear and he is dressed in a brilliant, golden cuirass. He has the purple buskins or boots which could only be worn by the emperor and wears a purple tunic, fringed with gold. On his brow an angel has placed a golden diadem, while another angel grasps his spear. Above him, in the sky, Christ holds the Gospels and a golden circlet. Beneath his footstool eight robed figures prostrate themselves in an act of obeisance. The whole impression is of pomp and grandeur, but also complex symbolism in which the emperor is displayed as the link between heaven and earth, between spiritual and temporal things, a representative of God on earth as revealed by his spear and his golden breastplate. He symbolizes holy war.[31]

In earthly terms the empire was surrounded by enemies of God, allies of Antichrist and the progeny of the Devil. These enemies would attempt to damage the Christian empire, capturing its lands, its cities and its people, and hope eventually even to take Constantinople itself, the first Christian city. In defence of God's empire on earth the emperor and his soldiers were justified in fighting in God's name and taking the lives of God's enemies. Thus the empire's campaigns were always designed to enact the will of God and were always holy. This meant that wars undertaken to protect the Christian populations of neighbouring states were both justified and sanctified. For the Byzantines, from the fourth to seventh centuries the neighbouring state with the largest Christian minority was Sasanian Persia and wars with the Persians, notably over Armenia, always had a strong religious element.

From the moment that Constantine created his Christian empire it was inevitable that relations between Rome and Sasanid Persia would be affected by the development of Christianity as a world religion. As an eastern rather than a European religion Christianity was bound to spread into areas beyond Rome's control. Large numbers of Christians were located in Persia even before Constantine's 'conversion'. In 410, a Christian synod was held at Seleucia at which six metropolitan sees and over thirty bishoprics were represented. Two centuries later the numbers had risen to ten metropolitan sees and ninety-six bishoprics. In the seventh century we know that several members of the Sasanian royal family were Christian and so were such high officials as the doctor and chief tax collector of King Khusro II. During his great wars with Heraclius, Khusro had a favourite wife, Shirin, who was herself a Christian. In northern Mesopotamia the majority of the Persian population was Christian and in other areas of the country the Christians formed a substantial minority. The fundamental problem for the Roman or Byzantine emperors was to realize and come to terms with the fact that these Christians were Persian and many of them proud of the fact. Their earthly allegiance was to the Shah not to the self-appointed representative of God on earth, the emperor in Constantinople.

During the successful wars of the Persian kings Shapur I and II during the third century, several large Roman armies came to grief in Persia and many thousands of Roman soldiers and civilians, including Syrian Christians, became prisoners. These Roman Christians were viewed by the Persians as being different from their own native Christians, whom they referred to as *nasraye* or

Nazarenes. The Roman soldiers or Syrian civilians who maintained their Christianity were called *kretyane* and, in spite of living within Persia, their descendants looked to Constantinople for salvation. The Christian community in Persia, whether native or Roman, suffered periodic persecution just as Christianity had in the Roman Empire before Constantine. During wars between the Persians under Shapur II and Bahram V and the Romans there was even suspicion that the Persian Christians were disloyal and favoured their co-religionists. Once it was clear that the 'kingdom of the west' had a Christian emperor in the person of Constantine, the lives of the Christians in Persia deteriorated permanently. [32]

From the fourth century onwards, the Byzantines interpreted their wars against Persia in a religious context. This view was taken up by the Syriac author Aphrahat:

The People of God have received prosperity, and success awaits the man who has been the instrument of that prosperity [Constantine]; but disaster threatens the army which has been gathered together by the efforts of a wicked and proud man puffed up with vanity [Shapur]. . . . The Roman empire will not be conquered, for the hero whose name is Jesus is coming with his power, and his armour will uphold the whole army of the empire.[33]

In the war that immediately followed the death of Constantine in AD 337 the Persian ruler Shapur suffered a humiliating defeat at the hands of the new Christian emperor, Constantius, who not only took the border city of Nisibis in 338 but in so doing captured the Shah's harem. Jews and Manicheans within the Persian army accused Persian Christians of betraying their comrades. Shapur, no doubt feeling bitterly humiliated, was also eager to place the blame on the Christians, accusing their leader Simeon of making his followers 'rebel against my kingdom and convert into servants of Caesar, their coreligionist'. A magus priest of Zoroastra, Mihrshabur, fearing the growing influence of Christianity in Persia, took up the same point in the fifth century in this address to the Shah:

From this moment on, my lord, all the Christians have rebelled against you: they no longer do your will, they despise your orders, they refuse to worship your gods. If the Shah will hear me, let him give orders that the Christians convert from their religion, for they hold the same faith as the Romans, and they are in entire agreement together: should a war interpose between the two empires these Christians will turn out to be defectors from our side in any fighting, and through their playing false they will bring down your power.[34]

Persian Christians were constantly torn by the problem of divided loyalties; even when they did not feel it themselves, they were accused of it or had it forced upon them. Both the Roman and the Sasanian empires were mixtures of many races and religions. From early times the idea of being a Roman was a proud boast for all who lived within the empire but no such nationalism existed in Persia, where religion rather than national origin was the defining feature. This increased the feeling that Christians within the Persian empire were certain to identify with the great Christian state that happened to be their immediate neighbour. The Persian Christians, struggling as a minority for an identity within an empire where Zoroastrianism was the state religion, made matters worse by emphasizing the differences between themselves and their pagan Mithran or Zoroastrian neighbours. They called themselves the 'People of God' or the 'People of Christendom' and adopted such an air of superiority over the followers of Persian religions that they courted persecution and frequently suffered it. As the divisions within eastern Christianity developed in the fifth and sixth centuries, reaching a climax in the early seventh century and opening the way for the spread of Islam, the identification of the Persian Christians with the Roman or Byzantine emperor as defender of Christians everywhere finally came to an end. It had already ceased in Syria and Egypt.

By the end of the sixth century the Roman Empire in the West was a memory only and the survival of the Eastern Empire, now the centre of the *Orbis Romanus* (Roman world), was based on a policy of defence against collapse in the Balkans and the eastern provinces, including Armenia, Syria and Egypt. Constantinople was the centre of both the empire and the Christian world. Yet the empire was united only in its struggle for survival against external foes. Internally it was riven by national and doctrinal differences. When the two differences combined, as in Syria and Egypt, the greatest danger presented itself.

Religion worked to both unite and divide the empire. In 451 the Council of Chalcedon reached a decision which sundered the empire, condemning the theory of Eutychius that Christ had a single nature. This decision alienated the people of the eastern provinces, who henceforth were known as Monophysites. They drew a sharp line between themselves and the Orthodox believers in the western provinces. Moreover, dissatisfaction in the East with the heavy-handed financial and administrative policies of Constantinople meant that separatist movements developed which combined nationalist and religious complaints into a general desire to break away from the centre. Monophysitism and the clergy who represented it thus became leaders of the struggle to break away from Constantinople. When foreign enemies, notably the Persians externally and the Jews internally, threatened the eastern provinces they found that the local Monophysite population either welcomed them as liberators or at least remained neutral, leaving the defence of those provinces to the overstretched Greek garrisons. This weakness was fundamental for any Byzantine emperor and was at its worst during the late sixth and early seventh centuries.

Byzantine policy in the east depended almost entirely on the relationship with the neighbouring Sasanian Persians. From their capital at Ctesiphon, close to present-day Baghdad, the Sasanians had ruled their vast empire since the third century when Ardashir overthrew the Parthians. The Sasanian empire stretched from the Indus river on the borders of India, to the Oxus river and the Caucasus mountain range in the north, Armenia in the west and to the Persian Gulf and Arabia in the south. Just like the Byzantines, the Sasanians faced powerful neighbours. In the east they abutted the Chinese, in the north the Turks and in the west Rome. To the south, not apparent until the seventh century but eventually the most dangerous neighbours of all, were the Arabs.

For much of the sixth century the Byzantines and Persians were involved in frontier warfare, tedious to relate and financially crippling to the economies of both states in view of the catastrophic climactic effects that followed the immense volcanic explosion of Krakatoa in 535.[35] When civil war broke out in Persia in 590 it was to have disastrous long-term consequences for both empires. The conflict originated from a defeat suffered at the hands of the Byzantines by the Persians under their general Bahram Chubin, a national hero and a great warrior 'as proud as a male lion' with 'a magnificent, stature, ready speech and clear intelligence'. Bahram had already won victories in the north against the Turks and the Khazars and so his defeat by the Byzantine general Romanus was both a surprise and a disappointment to King Hormuzd, who responded rather inappropriately by sending the great hero a woman's dress and a distaff. The insult was obvious. Bahram immediately rebelled against the king and marched on the capital, Ctesiphon. Hormuzd sent an army against him but Bahram, his ire fully roused, routed the royal force. In Ctesiphon Hormuzd was blinded, murdered and replaced by his son Khusro II. However, Bahram was not satisfied and drove the new king from the throne, taking it for himself and proclaiming himself 'Lord of the world'. Bahram's rule represented a break with the Sasanian royal family; he was a member of the Mihr-ran family of Rayy, and as such was resented by many conservative Persians, who preferred the legitimate heir, Khusro.

Khusro, meanwhile, fled across the border into Byzantine territory and sent a letter to the Emperor Maurice, calling on him to come to the aid of a legitimate ruler overthrown by a usurper. Khusro offered Maurice incentives, including the return of the recently captured Byzantine cities of Dara and Martyropolis, as well as Persian Armenia, over which the two empires had been fighting for fifty years. It was an attractive proposition. Bahram, when he heard what Khusro was offering, made his own approach to Maurice, asking him not to help Khusro in return for certain lands and cities. The Byzantines were divided. Most of the emperor's senior officials felt it was safer not to help Khusro, leaving the usurper on the throne and much in their debt. Maurice, on the other hand, felt he would rather have the legitimate Sasanian ruler in his debt. He overruled his advisers.

Maurice's decision was a disastrous mistake. It condemned the Byzantines to a new war with Persia.[36] At this time financial constraints were extreme: the empire was slowly recovering from a severe outbreak of bubonic plague, second only in intensity in the whole of human history to the Black Death of the 1340s. It has been estimated that the population of the Byzantine Empire fell by at least a third in the second half of the sixth century, with a consequent collapse in tax revenue. Moreover, the continued threats from the Avars in the empire's Balkan region meant that if troops were to be transferred to the eastern front for use against the Persians, the only policy available against the Avars was to buy them off with huge payments of gold which the empire could not afford.

Nevertheless, Maurice committed himself to restoring Khusro to the Persian throne and by doing so virtually signed his own death warrant. At first, all seemed to go well. As the Byzantine army under Narses invaded Persia, many troops flocked to support Khusro against Bahram. The usurper abandoned Ctesiphon and made a last stand in Atropatene where he was defeated in a decisive battle by Narses and Khusro. Bahram fled to his erstwhile enemies, the Turks, who murdered him once they saw no further use in supporting him. Khusro regained his throne and rewarded his Byzantine allies with treasure and territory. For the rest of Maurice's reign relations with Persia remained peaceful. However, in the Balkans the Avar threat had grown.

Maurice had made financial cutbacks in the army so that he could bribe the Avars to keep the peace while he was at war in Persia. The effect of this on his soldiers was obvious. While he remained victorious they would hold their hand but if matters took a turn for the worse in the Balkans he would face mutiny and perhaps even overthrow. Maurice continued to try to cut the costs of his wars in the Balkans, campaigning through the winter and ordering his troops to live off the country and feed themselves. The army commander, Priscus, tried to countermand the emperor's orders and lead his forces into winter quarters at Odessa on the Black Sea, but he was dismissed by Maurice and replaced by the emperor's brother, Peter. The new commander soon recognized that Maurice was asking too much of his men and when he pressed the emperor for improved conditions he too was dismissed and Priscus was reinstated. Byzantine troops were dispersed all over the Balkans on foraging expeditions and were in no position to resist a massive invasion by the Avars, who advanced almost to the walls of Constantinople.

Maurice prepared the city garrison and the Blues and Greens, the circus factions, to defend his capital but fate intervened and they were not needed. The Avars began to contract bubonic plague (in fact the khagan lost seven of his sons to the disease) and agreed to withdraw from Byzantine territory in return for the enormous sum of 120,000 gold pieces. Maurice agreed to pay, virtually bankrupting the state in the process. However, the emperor had no intention of letting the Avars get away with his money. Once they had withdrawn from the environs of the capital he sent Priscus after them to exploit the weaknesses caused by the plague. He won four victories over the Avars and removed them as an immediate threat.

Maurice next ordered his brother Peter to campaign north of the Danube against the Slav (Sclaveni) tribes there, which meant that the troops would have to spend another bitter winter in enemy territory. This was the final straw and the army mutinied. Peter fled back to Constantinople and a centurion named Phocas was raised on a shield by his comrades in the fashion employed when selecting a new emperor. We will never know how serious the centurions were in their intentions. Suffice it to say that events moved fast and Phocas was swept along with them. To make matters worse, the Constantinople masses were enraged when the grain ships from North Africa were delayed by bad weather; food shortages were always likely to bring the people onto the streets demanding the overthrow of the emperor. When news of the army mutiny reached the capital the Blues and the Greens organized opposition to the emperor. Although they had originally taken their names from the colours worn by chariot teams in hippodromes throughout the empire, by this time the factions had become almost political parties and had other ceremonial and even military functions.[37] They could make or break emperors and that is what happened in 602. When Maurice fled with his family from Constantinople to the Asian shore, taking refuge in the church of Autonomus the Martyr, the Green faction, favouring Phocas because he was a relatively junior officer and not one of the aristocratic gang who had brought the empire to its knees, had their man proclaimed emperor. This was a death sentence for Maurice, and Phocas sent one of his cronies, Lilius, to carry out the killing. However, before Lilius arrived, Maurice sent a letter to the Persian Shah Khusro II asking for his help, and reminding him of how he had once needed help himself. Maurice did not live to get a reply for he was trapped with his children on the harbour side where he and his five sons were murdered. His wife and three daughters were dragged off to a nunnery.[38]

The events that followed during the reign of Phocas fill some of the blackest pages in Byzantine history. It was as if the excesses of the Roman emperors Caligula and Nero had returned, with the added element of foreign invasion from both east and west. In the eyes of both contemporary chroniclers and of modern historians Phocas came close to destroying the empire nearly a thousand years before its eventual fall in 1453, and eastern Christianity along with it.

Genetics as well as the pen of the chroniclers typecast the two main protagonists in the events of 602–10. The villain – Phocas – was elderly, ugly and red haired, we are told. He had thick eyebrows and an scar on his cheek which throbbed and darkened when he was angry. He was a drunken killer, a devourer of women and an irreligious beast.[39] In contrast, the hero – Heraclius – was golden haired, blue eyed, with a golden beard. Naturally he wore white armour and took the icon of the Mother of God with him on his 'crusade' to overthrow Phocas in 610.

Reading between the lines, Phocas was cunning and sly, and not absurdly ambitious. He was no megalomaniac as the insane early Roman emperors had been. He knew his limits and tried to operate within them. Events were just too big for him to control. He had probably been an efficient soldier in the army but his level of command was no preparation for the task of being emperor. He was a 'small' man with 'small' vices, overwhelmed by the opportunities that suddenly came his way. Unable to intellectualize the problems he encountered, he fell back on what he knew best – ferocious force and bullying cruelty. When Phocas heard that the dead emperor had sent a request for help to the Persian king Khusro, he was faced with the problem of how to cope with such a powerful ruler who would inevitably view him as a usurper and a regicide. His solution was typically cunning and utterly disloyal to those who had supported him. He appointed his companion Lilius, the man who had been sent to slaughter Maurice and his children, as ambassador to Persia. Then he sent this veritable scapegoat to Ctesiphon to present his credentials. Lilius was either very brave or very stupid. Khusro, bitterly angry at Maurice's fate, simply threw him in prison and treated him so badly that he quickly died. It was just the first death in what Khusro planned to be a very bloody revenge, for he honestly regarded the murdered Maurice as his 'father' and was determined to punish those who had killed him and usurped his throne.

The complex machinations which preceded the last and greatest Romano-Persian war do not concern us here. Suffice it to say that Khusro began in all good faith what he saw as an honourable war to destroy Phocas. Unfortunately, he got so used to the part of 'avenger' that he continued to play it when the Byzantine 'saviour' Heraclius arrived. Ultimately he became a conqueror in the style of his great ancestors Shapur I and Shapur II. Khusro initially claimed, and later convinced himself, that his war was not with the Byzantine people but merely with Phocas. However, to his mind one usurper was the same as another and he viewed the overthrow of Heraclius as just as much part of his vengeance as the destruction of Phocas himself. Soon Khusro began to see himself as the sword of history, putting an end to a millennium of warfare between East and West, reversing the conquests of the Devil – Alexander the Great – and putting an end to Rome and Christianity in a single stroke by taking Constantinople. It was not a mad vision at all. Between 622 and 626 the Persian king came closer to crushing Byzantium than anyone until the Ottoman Turks 800 years later.

Claiming to represent Theodosius, son of the dead emperor Maurice, who it was rumoured had somehow escaped the slaughter on the quayside, Khusro tested out the Byzantine defences in the east by a series of destructive raids, during which the great city of Dara fell. Dara was a powerful strongpoint and should have been able to withstand a Persian siege. A Byzantine army sent to break the attack was soundly beaten by Khusro near Edessa. Phocas, panicking at this first setback, made a catastrophic agreement with the Avars in the Balkans and moved all his troops to the eastern front. Here, in another great but thinly documented battle, the Byzantines were overwhelmed by the massed elephants of Khusro's army and thousands were taken prisoner. The huge payments Phocas had made to keep the Avars quiet had precisely the opposite effect: realizing that the new Byzantine emperor was not the man his predecessor had been and that Phocas was acting out of weakness, the Avars broke their agreement with him and swarmed into Byzantine territory, brushing aside the now pitiful military forces available to guard the region.

Once Khusro found that the morale of the Byzantine army had virtually collapsed and that its best generals were no longer available, he changed his strategy from raiding to long-term conquest. The absence of Maurice's most able commanders was perhaps the greatest problem Phocas faced. He could hardly leave such men in command of his forces without facing an immediate attempt to remove him. Yet without them his eastern armies were no match for the Persians. Ironically, one of Maurice's best generals, Heraclius the Elder, had taken up the post of Exarch of Africa just before Maurice's fall in 602 and so had been out of Phocas's reach when he seized the throne. While his absence from the battle fronts in the east may have cost the empire dear, in the long run his safety in Africa enabled him to make the eventually decisive move to overthrow the tyrant and save the empire.

Between 607 and 609 Khusro concentrated all his forces on major invasions of Byzantine Mesopotamia. His most able general, Ferouk Khan, nicknamed Shahrvaraz or the 'Royal Wild Boar', led the main army, capturing all the Byzantine territory south of the Euphrates river, including the great city of Edessa. Khusro was surprised not only by the feeble resistance of the Byzantine armies but by the hostility shown by the local Monophysite population to their Greek Orthodox rulers and the welcome the inhabitants of the captured towns gave to Shahrvaraz. The latter, more astute than his master, responded by handing over the captured Orthodox monasteries and churches for the use of the Monophysites.

Meanwhile, a second Persian army commanded by Shahen Patgospan, advanced across the Anatolian plateau, reaching Chalcedon, just a short sea journey from Constantinople itself. No enemy had ever penetrated so deeply into Byzantine territory and but for the lack of a fleet Shahen might have taken the capital in 609. However, he had to withdraw from this advanced position because his supplies were not adequate to maintain a siege at that time. The southern wing of his huge army had, meanwhile, captured Caesarea in Cappadocia, one of the pivots of the entire Byzantine

defensive system. However, lack of supplies now forced the two
Persian armies to pull back to Persian territory to reorganize and
prepare for the following year's campaigns.

As well as boosting the confidence of his eastern enemies through
the feeble resistance shown by his armies, Phocas had unwittingly
saved his Balkan enemies, the Avars, from virtual extinction. Under
pressure from the Emperor Maurice their confederation of tribes
had begun to disintegrate and various Slavic groups, notably the
Gepids and the Bulgars, had begun to assert their independence.
However, the accession of Phocas to the imperial throne in 602 had
transformed the situation, removing the Byzantine threat from the
Avars and allowing them to re-establish their control over their Slav
vassals. The Avars could hardly believe their luck. As they and their
Slav allies now poured across the Danube they encountered no
resistance from the Byzantine authorities, Phocas having moved all
his troops to the eastern front. They were able to plunder Roman
territory before settling in the deserted towns and villages. The
situation in the Balkans was virtually beyond repair, with even the
great city of Thessalonika being besieged by Slav troops for the first
time in generations.

Discontent with Phocas had reached boiling point by the beginning of 609. A hard winter – we are told that the sea froze – combined with the non-arrival of the usual grain shipments from Africa
and from Egypt to make life almost intolerable for the poorer classes
of Constantinople. Public discontent, centred on the Green faction,
broke out when the emperor's late arrival at the hippodrome delayed
the start of the races. When he eventually entered the stadium he
was met with angry chants accusing him of drunkenness. Phocas lost
his temper and ordered his troops to attack the Greens. There followed a massacre of Green supporters: many were cut down where
they stood, others were tortured and strung up to die slowly in the
hippodrome itself. The hostility between Phocas and the Greens now
spilled over into the streets as a state of virtual civil war gripped the
city. As buildings burned all around him Phocas panicked, trying to
buy off his enemies and undo some of the harm he had done over
the previous seven years. But it was too late for that.[40]

Outside the capital, enemies queued up to demonstrate their
contempt for how far Roman greatness had fallen since the heady

days of Justinian and Belisarius, even of Maurice. Inside Constantinople Phocas fought a microcosmic version of the external struggle against enemies both real and imagined. Maurice's generals Germanus and Philippicus became monks and entered monasteries to escape execution. In the streets the Blue and Green factions fought, setting fire to parts of the city and ultimately destroying the central area of Constantinople. Phocas had no answer except to have John Kroukis, one of the leading Greens, burned alive. Attempts to overthrow the emperor failed because like so many tyrants he seemed to have a charmed life. When one plot failed Phocas had Constantia, the ex-empress and wife of the murdered Maurice, tortured and then killed, along with her three daughters. Other suspected plotters were eliminated with extreme brutality. The Patricians Theodore and Anastasius were respectively whipped to death and beheaded, while the Governor of Sicily, Elpidius, was mutilated by having his hands, feet, ears and tongue cut off; he was then burned alive. As both foreign and domestic affairs grew more desperate it was almost as if Phocas wished to bring the whole state down with him. It was a contest to see whether the Avars, the Persians or Phocas himself would achieve the final overthrow of the empire. Having already reversed Maurice's wise policy of religious toleration Phocas began to persecute both the Monophysites and the Jews, driving the latter to welcome the Persian invaders of the eastern provinces with open arms.

When he overthrew the Emperor Maurice in 602 Phocas had swept away all those who had supported the old regime. However, he had not dared to remove the immensely able and popular Exarch of Africa, Heraclius the Elder, who was one of Maurice's best generals and the man who controlled much of the grain shipment to Constantinople. Phocas clearly underestimated Heraclius, assuming that at sixty-eight he was too old to be a real threat in person and that his loyalty to the empire would prevent him from supporting rebellion against the established emperor. As events were to prove, Phocas had misjudged his man. In the first place, Heraclius's loyalty was to the empire rather than the emperor. He had been a friend and loyal colleague of Maurice and had received the Exarchate of Africa as a reward for his services during the extensive Persian wars. When Maurice fell in 602 Heraclius's lack of action was not an acceptance of a *fait accompli*, it was based on a realization that he was not strong enough to face the usurper. To control his huge territories in North Africa he had an army of just 18,000 men, hardly adequate to keep the desert tribes in order let alone invade Europe and overthrow Phocas and the full might of the empire. The decision to bide his time was also to be a feature of his son's policy at times of crisis.

During Phocas's orgy of terror in the capital, Heraclius the Elder was approached by members of the Senate and established contact with Priscus, the military strong-man whom Phocas had attempted to win over by marrying him to his daughter Domentzia. Something of a trimmer, Priscus waited to see who would emerge the winner in the coming crisis. More important even than Priscus was the Green faction, which Phocas had alienated and which willingly offered support when Heraclius sent emissaries. In one respect, however, Phocas had been right: Heraclius the Elder was too old to lead the rebellion except symbolically. Nor would he be a candidate for the throne once Phocas was overthrown and Priscus saw himself as the likely winner, whatever the outcome of the African revolt. If Phocas won then Priscus as a close relative, his brother-in-law, might easily succeed him. If Heraclius won then Priscus was the strong man on the scene and would certainly be offered the throne.

At this time little had been heard of Heraclius the Younger, at thirty-three no stripling, but still a man with no great victories to his name. The Exarch, probably on the advice of the Senate, appointed his son as Consul and issued coins in Carthage with both himself and his son represented. The aim of making the younger Heraclius consul was to elevate him to a position where he could be seen as a legitimate alternative to Phocas as emperor. Phocas, having simply been a usurper, would have his legitimacy reduced and Heraclius, supported as he was by the Senate, would have his increased.

Unknown to Phocas the plotting continued in both Carthage and Constantinople. Heraclius the Elder and his brother Gregory, who acted as his second-in-command, planned the strategy for a land and sea operation against the capital, using their economic weapon, the grain supply, to impose a stranglehold on Phocas. Egypt, notably the great city of Alexandria, was the key to the campaign. It was agreed that Gregory's son Nicetas would lead an army along the coast from

Carthage and overcome the pro-Phocas forces in Egypt. While he did this Heraclius the Younger would take the fleets of Mauritania and Africa to Constantinople and, hopefully, overthrow Phocas in person. What was to happen next remained undecided. As leader of the elite Excubitores, Priscus would seem to have been the obvious choice for emperor and, indeed, it is reported that the younger Heraclius offered him the throne but, as we shall see, the Greens would not accept Phocas's son-in-law and so by default Heraclius was chosen.

The land operations under Nicetas have, not surprisingly, been overshadowed by the glamour that surrounded his cousin's triumph. Nevertheless, it should not be overlooked that Heraclius owed much to Nicetas at this stage. Militarily it was a touch-and-go situation for the pro- and anti-Phocas forces.[41] Neither Nicetas nor the imperial governor of Egypt had large forces and opinion inside Egypt was divided, some seeing one usurper as little better than another. As Nicetas moved along the African coast he gained support from the governors of Libya and Mauritania but in other places he had to fight his way through hostile troops. The first major battle was fought near the Drakus Canal to the west of Alexandria and resulted in a close victory for Nicetas. The head of the imperial governor was struck off and sent to Alexandria where it prompted an immediate rising of the people led by the Coptic Christians who murdered the Patriarch, symbol as he was of the hated Orthodox Church in Constantinople.

Nicetas appeared to have won control of Egypt but now a more formidable enemy appeared in the shape of Bonosus, one of Phocas's best generals, who had been sent with reinforcements to the coastal city of Caesarea. The tide of war suddenly turned against Nicetas as Bonosus invaded the Nile Delta and began a reign of terror there, massacring Copts and rebels alike. Near Athrib the rebels suffered a disastrous defeat after which four of their senior generals were executed. Meanwhile, imperial ships under Pavlus besieged Alexandria where Nicetas was trapped with the remnants of his small army. The future of the whole rebellion now hinged on how effectively Nicetas could organize the local forces there. Aware that the rebellion would fail if he was bottled up for too long in the city, Nicetas decided to fight Bonosus outside its walls. He packed the battlements of Alexandria with stone-throwers and various missile-firing soldiers while he arrayed his local troops in front of the Gate of the Sun on the road that led to Heliopolis. Taking personal control of his regulars from Carthage, he held them in reserve. Bonosus was as desperate as Nicetas to achieve an immediate victory and launched a frontal assault on the rebel troops. Before the imperial soldiers could come to grips with the inexperienced local levies they were hit by missiles fired from the city walls and suffered heavy casualties. Seizing his opportunity, Nicetas had a side gate to the city opened and led his reserves, his best troops, into the confused imperial ranks. This was the decisive moment and Bonosus was forced to flee the field, leaving the rebels in complete command of the Nile Delta.

Bonosus was a doughty opponent and tried to keep the war going but his numbers were now too few to risk a battle. He therefore tried to assassinate Nicetas and when this attempt failed he fled to Constantinople. This was a signal for a bitter internecine struggle between followers of the factions, the Greens and the Blues in Alexandria. The Greens had supported the rebels throughout and after Nicetas's victory they could now settle old scores with their Blue enemies, who had sided with Bonosus. Only the personal intervention of Nicetas and his victorious troops prevented a bloodbath. As ruler of Egypt, Nicetas showed greater wisdom than any preceding Roman governor, and he was greatly loved by the people.

Meanwhile, Heraclius the Younger, from this point to be known simply as Heraclius, was on the African coast preparing the naval operation against Phocas in Constantinople. The deeply religious nature of the operation, little less than a crusade even though the word is hardly appropriate at this early stage, was clearly demonstrated by the choice of the Virgin to be the icon raised to the topmast of all the ships in the fleet. Heraclius was coming as the much awaited saviour of his people and the city of God from the foul atrocities of the tyrant Phocas.

Heraclius sailed in late spring 610 with a fleet of vessels manned by local Maroi berbers, but did not make directly for Constantinople. He needed to prepare the way by advertising himself as the 'coming man' so that by the time he struck against Phocas there would be an air of inevitability about it. He sailed from island to island working up support and gaining many reinforcements, mainly from the Green faction. In September he captured Abydos at the mouth of the Hellespont and began making public approaches to senators in the capital. At Calonymos he was publicly blessed by Stephen, Bishop of Kyzicos, and some kind of crowning process took place amidst public acclamation.

Phocas was already psychologically a beaten man. News from Egypt of Nicetas's victory over Bonosus prepared him for what was about to happen. The loss of his fleet in the fighting around Alexandria meant that he could not now challenge Heraclius at sea and his eventual response had a fatalistic air. He took as hostages Epiphaneia, Heraclius's mother, and Fabia, his fiancée, and had them conveyed to the Monastery of Nea Metanoia under guard. The Phocas of 602 had inspired terror in his enemies and one can only wonder in disbelief that Heraclius could really have left his womenfolk to be taken hostage in this way. As commander of the Excubitore guards, Priscus remained Phocas's best hope of resisting Heraclius's rebellion. But Phocas could not be certain of the general's loyalty. When he ordered Priscus to guard the Hippodrome the general refused on the grounds of ill-health. Bonosus, returned from defeat in Egypt, stayed loyal to Phocas and advised the emperor to have Priscus killed. Phocas demurred and the moment passed. He then made the cardinal error of calling out the Greens to guard a section of the city walls even though he must have known that as soon as these men saw Heraclius approaching they would desert to him. It was as if the emperor was acting the part of the scapegoat in a Greek play: his fate was sealed but he must follow the proprieties.

News that Heraclius was approaching the city was enough to bring the Greens thronging from the city walls they had been left to guard. To prevent any harm coming to Epiphaneia and Fabia, Green soldiers stormed the monastery where they were being held and freed them, taking them to Calonymos to be reunited with Heraclius himself.

Eventually, on Saturday 3 October 610, Heraclius sailed within sight of Constantinople. For the last few miles the shores were lined with multitudes cheering the blond warrior in his magnificent white armour who was coming under the icon of the Virgin to save his people. Phocas, like the archetypal villain that he was, mounted his warhorse and rode back within the city walls, having watched his nemesis approaching.

Aboard his flagship, Heraclius received precise details of his enemy's movements from within the city. When he heard that the Greens were garrisoning the harbour at Sophia he took his ships in, certain of a friendly welcome. When the vessels hove into sight of Sophia the favourite charioteer of the Greens, Kalliopas Trimolae-mis, resplendent in the silver regalia of his exalted rank within the faction, had himself rowed out to the tip of the mole to give the signal to all the Greens that the revolt was to begin. At once fighting broke out between troops loyal to Phocas and those who were in favour of Heraclius. Bonosus, as usual, was in the thick of the fighting, burning part of the harbour area to keep the Greens at bay. But it was too late for countermeasures. Support for Heraclius spread throughout the city like a tidal wave. Bonosus, trying to escape in a boat, was transfixed by a lance and lifted, wriggling like a fish, into the air. With his death, support for Phocas crumbled and the Greens began settling scores with their Blue enemies, many of whom fled and took refuge in Hagia Sophia. Phocas was arrested by senators and officials, stripped of his finery and bound in chains. He was then dragged down to the Sophia harbour where Heraclius's fleet was now anchored. The ex-emperor was rowed out to the ship that carried Heraclius.

The scene on the deck has an almost Shakespearian theatricality about it. The wretched Phocas sprawled at the feet of his conqueror while Heraclius carried out the *calcato colli*, or ritual trampling.[42] Nevertheless, Phocas showed more courage now than at any stage of the revolt.

'Is it thus', Heraclius is reported as saying to Phocas, 'that you have governed the Empire?' It was easy for him to stand there, secure in the knowledge that every eye was on him and every arm at his service. But Phocas was defiant. He looked up at the face of Heraclius and asked coldly, 'Will you govern it any better?' It was a bitter question but in the years to come it must have often occurred to Heraclius that only minutes before his execution, Phocas was inspired. Whatever doubts Heraclius may have had, they were to be reflected upon in solitude and were not for that glorious moment. He found himself grinding his teeth. He wanted to kill Phocas himself, there and then, hacking the body with his own strong arm, but now that he was the emperor he was God's representative on earth. His word was law and at his command the wretched Phocas was dragged away to execution. Other hands did the killing, but they acted with Heraclius's authority. It was his first command as emperor.

In the euphoria of the moment Heraclius was swept up and carried along by a popularity that few emperors – indeed, few men – ever know. He was acclaimed the new Constantine, chosen of God and protected by the Virgin herself. The Patriarch Sergius lost no time in carrying out the ceremonies that established the new regime. The next day, 5 October, Heraclius was crowned emperor in the Palace Church of St Stephanus and then immediately married the exquisite Fabia, who henceforth was known by the name Eudokia (Esteemed). With the private ceremonies completed, Heraclius went to the great Hagia Sophia, where he was welcomed by the thronging crowds of well-wishers. It would have been easy for him to lose contact with the reality of the situation in the presence of such acclamation. Everyone was willing him to succeed but would that be enough in the difficult days ahead?

We know virtually nothing of Heraclius before his expedition to Constantinople. It is likely that he served with his father in the Persian wars, though latterly he had been with the Exarch in Africa. He was not noted for having independent commands, though in view of the fact that much of the previous decade had been dominated by the unpopular rule of Phocas, it is likely that Heraclius had confined himself to the warfare in the deserts of North Africa. His chief friend and adviser seems to have been his cousin Nicetas, but when Heraclius was crowned emperor Nicetas remained in Egypt. Heraclius had proved to be a worthy son to his father but the latter did not live to act as adviser to the new emperor. No sooner had Heraclius sent the joyous news of his success back to Carthage than his father was taken ill and died. His uncle, Gregory, father of Nicetas, might have filled the role of adviser but the new emperor realized that he was too important to bring back from Africa and appointed him Exarch to succeed Heraclius the Elder. The chief advisers of the Emperor Maurice had not survived the tyranny of Phocas and so for a while Heraclius had to look to younger, more inexperienced men. It was an unenviable position for any new emperor in view of the external threats to the empire.

The chroniclers of the period have left us a fairly full picture of the man. At thirty-five he was already middle-aged by the time he came to the throne, and he is presented as mature rather than callow, manly rather than boyish. Although we know that his family was Armenian, or at least Cappadocian, the chronicles present him as almost 'Nordic', with beautiful blue eyes, fair skin, blond hair and a blond beard. Although not tall he was noted for being very strong and unusually athletic. He was obviously trained as a warrior but was still singled out for his immense feats of strength. He was by no means stolid, in spite of his strength, but had something of the 'beau sabreur' about him at certain moments and was a daring if thoughtful commander. The poet George of Pisidia, not surprisingly, presents his emperor and patron as a perfect human being, both a soldier and a scholar in the tradition of great emperors like Marcus Aurelius.

During his triumphs in the 620s Heraclius was to be equated with the biblical figure of David, both as a triumphant warrior-king and as the man who united the nation of Israel. Like David, Heraclius had not come to his throne by orderly succession but by slaying a tyrant; for Goliath, read Phocas or indeed Khusro. Whether such a biblical image was in anybody's mind in October 610 as they saw the blond-haired hero in the prow of his ship, under the icon of the Mother of God, is doubtful. But after the dark times endured since the reign of Justinian, the Christian empire had every reason to hope for better times under this 'New David'.

FOUR

The Wild Boar

The reign of the Emperor Heraclius began with a huge earthquake in Constantinople and its meaning was interpreted in many different ways. The emperor, something of an astrologer himself, never made public his view of its significance. The Patriarch Sergius responded to the natural disaster with prayers and litanies. The people of the capital waited until the dust settled.

In his search for advisers Heraclius began by turning to one of the few men who had survived the reign of Phocas with his reputation still intact, the late emperor's son-in-law, Priscus. With the military situation on the Persian border close to catastrophe Heraclius appointed Priscus commander-in-chief. Priscus misjudged the new emperor and began to assume that the friendship sought by Heraclius was a sign of weakness. When matters did not improve in the East the emperor offered to come to visit Priscus in his camp. As he had with Phocas, Priscus claimed he was too ill to receive him but Heraclius turned up anyway only to receive an unfriendly reception from his commander. He retired to Constantinople to consult the Patriarch Sergius and his cousin Nicetas who, by chance, was visiting the capital. The three men decided to summon Priscus to the city to confront him before the Senate. When Priscus arrived he found that Heraclius had surrounded himself with friends. The emperor now upbraided his commander for insulting him. He is recorded as taking a copy of the Gospels and, lightly tapping his general on the head, he said, 'You were a bad son-in-law; how can you become a good friend?'[43]

Heraclius passed his first test. He had anticipated that Priscus might raise a revolt against him and had pre-empted him. All was enacted within the law and without undue drama. The Senate decreed that Priscus should give up his command and retire to a monastery. Nicetas was given command of the Excubitores, the imperial guard, and when he returned to Egypt the powerful unit was incorporated within the regular army. There were to be no praetorians to make or break emperors as in the days of ancient Rome.

On the battlefront, the Persian invasion of Syria culminated in the capture of Antioch in 611 by Shahrvaraz, greatest of Sasanian generals. Nicetas hurried northwards from Egypt with the forces he could muster to try to stop the Persian advance. Near Emesa the Byzantines and the Persians met in a sanguinary drawn battle at the Monastery of St Thomas. The result was the best Heraclius could have hoped for. The battle halted the Persian advance but it did nothing to regain territory lost in the last years of Phocas's disastrous reign. In fact, Byzantine territory between Emesa and the Euphrates, once an area of urban development and brilliant civilization, had been turned into a desert with Greek towns and religious buildings left as ruins.

Meanwhile, Cappadocia suffered a devastating Persian invasion under Shahen. With his resources stretched to breaking point Heraclius could do nothing to regain the ground lost here. By the start of 613 the Persian king Khusro II believed that he was close to overthrowing Roman power in Asia. At Constantinople Heraclius was cut off from any land route to Syria, Palestine and Egypt. Only the survival of the Byzantine navy enabled the empire to avoid being broken in half and losing control of its grain supply from Africa. In 613 the Byzantine state was at its nadir. Invasions by Persians, Slavs and Avars were widespread and the army had almost disintegrated. The best officers had been purged in the overthrow of Maurice and the soldiers, many of them mercenaries, were accustomed to defeat. Chroniclers record that many soldiers sought refuge in monasteries.

Personal tragedy now struck the emperor. One of the happiest results of his overthrow of Phocas had been his marriage to the beautiful and much-loved Fabia-Eudokia, by whom he had two children in their first two years of marriage. However, in August 612 Fabia died suddenly and was buried in the imperial mausoleum at the Church of the Holy Apostles. Her funeral included a curious incident which shows the volatility of the Constantinopolitan crowd. The open coffin of the dead empress was being taken through the streets of the capital, which were crowded with grieving onlookers. In one street, presumably narrower than most, a servant girl spat from an upstairs window just as the open coffin passed underneath; her spittle landed on the dead face. Pandemonium broke out at this unintentional but deeply insulting incident and the crowds dragged the wretched girl from her house and burned her alive.[44]

What followed the death of Fabia has divided historians of the period. The grieving emperor either made an immediate and catastrophic marriage to his niece, Martina, breaking the laws of incest and alienating the Church and his people and, in direct consequence, bringing down disaster on the empire, or he remained single for eleven years before his incestuous marriage to Martina, leaving just one son to succeed him and that boy, no more than a year old, susceptible to all the ailments of childhood. Without new evidence one is left with a choice between two unsatisfactory options. We simply do not know whether Heraclius married his niece, apparently at the suggestion of his mother, in 613 or in 623. Strong cases can be made for both dates but each contains fatal flaws. The coins issued in the year 616 contain a female face alongside the emperor; is this the face of his new wife Martina or is it the little princess Epiphaneia, then just fifteen months old? It was not unknown for children to be displayed on coins with 'adult' faces, so the answer is not as obvious as it seems. All that we know for sure is that when Heraclius did marry Martina it earned him the hostility of the majority of the people, who viewed the union as incestuous.

Theophanes records the 'earlier' marriage of Heraclius and Martina in 613; Nicephorus the 'later' one in 623.[45] Probability and common sense have to guide us here in the absence of historical evidence and they tend to favour an earlier marriage for a number of reasons. While not universally true, it was usual for a royal head of state to provide for the succession by marrying and fathering a number of sons. It was also common for leading members of the government and the army to prefer a legitimate succession by the eldest son or the chosen blood relative of the ruler to avoid the inevitable civil war that results from a disputed succession. In this case pressure might be brought to bear on a ruler to marry and provide heirs.

Heraclius was a middle-aged bachelor of thirty-five when he came to the throne. We do not know enough about his family background to do more than hypothesize as to why such an attractive personality, and one who obviously enjoyed marriage when it eventually came, should have remained single for so long. The likeliest explanation is that he was a career soldier who was 'married' to the army. Events in Constantinople, however, during the reign of Phocas, brought him into the limelight once it was agreed that his father would be too old to lead the revolt against Phocas and succeed to the throne. From 608 onwards, marriage became a necessity for Heraclius. He and Fabia-Eudokia were very happy and had two children, including a son named Constantine, who was born in 612 and was obviously destined to be his father's eventual successor. However, it is virtually unknown for a royal head of state to rely on just one son to survive to adulthood and assume the throne. Plague was common in sixth and seventh century Constantinople, and the epilepsy suffered by his mother might strike down the baby son. The likelihood is that Heraclius hoped for further sons from his beloved Fabia, but when Fabia died in August 612, he was left alone with his two young children. We have evidence that his infant daughter Epiphaneia was crowned Augusta in early 613.

Having been on the throne for just three years, Heraclius found himself a widower with just one son. At thirty-eight he was no longer a young man and had to face the danger of failing to provide for the succession. We know that his mother Epiphaneia was still at court and likely to be influential, at least in the domestic side of the emperor's life. It would have been surprising if neither she, nor the Patriarch Sergius, nor even his closest friends like his cousin Nicetas, did not encourage him to marry again. Whatever his emotional state, he would have realized that he had a duty to God to preserve the peace and order in his lands which a secured succession would facilitate.

Heraclius must have known Martina as a niece before he considered her as a wife. Assuming that his sister Maria, Martina's mother, was three to five years younger than the emperor himself, then Martina was probably in her mid teens when she became empress, young but not uniquely so. It was Heraclius's mother who first suggested Martina as a wife to her son and, once his mind was made up, he apparently became infatuated. He faced up to the severest criticism of the Church and of his people in order to marry her. When he heard what the emperor intended to do the Patriarch Sergius told Heraclius that the marriage to Martina would be illegal and incestuous in the eyes of the Church. There was also opposition from within the family, presumably on the same grounds, from the emperor's brother Theodore, one of his most powerful supporters. We do not hear what his influential cousin, Nicetas, thought of the marriage. Significantly, Constantine, Heraclius's son by Fabia-Eudokia, married Gregoria, the daughter of Nicetas, in 629, also an incestuous union of second cousins.

At first, Sergius refused to perform the marriage of Heraclius and Martina. However, once he realized how determined Heraclius was to go through with it the patriarch adopted a more pragmatic approach. There was no doubting the popularity of the emperor or of his dead wife and his two children, particularly the infant Constantine. This side of the equation would have to be balanced against the inevitable unpopularity of the incestuous couple, of the new empress Martina and of the emperor's subsequent children by her. In view of the disastrous reign of Phocas the empire needed a man like Heraclius and therefore the Church must compromise on the marriage, although the people never would. Thereafter, the unpopularity of the union was made clear whenever the imperial couple appeared in public. Even the Greens, who had always favoured Heraclius and had made a major contribution to his successful revolt against Phocas, jeered the royal couple at the Hippodrome.[46]

The first two sons born to Heraclius and Martina after 613 had disabilities, something everyone assumed to be God's judgement. Fabius, the first child, had a paralysed neck and the second, Theodosios, was a deaf mute. Of their subsequent children, at least two more had severe problems and four died between 624 and 628. These domestic setbacks were merely a microcosm of what was happening in the empire as a whole with the fall of Jerusalem and the loss of the True Cross. Was Heraclius's incestuous marriage bringing disaster on the empire? If God was punishing the couple, however, he must have relented because from the 620s onwards Martina continued to provide the emperor with children, some of them healthy like Heraclonas, born in 626, who was eventually to become emperor. The empire as a whole was enjoying some of its greatest days by then.

I have rejected the view expounded by C. Mango and others[47] that Heraclius spent the period from 612 to 623 as a single man with just one son. The old argument that the incestuous marriage took place in 613 and was used by the Church and the citizens of Constantinople to explain the disasters of the period 612–19 seems sound. The profound unpopularity of Martina during the lifetime of the emperor and immediately after his death simply would not make sense if the marriage took place in 623. The whole mood in the 620s was different. The empress joined Heraclius on most of his campaigns and bore his children away from the capital, alienating army leaders, of whom the emperor's brother Theodore was the most important. However, they had known about her since 613 and had resented the way in which she seemed to be trying to oust Constantine, the emperor's son by his first marriage to Fabia. I suspect that it was Martina's personality rather than the mere fact of her incestuous relations with the emperor that was at the root of the problem. Had Fabia been the emperor's niece in 610, I do not believe the matter would have arisen at all.

Another major factor in the anarchy that beset the empire after the reign of Phocas was the religious schism between the ruling Orthodox Church in Constantinople, and the Monophysites of Syria and the Copts of Egypt. Resentment among the Monophysites prevented the people of the southern and eastern lands feeling devoted to those who ruled them from distant Constantinople, something the Greeks did little to rectify. Even more divisive in Syria was the age-old conflict between Christian and Jew, particularly concerning Jerusalem and its environs.

Syria remained the battlefield. Heraclius knew that he must break the Persian grip on the province and so he looked for an experienced commander to replace Priscus. His choice was Philippicus, a general who had taken refuge in a monastery after Maurice's fall.

Philippicus arriving from the north and Nicetas advancing from Egypt planned to free Syria from the Persian grip. At first they were successful in forcing Shahen to abandon his hold on Cappadocia, allowing Heraclius himself to lead another army to relieve Antioch. In front of the city walls a great battle was fought in 613 which again proved indecisive. The Persians, able to call up reinforcements more quickly than the exhausted Byzantines, recovered their strength and drove Heraclius back. The new emperor, bloodied and depressed, was forced to retire through Anatolia to Constantinople.

It was in Syria that the greatest disaster took place, one so terrible that it rocked the foundations of Christianity itself. Although the chronicles do not help us here, the fact that Shahrvaraz was able to penetrate as far south as Jerusalem indicates that Nicetas, advancing from Egypt, must have been defeated by the Persians and pushed as far as Sinai. Shahrvaraz rampaged down the Orontes Valley and into Roman Palestine. On the way he captured Damascus without resistance and his progress was made even easier by the thousands of local Jews who flocked to join the Persian army, eager to settle scores with their Christian neighbours. Advancing through Arsuf he reached Jerusalem, which was crammed with refugees from the Christian towns to the north who had fled south to escape the killing. The Persians destroyed hundreds of monasteries on the march, leaving southern Syria and northern Palestine dotted with burned-out churches and covered in crosses where monks and nuns had been nailed and burned.

When Shahrvaraz arrived at the walls of Jerusalem he was met by an embassy from Patriarch Zacharias, who hoped to prevail upon the Persian general not to destroy the centre of the Christian faith. Shahrvaraz was content to occupy Jerusalem peacefully and placed a Persian garrison there. However, Zacharias was regarded as a traitor by some of the more warlike Christians who wanted to continue the fight and who were not content to see Jews re-entering the city in triumph. Once Shahrvaraz had withdrawn his army and crossed the River Jordan, Christians and Jews began fighting and the Persian occupiers where helpless to control the civil strife. After many of the Persians were killed by the Christians the survivors fled to tell Shahrvaraz of the disaster. His fury knew no bounds. At the urging of the Zoroastrian priests who travelled with his army and directly represented the Persian high king Khusro himself, the 'Royal Wild Boar' vowed to annihilate the treacherous Christians.

We have eyewitness accounts of what happened next. Antiochus Strategus, a monk from the Abba-Savas monastery, survived the disaster and recorded what he had seen.[48] Although this siege is one of the least known of all those that the holy city endured during the Middle Ages it was undoubtedly the most terrible, exceeding in destructiveness even the fall of the city to the First Crusade in 1099. Shahrvaraz showed no mercy, destroying everything in his path as his army rolled back towards Jerusalem. Dozens of monasteries and nunneries in the Jordanian hills were burned and their occupants put to the sword. Aware of what was coming, the people of Jerusalem defended the city with desperate courage. They could expect no help from the Byzantine garrisons in Syria and Palestine which had already been defeated and whose survivors flooded all the roads southwards to Egypt. And in Egypt itself Nicetas was at his wits' ends to stem the inexorable progress of the Persian juggernaut.

Shahrvaraz surrounded Jerusalem, cutting off all escape routes, and then concentrated on the western walls, near the Gate of David. Bitter hand-to-hand fighting raged on the battlements, with the Christian defenders fighting with the ferocity of despair. While their great stone-throwers battered at the walls, the Persian miners dug long tunnels towards the city and then began excavating galleries under the fortifications. Inside the doomed city the defenders listened for the tell-tale sound from below the ground which indicated that the Persians were burrowing beneath their feet. The Christian soldiers dug counter-mines, occasionally breaking into the subterranean passages and fighting the Persian miners in pitch darkness. But the defenders could not detect every tunnel and soon the Persians had completed their preparations, propping up the walls of the city with wooden beams until they were ready to strike. Now, at a given signal, they ignited the wooden props and in a vast cloud of dust and smoke the stone walls crumbled. The eerie silence that followed the collapse of the city walls was broken first by a dreadful communal groan from the Christian defenders, who knew their time had come, and then by joyful cheering from the Jews, who saw their revenge was at hand.

The Christian commanders pulled back most of their men who had been defending the ramparts and drew them up behind the breach in the western walls. This was the moment for which the Persians had been waiting. Opposite St David's Gate they had set up forty wooden crosses and now, in a cruel mockery of their Christian enemies, they nailed to each one of the monks they had captured at the monastery of Abba-Savas. Five white-robed and white-turbaned Mobad priests unfurled the *Drafsh-i-Kavyan*, the huge Sasanian royal flag, stretched on crossed timbers and reputedly fifteen feet by twenty-two, its golden and silver cloth embedded with gems. It was protected by a flag party surrounded by archers and a ring of spearmen. Other magi, carrying flaming torches, ignited brush fires at the base of each cross, demonstrating the triumph of the great god Ahura Mazda and the sacred fire over the Christian god.

To the beat of drums and cymbals companies of Persian assault troops, the *Jan-avaspar*, who were always first into the breach and who were known in the army as 'the men who sacrifice themselves', rushed forward through the piles of smoking ruins, oblivious to the storm of arrows that hit them from the last defenders. Behind the *Jan-avaspar* came heavily mailed Sughdian warriors and Epthalite knights, all armed with heavy battle axes, who forced their way past their own assault troops and into the streets of Jerusalem, now filled with fleeing crowds and screaming women and children.

For the rest of the day and through the night the killing went on as the Persians hunted down every living thing: man, woman, child, even animal. Much of the slaughter was carried out by the Jews who had volunteered to join Shahrvaraz and now fell to their work with any weapon that came to hand: axes, clubs and even sharpened staves. Almost intoxicated by the killing, they hacked at everything in their path. Even by torchlight the Christians of Jerusalem were hunted down, some dying by fire, some by the sword. Others, abandoning hope, chose to leap to their deaths from the highest buildings.

Any intention Shahrvaraz might have had to take the city peace-fully was forgotten as he lost control of his troops and the Persians massacred the Christian inhabitants. Many had taken refuge in the holy buildings around the site of the Holy Sepulchre but even here they found no respite. The Persians set fire to Constantine's magnificent Martyrion and in their despair the Christians watched as even the roof of the Anastasis was destroyed. Thousands of

Christians sought refuge in the underground cisterns only to die of suffocation or to be smoked out by their relentless enemies.

Shahrvaraz, aware of the fundamental significance of the city, made the capture of the True Cross his target. Once he had taken the Patriarch Zacharias alive he knew that Christianity's holiest relic was within his grasp. Many of Zacharias's priests were tortured to reveal the hiding place of the Christian relics but to no avail. Eventually, even the patriarch was tortured. The Persians found what they were looking for, buried in a kitchen garden near the patriarch's palace. The wood from the True Cross was kept in an ornate box. Once passions had cooled, Shahrvaraz allowed Zacharias to accompany the relic into captivity in Persia.[49]

When all resistance had ceased, Shahrvaraz tried to impose some order on his troops but without success. Those Persians who took Christian prisoners found that the Jews insisted on ransoming them so that they could kill them all.[50] The number of people slaughtered in the sack of Jerusalem will never be known. Figures in medieval chronicles are notoriously unreliable and there is no general agreement on how many died in 614. From a lowest figure of 34,000 to an unlikely high of 90,000 the chroniclers recorded one of the great slaughters of history. A point that needs to be considered is that the normal population of Jerusalem had been immensely swollen by the refugees fleeing from Syria. One of the survivors, a monk named Thomas, had the task of burying the bodies and he made a fairly detailed list of the victims, amounting to 66,509. During Shahrvaraz's campaign it is estimated that more than 300 monasteries and Christian foundations were destroyed in and around Jerusalem. Syrian Christianity never recovered from this holocaust.

Those who were captured, and as many as 30,000 survived the killing, were marched into Persia as prisoners. First they were taken up the Jordan Valley to Damascus and then on the long march into the Land of the Holy Fire. Even here the killing did not stop. Jews carried out a policy of genocide, aided by Bedouin tribesmen, killing any Christians they found sheltering in caves. Before turning back across the River Jordan Shahrvaraz handed over the administration of Jerusalem to the Jews, in payment for their contribution to the campaign.

When news of the fall of Jerusalem reached Constantinople it fell upon a despondent people; it was the greatest blow Christianity had suffered since the death of Christ himself. The impact of the loss of the True Cross to the worshippers of the Holy Fire cannot be understood by modern minds. The shock was felt almost as severely by the Christians inside Sasanid Persia. Khusro's favourite wife Shirin was a Christian as was Yiazdin, his doctor. They believed Persian soldiers had gone too far in destroying God's holy city and carrying off the supreme symbol of their religion. They pointed out to Khusro that his fight had been with the Byzantines not with the Christians of Syria, most of whom were Monophysite and actually hated the Orthodox Byzantines. His action in Jerusalem would make it harder rather than easier in future to conquer Christian lands, notably Egypt. Khusro saw the power of their argument and in the aftermath of the holocaust he sent orders to Shahrvaraz instructing him to adopt a more conciliatory policy towards the Christians of the conquered lands. Permission was given to them to rebuild the churches that had been destroyed in the conquest. The Jews once again lost control of Jerusalem and were forbidden to stay there. But the glory of Byzantine Syria was gone forever. The destruction of both agriculture and town life in the province made it an easy prey for the future Muslim conquerors.

Once Shahrvaraz had consolidated his conquests and reorganized the Byzantine lands into Persian satrapies, he prepared to attack Byzantine Egypt. There Nicetas awaited the inevitable, short of troops and with the country bitterly divided between Greeks and Copts. Although the people loved him they had different feelings for the Byzantine state he represented, which had exploited the native Copts for generations.

At the beginning of 617 the Persians were ready to advance into Egypt by the coast route through Gaza, while a Persian fleet moved against Alexandria. The sources of information about this campaign are so thin that it is almost impossible to plot a coherent strategy for either the Persians or for Nicetas and the Byzantines. What is certain is that the Egyptian troops showed little spirit and Nicetas had to rely on his Greek and mercenary soldiers, who were totally inadequate to face the power of Shahrvaraz. Alexandria was besieged. Viewing the situation as hopeless, Nicetas and the Greek patriarch escaped to Constantinople by sea. When the city fell the Persians showed some of the ferocity that had followed the fall of Jerusalem but it was selective, aimed almost entirely at the Greeks and not the Copts. Indeed, they installed a Coptic patriarch in Alexandria to win the support of the Egyptian people for the new regime.

With the loss of Egypt, Heraclius faced almost total ruin. Alexandria had been the port through which Egyptian grain came to Constantinople; now it was only a matter of time before starvation in the capital brought Heraclius to his knees. The Persians, meanwhile, had adopted a dual strategy of sending one army under Shahen into Anatolia to keep Heraclius busy while Shahrvaraz did the damage in Syria and Egypt. Time was not on Heraclius's side and as the victorious Persians made ever deeper gains in the Greek heartlands he decided to seek peace on almost any terms. Shahen was entrenched at Chalcedon, on the Asian side of the Sea of Marmara, and Heraclius went to meet him to sue for peace. Shahen told the emperor that he was not empowered to make peace but that if the Byzantines sent an embassy to Khusro, he would guarantee its safety. Heraclius had no choice. An embassy of five or six senior figures, including the Patrician Olympius and Leontius, Governor of Constantinople, left with Shahen, who showed them almost exaggerated respect until he reached Persian territory, whereupon he had them bound in chains and threw them in prison where they later died. When Shahen came face to face with his own king, Khusro was apparently furious with his general because although he had met Heraclius, he had not arrested him as well![51]

With an empty treasury and a beaten army, with his European lands overrun by Slavs, Avars and Lombards, and with the eastern provinces lost to the Persians, with the great cities of Antioch, Damascus, Jerusalem and Alexandria all in the hands of the enemy, and with the True Cross carried off to the land of the Holy Fire, no emperor before or since Heraclius had faced such a hopeless situation. The empire of Augustus, Hadrian, Marcus Aurelius and Constantine, it seemed, was now only months away from total collapse and extinction. Greek and Roman civilization, along with Orthodox Christianity itself, was about to be swept away by a torrent from the East. The chronicles report that Heraclius was plunged into despair after the loss of Egypt. It was said that he planned to abandon Constantinople and return to Carthage where he would establish his new capital. It was even reported that he loaded his personal treasure aboard ships bound for Africa but that these were lost in a storm.[52] There is an air of unreality about this story. Nevertheless, true or not it symbolizes the desperate nature of the situation the Byzantines faced in 620. Ten years of Heraclius's rule had not brought the triumphs everyone expected after the overthrow of the evil Phocas. Instead, matters had grown so much worse that one might almost have supposed God wished Heraclius to fail. At this moment of supreme trial, the emperor made a decision that was to determine the direction of European history for the next millennium: trusting in God and appealing to Christians everywhere to come to the aid of their religion, he would take the offensive against the Persians and carry holy war into the enemy heartland.

Since his accession to the throne a decade earlier Heraclius had enjoyed an unusually close relationship with the Patriarch Sergius. They were colleagues in the great business of state, but they almost seemed to be friends too, and the loss of his father within days of coming to the throne meant that Heraclius needed a wise shoulder to lean on from time to time and, one suspects, to cry on occasionally. In Sergius he was fortunate to find not just a great theologian but also a statesman who understood the needs of the empire. Sergius recognized that in Heraclius he had a man who could save his people but he knew that the emperor had first to regain the confidence which had taken such heavy blows in the previous ten years. The loss of his powerful and wise father, the untimely death of his beautiful and gentle wife, the shock of the sack of Jerusalem, the removal of the True Cross and, finally, the fall of Egypt would have broken almost any man, however strong. Sergius therefore asked the emperor to come with him to Hagia Sophia and, as they stood together in the great church, he asked Heraclius to swear that he would never abandon his people. Heraclius, probably overwhelmed by the solemnity of the occasion, offered up his oath in the form of a prayer.

However, Sergius was aware that it would take more than good intentions to turn back the tide of defeat and despondency. What the emperor needed was enough money to equip an army – an army of redemption, fighting like that of Constantine under the symbol of Christ's cross. Although the concept was as yet undeveloped, the army of Heraclius would be made up of soldiers of Christ, fighting to regain the land that God had decreed the Greek Christians should rule. They were charged with regaining the True Cross, the holy city of Jerusalem and the Holy Land where Christ had walked on earth. In the euphoria that followed the sanctifying of a war of redemption Sergius decided to offer the wealth of the church for the equipping of a holy army.

By all accounts Heraclius himself was a deeply religious man. Once Sergius's influence overcame the natural despair he felt at the catastrophic events of the period 610 to 620 he acted as a man inspired, a leader of titanic power, like Constantine after the battle of the Milvian Bridge. The war ahead was no longer seen as merely a continuation of the territorial disputes that had characterized Romano-Persian relations for many centuries. It became part of the eternal struggle between Good and Evil, with the Sasanian king Khusro cast as Satan, enemy of God. The poet and court chronicler George of Pisidia described Heraclius (his paymaster, of course) as the instrument chosen by God to punish the evil-doers, the fire-worshipping Persians. Like the biblical David, Heraclius was the man God had chosen to lead the Romans – now the chosen people – in their struggle to regain Jerusalem and the True Cross. To modern eyes this looks like a masterful propaganda exercise but in those days of supreme faith it appealed to the deepest recesses of the human heart. To ensure that he controlled the moral high ground Heraclius made what he realized could be only a gesture but it was necessary, nevertheless: for the last time he offered Khusro peace. When this was spurned he declared, in the words of George of Pisidia, that 'the source of all evil is Persia'. From that moment it was a fight to the death between the Byzantines and the Sasanian Persians.

When Sergius decided to fund the coming campaigns he was, in a way, setting the agenda. And yet what we know of Heraclius himself suggests that he was happier taking the initiative rather than standing on the defensive. Even before 622 he had already shown a predisposition to employ mobility and surprise against the Persian juggernauts of Shahrvaraz and Shahen. Sergius and Heraclius were at one in their decision to take the war to Persia and to remove

Khusro's ability to inflict suffering on Byzantine territory and civilians.

To fund the enormous cost of such major military operations Sergius ordered Church plate and candelabra to be melted down and turned into coin. With charitable funds being turned over to the war effort, everyone in Constantinople, both rich and poor, could feel that they were contributing to this unprecedented struggle against the enemies of God and His people. It is said that even the great bronze ox which had stood in the Ox Forum and had been used as the site to burn the body of the hated Phocas was melted down and minted. The symbolism adopted for the new coins was very significant. On one side the emperor was depicted seated on the throne and his son with him; both have their hands upon an orb. On the other side is the cross supported by an orb on three steps. The symbolism is clear: the world was dominated by Christ and by the Christian empire. This propaganda was not so much directed at the Persians themselves but was to be circulated among the Transcaucasian peoples, of whom most were Christian. The message 'God has chosen the Romans' was printed on each coin and could not have been emphasized in a more effective way. Even the numerous Persian Christians must have found their loyalties challenged by this provocative message.

After the decision to carry the war into Persia was taken in 620, Heraclius and his advisers faced an awesome responsibility. The campaign that lay before them promised greater risks than any the Romans had faced since the Punic Wars. As an exercise in grand strategy its like had not been seen since the days of Alexander the Great and the consequences of defeat were too terrible to contemplate: nothing less than the end of Greco-Roman civilization and the collapse of eastern Christianity.

Faced with such pressures, Heraclius can be excused for moving slowly. Determined to lead his armies in person, something no emperor had done for more than two centuries, he was adamant that he must out-think his opponents as well as out-fight them. As a result, he left the royal palace at Constantinople and retired to Hiereia, where he found the peace necessary to prepare for the forthcoming challenge. Isolating himself for long periods he studied all existing military manuals and once he was satisfied with his own fitness to lead, he summoned his senior commanders and together they spent days poring over maps and intelligence reports. In the phrase of the poet George of Pisidia, Heraclius 'gave battle before the battle'.

Years of unbroken failure had undermined the morale of the Byzantine army. Heraclius knew that his troops were already half beaten each time they took the field against the all-conquering Sasanian armies. Yet it had not always been like this. In the previous century, under the leadership of Justinian's generals, notably the great Belisarius, Byzantine arms had enjoyed as great a superiority over the Persians as they now endured inferiority. Fortunately for the Byzantines, in Heraclius they now had not just a hard fighting warrior as their leader but a student of history and warfare, who had learned his craft under an able father and in an army which, in the reign of Maurice, marched with the confidence generated by frequent victories. The disasters of the period 602–22 destroyed the spirit of the Constantinopolitan rank and file, and the purges of Phocas had eliminated the middle and higher ranks of command, but the army in Carthage had survived virtually untouched, saved by distance and by the personality of the elder Heraclius from the damage it would have suffered closer to the capital. Heraclius the younger, Nicetas and many nameless officers had survived untouched through the worst excesses of the Phocas era and had returned to Constantinople in the successful revolt of 610 to form a cadre for the future.

After Heraclius reached the capital in 610 he needed time to bring about his military revolution. The dependence on mercenaries which had been the preferred Roman system of recruitment for centuries (since the supersession of the legionary system) had to be ended once and for all. Heraclius adopted the principle of getting to know his enemy in order to copy its strengths and exploit its weaknesses. His father, and possibly he himself, had fought the Persians during the reign of Maurice and thus knew that the traditional strength of the Persian army had been its heavy cavalry, forerunners as they were of the heavily armoured medieval knights. Built on the traditions of the Parthian cavalry, with their lamellar mail armour, the Persian horsemen relied on strength and impact rather than mobility. They were most susceptible in desert lands – just as the western crusaders later proved to be when they encountered the mobility and speed of the lighter cavalry of the Saracens and Turks. None of this was new, of course, to Byzantine military planners. The Persian military machine was very traditional in its outlook and rarely sought to initiate change, particularly in a period like the early seventh century when it was enjoying almost unbroken success under a warlike king and able generals.

Heraclius, however, had to change a losing system. Historians have been unable to agree on the precise nature of his reforms. Certainly the military manual known as the *Strategicon of Maurice* dates from the period 618–28 when Heraclius was rethinking his military options, but the extent to which the Theme – or regional – system of organization originated with him is uncertain. The period was conducive to original thinking by talented, possibly young officers under an emperor whose intellect was still active. Those historians who, like Warren Treadgold, question Heraclius's development of the Theme system on the grounds that what had apparently worked against the Persians later lamentably failed against the Arabs, miss the point that leadership against the Persians and the religious factor contributed much. In 622 Heraclius was forty-seven and the chosen one of God. In 634 he was fifty-nine and exhausted by religious schism. Moreover, he never led an army against the Muslims.

The combination of regional – Theme – and central – Tagmata – armies was the basis of Byzantine military reform under Heraclius and his successors. The Thematic armies were made up of soldiers who farmed land in peacetime but answered the call when war broke out. In many cases these men were more than simply feudal peasants in the western European fashion and were more like the knights who lived off the produce of land farmed by a regular peasantry. Where the region was agriculturally poor and the soldiers less able to fund their own equipment they were often supplied by their fellow villagers or by richer local magnates. Most of the Thematic troops would have been heavy infantry but there was always an aristocratic cavalry which supplied the officers of the regional force because they occupied civilian offices in peacetime.

Heraclius knew that his army needed more than administrative changes to reverse the losing habits of a generation. The basis of the revolution he was proposing was to raise individual and group morale through specialized training and inspired leadership. Above all, however, was the appeal to every soldier as a Christian warrior, not just the paid servant of the state. Each man must believe that he was a part of God's purpose and that should he lose his life in the holy war ahead, he would enjoy the rewards of the martyr in the after-life. Every man in the army, from the emperor down to the common soldier, was a single, individual Christian soul who mattered in God's eyes.

FIVE

The First Crusader

Between 622 and 628 Heraclius was to achieve a military reversal without parallel in history. Great commanders like Alexander of Macedon or Napoleon Bonaparte won greater victories than Heraclius, though it is doubtful if anyone began from such a low point as the Byzantine emperor. The achievements of Alexander the Great cannot be understood without appreciating the important work done by his father, Philip, who developed the Macedonian army into the superb machine that his son was to employ. Napoleon inherited the French revolutionary armies created by Lazare Nicholas Carnot. All Heraclius inherited was the detritus of the unsuccessful wars of Phocas. Deprived even of good raw material with which to work, Heraclius had instead to mould a new army from a broken, spiritless force. In this sense, his greatest achievements were won on the parade grounds of Anatolia rather than the battlefields of Persia: he was both Philip and Alexander, Carnot and Napoleon.

Like Winston Churchill in 1940, initially Heraclius could not wage war as he would have liked but only as he was able to. Much as he would have preferred to defeat the main Sasanian armies in open battle he knew that this was impossible given the prevailing conditions in 622. The Byzantine army was both quantitively and qualitatively inferior to the Persian force, and it was suffering from lower morale. Consequently, the strategy that Heraclius adopted for his counter-attack on Persia was a subtle one. If Khusro had detected the Byzantine soft underbelly in Monophysite Syria, Heraclius responded by finding the weakness in the Sasanian defences: the north-western provinces of Transcaucasia. Here, a strong Christian message and appeals for a holy war against the dominant but hated fire-worshippers would find many willing listeners. Constant emphasis on the loss of the True Cross and the Christian holy places would, at least temporarily, break down national differences and sweep up the Christian tribes in a greater cause.

Until 622 financial and military difficulties kept Heraclius on the defensive. In one way alone had he been able to take the offensive and that was through the use of propaganda. There were two ways of deploying this weapon: to undermine the enemy's confidence or to boost your own. It was in the second way that Heraclius triumphed and in doing so he built up a concept of holy war that was to have enormous repercussions, not just in the Christian world. Heraclius reasoned that disunity had been at the root of Byzantine difficulties. During the reign of Maurice the empire had been united and had preserved a state of equilibrium with adjoining Persia. The loss of unity through civil war and religious schism had made it easy for the Persians to attack and had encouraged Khusro to think the previously unthinkable: that the Roman Empire could be dismembered. Heraclius appreciated the need to restore unity by offering leadership and by raising morale. If the empire were to survive the crisis, it would be because everyone could look to a single leader with confidence, just as every Christian looked to God. As emperor he must remind his people that they were the chosen ones and that he was God's chosen representative on earth, just as Constantine had done three centuries before. Arguments over minor matters of belief were less important than the fact that the Christian faith was in danger of destruction by barbarian Avars and fire-worshipping Persians. The True Cross, the holiest relic of the faith, had been captured by the Persians and taken away from Jerusalem, the holy city that was now in the hands of the ancient enemies of Rome. If the Byzantine people would not rise up and fight for such things then they were lost.

The year 622 saw a new concept added to the vocabulary of human conflict – holy war or jihad. The historian James Howard-Johnson has suggested Heraclius's first campaign against the Persians in 622 may have had unexpected side-effects for the whole area covered by the vast Romano-Persian conflict.[53] The Persian conquests of Palestine and Egypt had disrupted the whole Arab world, hinged as it was on the trading routes between the Hijaz and Syria, and between the Red Sea and the Persian Gulf. Such a cataclysmic contest, during which cities such as Alexandria, Jerusalem, Damascus and Antioch changed hands and whole tribes were uprooted, cannot have failed to produce ripples spreading far and wide. Arabs from Mecca were accustomed to passing through Byzantine territory on their way to Damascus and must have witnessed terrible sights around Petra and in the Jordan Valley as the Christians and their priests were slaughtered by Persians and by Arabs in the pay of Khusro, notably Lakhmids. And when the Byzantines began their counter-attack in 622 many Christian Arabs, Ghassanids in the main, travelled north and east with them as their allies. For the Arabs of the Hijaz, the removal of the Ghassanids and the Lakhmids produced uncertainty as well as opportunity for those who remained behind. Above all, news from the respective camps, Byzantine and Persian, must have been of vital interest to the Arabs of Arabia, provoking a restlessness, notably among the younger men.

Howard-Johnson asks the question: 'To what extent was the Prophet [Mohammed] influenced by news of the great war in the north (which was taken by other observers to presage the end of time) and by the threatening advance of Persian power into Arabia which had followed the conquest of Syria, Palestine and Egypt?' In other words, was Mohammed influenced in the development of his concept of jihad by the way Byzantine propagandists, acting through Heraclius, used religious arguments to inspire Christian warriors with a willingness to sacrifice their lives in exchange for a martyr's crown? Mohammed first articulated jihad at the battle of Badr in 624, but it had already been used by Heraclius to inspire his troops two years or more before.

For Christian warriors of the Middle Ages Heraclius was the 'first crusader'. For medieval writers he was a paladin, one of the heroes of Christianity along with Roland, Charlemagne, Godfrey of Bouillon and Richard *Coeur de Lion*. Five centuries after his great Persian campaigns Heraclius became part of the history of the crusades written by William of Tyre, who entitled his book *L'Estoire de Eracles, Empereur, et la Conquete de la Terre d'Outremer*. None of the other paladins of chivalry contributed quite so much to the crusading movement as Heraclius: he reconquered the Holy Land and returned the True Cross of Jesus to Jerusalem – thereby adding the Feast of the Holy Cross to the Christian calendar on 14 September.

However modern academics view Heraclius, he was an integral part of 'crusading' history. If the word 'crusader' had existed in 622, he would have used it to describe himself and his men.

Heraclius became a holy warrior in 622, leading the chosen people against the enemies of God. His soldiers had to become agents of the holy will and in return, he told them, 'Be not disturbed, O brethren, by the multitude of the enemy. For when God wills it, one man will rout a thousand. So let us sacrifice ourselves to God for the salvation of our brothers. May we win the crown of martyrdom that we may be praised in future and receive our recompense from God.' The message was clear: death in battle against the enemies of Christianity meant martyrdom and martyrs were rewarded in heaven with everlasting life. James Howard-Johnson has shown that this message had been used in Armenia to boost Christian resistance there to threats of Zoroastrian conversion in the fifth century. Significantly, much of the religious propaganda deployed by Heraclius between 622 and 624 was directed towards the Armenians and other Christian people of the Caucasus to win their support against Persia as the enemy of their religion. As Christian emperor and defender of the faith Heraclius felt that he spoke *ex cathedra* on this issue and, because he had the support of the patriarch, his words carried the assurance that they were God's will. From this point onwards, even the weather seemed to be used by God to favour the Byzantines: Theophanes points out that at various times heavy snowfall impeded the Persians, 'dewlike air' refreshed the Byzantines and a violent hailstorm struck the Persians but spared the Romans.

In addition to religious propaganda, Heraclius had another strategic option in the forthcoming campaign. If the Persians were able to exploit Byzantine weakness in the Balkans by persuading the Avars to attack the empire from the west, Heraclius could approach the Transcaucasian Turks to the north and persuade these people, Persia's nemesis, to join him in an invasion of Persia to the south. In this Heraclius adopted remarkably modern strategic imperatives, mixing guerrilla with regular warfare, sea and land operations, propaganda and economic warfare and, above all, a policy of political and military annihilation that was almost Napoleonic. The advance on Ctesiphon while vast areas of Byzantine territory remained under

Persian control and three huge, unbroken Persian armies were still in the field, brings to mind Napoleon's 1805 campaign which led to the battle of Austerlitz and the capture of Vienna.

Deliberately choosing Easter for the start of his campaign, Heraclius imbued every part of his preparations with a deep religious significance. Taking upon himself responsibility for the lives and welfare of all his people and of God's empire on earth, Heraclius used the great ceremony held at Hagia Sophia to make the spiritual purpose of his war apparent to everyone. Heraclius and his army took on the mantles of the 'elect of Christ' (Philochristus), warriors of the faith in a battle against the evil fire-worshippers who threatened the very existence of all they believed in. According to the sources, Heraclius entered the great church and having received Holy Communion in full view of his people, he knelt and prayed. He then spoke in a loud voice so that everyone could hear. 'Lord God and Lord Jesus Christ. Do not deliver us to our enemies in disgrace because of our sins. But be merciful to us and give us the victory over our foes that the ungodly may not rejoice.'

During his speech the crowd was deathly quiet but, as he concluded, a great roar began to well up from the throats of the assembled masses. Those close to the front saw that Heraclius was holding up the Image of Camuliana, a portrait of Christ 'not made by human hands'. This was to be the emperor's palladium throughout the forthcoming campaigns and until the restoration of the True Cross it was the spiritual symbol of the crusade. Amidst the acclamation of the people Heraclius bid farewell to his family and friends then made his way through the thronging multitudes who were held back by his guards. At the quayside he went aboard the imperial flagship, a great dromon bedecked in flowers bearing at its prow an icon of the Theotokos, the Mother of God. All around him his guards and household troops boarded other dromons and transport vessels. Trumpeters and musicians added to the cacophony of sounds in the harbour and soon the fleet set sail for the brief journey to Pylae on the Asian shore where the emperor would disembark and join his first army corps which was waiting near Pythia. At this stage Heraclius had come to play not to fight. He was planning nothing less than an immense war game to hone the fighting skills of the new armies he was to lead in battle.

Anyone less confident than Heraclius that he was doing God's work might have been depressed by the early omens. No sooner had his fleet left harbour than it was hit by a storm and one of the dromons was driven ashore. George of Pisidia – the poet who accompanied the emperor on his first campaign and who is one of the most vivid, if somewhat confused, commentators on the Persian crusade – relates that Heraclius himself joined the salvage efforts, working alongside his subjects. In doing so he injured a toe and lost blood. Disembarking on Asian soil Heraclius lost no time in assembling the various army corps that had been gathering on his orders throughout Anatolia.

During the military exercises that took place in Bithynia in the spring of 622 we know that the emperor instigated a period of spiritual indoctrination alongside the troops' physical and military training. Priests were as much in evidence as NCOs and Theophanes shows how the emperor combined 'miraculous' holy symbols with religious imagery in his speeches:

Taking in his hands the likeness of the Man-God – the one that was not painted by hand, but which the Logos, who shapes and fashions everything, wrought like an image without recourse to painting, just as He experienced birth without seed – the emperor placed his trust in this image painted by God and began his endeavours after giving a pledge to his army that he would struggle with them unto death and would be united with them as his own children; for he wished his authority to be derived not from fear but rather from love. Having found, then, the army in a state of great sluggishness, cowardice, indiscipline and disorder, and scattered over many parts of the earth, he speedily gathered everyone together. As by common agreement, everyone praised the might and courage of the emperor. And he spoke to them these words of encouragement: 'You see, O my brethren and children, how the enemies of God have trampled upon our land, have laid our cities waste, have burned our sanctuaries and have filled with the blood of murder the altars of the bloodless sacrifice; how they defile with their impassioned pleasures our churches.'[54]

The emperor was to develop and elaborate on his theme in the years ahead. In 624, during his devastating campaign in Atropatene,

Heraclius was to address his troops with the following words, as Theophanes records:

> Men, my brethren, let us keep in mind the fear of God and fight to avenge the insult done to God. Let us stand bravely against the enemy who have inflicted many terrible things on the Christians. Let us respect the sovereign state of the Romans and oppose the enemy who are armed with impiety. Let us be inspired with faith that defeats murder. Let us be mindful of the fact that we are within the Persian land and that flight carries a great danger. Let us avenge the rape of our virgins and be afflicted in our hearts as we see the severed limbs of our soldiers. The danger is not without recompense: nay, it leads to eternal life. Let us stand bravely, and the Lord our God will assist us and destroy the enemy.[55]

Within a matter of weeks the soldiers of Byzantium, fanatics, zealots, martyrs and holy warriors, wrecked the most sacred religious site in Persia, the Fire Temple at Takht-i Sulaiman. The systematic destruction of this site, combined with the pollution of its holy lake was as clear a demonstration as was possible of the religious nature of the war and was a direct response to the destruction of the Holy Sepulchre at Jerusalem and the seizure of the True Cross by Shahrvaraz ten years before. The symbolic nature of Heraclius's crusade cannot be better exemplified than by this single action.

As Heraclius embedded his army like a single weapon into the body of the Persian state, the religious impulse became ever more urgent. By 625, he was addressing his troops with the words: 'So let us sacrifice ourselves to God for the salvation of our brothers. May we win the crown of martyrdom so that we may be praised in the future and receive our recompense from God.' The emperor's reference to 'praised in the future' is an interesting pointer to posterity and is certainly the cry of the potential martyr. Significantly, as we shall see, this form of holy war became a feature of aggressive Byzantine policy in the tenth century under John Kourkuas, Nicephorus Phocas and John Tzimisces.

The main difference between the form of indoctrination used by Heraclius from 622 onwards and that employed by countless military leaders of the ancient world was the way in which his words spoke to men as individuals rather than simply as parts of an indivisible army; he addressed them almost as if they were volunteers. In this way, they were closer to the crusaders of the eleventh century than to the warriors of other Byzantine holy wars. Byzantine armies in the age of Justinian had been equipped with religious images in the form of icons or ornamental crosses yet no commander in the sixth century ever thought to approach the mind or soul of the individual soldier. This is what Pope Urban did at Clermont, when he preached to the medieval crusaders in 1095. It is also what Mohammed did with the jihad but Heraclius deployed this tactic before either of them as he was about to launch his invasion of Persia. Theophanes tells us Heraclius observed: 'Danger is not without its reward but opens the way to eternal life.' Compared to duty, obedience or fear, 'eternal life' was an attractive motivational force for the soldier facing danger and probable death. Rape, loot and slaughter might have a transitory appeal for the pagan warrior, but to the Christian soldier 'a martyr's crown' was infinitely to be preferred.

Those academics who have rejected the concept of the Byzantine 'holy war' and have ridiculed the idea of Heraclius as the first crusader have done so because the concept of a 'crusade' is a medieval western idea. They do not believe that the Byzantines had a doctrine of holy war. However, the doubters are not seeing the wood for the trees. In a sense all Byzantine wars were holy wars and thus to search for individual examples is to miss the point entirely.[56]

During the spring and early summer of 622 Heraclius reverted to the role of 'sergeant-major' to thousands of new recruits and dispirited old lags. Theophanes gives us a substantial account of the military training in Bithynia that Heraclius set in motion but the simple statement 'He began to train them and instruct them in military deeds' only hints at the revolution that was taking place. Heraclius was developing a force to fit exactly the requirements of the campaign he had in mind. The emphasis was on speed and mobility rather than strength and weight in the attack. If the Persian 'heavies', the *cataphractarii*, could not be challenged directly, they must be lured into terrain where their weight and strength were positive disadvantages. Persian strengths must be turned against them; Byzantine weaknesses masked or turned into strengths.

Theophanes says that Heraclius, 'taught them [his soldiers] the battle cry, battle songs and shouts'. There were no longer the profanities of the Roman legionaries but the prayers and utterances of warrior priests. Like Cromwell's men of piety, this was Heraclius's 'New Model Army'. The atmosphere on the training grounds was dominated by the presence of the emperor. Heraclius set the agenda for the coming campaign in his stirring speeches. Such harangues were part of the repertoire of every military commander before the modern age. Only constant repetition could translate such words into deeds and only tangible rewards, in terms of battles won, could make them as much a part of a soldier's life as his boots.

It is doubtful that the versions of Heraclius's speeches to his troops are any more accurate than any of the four versions we have of Pope Urban II's great speech at Clermont in 1095. But the words are less important than the spirit in which they were spoken and the effect they had on listeners. George of Pisidia included verse summaries of Heraclius's speeches in his *Expedition Persica* and Theophanes has quoted most of these verbatim but, written at least two centuries after the event, his account cannot be free of the hindsight that all later commentators enjoyed – or suffered – with regard to these dramatic days in the history of the empire.

Heraclius assembled most of what strength remained to the empire on the training grounds of Bithynia. Perhaps half of the Egyptian and Syrian garrisons had been saved and transported by sea from Egypt after the fall of the province, while Armenian and Anatolian troops were present in large numbers. Even the remnants of the western armies from Illyricum and Thrace had been transferred to Anatolia, leaving the Balkans virtually defenceless. All that stood between the Avars and Slavs and Constantinople was the treaty they had signed with Heraclius the previous year. It was a time for taking risks. Never since the formation of Rome 1,300 years before had the entire strength of the Roman world paraded as one body before its ruler. From Spain to Armenia, the Byzantine Empire lay unguarded. Only Constantinople, with its powerful garrison and its tremendous walls stood like a rock against a raging sea of pagan fury.

By the summer of 622 Heraclius felt ready to challenge the Persian army of Shahrvaraz which had invaded eastern Anatolia, advancing into Cappadocia. Shahrvaraz had occupied the Cilician

Gates with a strong force, expecting Heraclius to try to force a
passage and move south to liberate Syria. For the first time, but
hardly the last, the Persians completely misread the intentions of the
Byzantine commander. Instead of heading south, Heraclius moved
north-west towards Armenia, threatening to outflank Shahrvaraz.
The Persians, assuming that Heraclius was manoeuvring against
their army, pursued him. In fact, the emperor was ignoring
Shahrvaraz and moving towards Persian-held Armenia in pursuit of
the strategy that he and his generals had already determined to
follow in the Caucasus region.

Theophanes describes what happened when the pursuing Persians
caught up with the Byzantines on what they had hoped would be a
dark night. We know the date of this first encounter between
Heraclius's 'new' army and the Persian invaders – 28 July 622 –
because the Persians got more than they bargained for in the shape
of a full eclipse of the moon, which terrified many of their soldiers.
Shahrvaraz apparently retreated into the mountains and for ten days
conducted a series of raids against the Byzantine troops. This was
exactly the sort of fighting for which the Byzantines had been
specially trained and the Persians came off distinctly worse.
Theophanes records that even during this skirmishing Heraclius
took the lead in repelling enemy attacks and won the admiration of
his men, an important step in building up their morale.

Shahrvaraz, realizing that skirmishing tactics were getting him
nowhere, decided to confront the Byzantines on the plain, where he
knew his heavy cavalry should prove decisive. Before dawn the
Persians came down from the mountains in full panoply and
arranged themselves in their traditional formation of three divisions.
With their Zoroastrian Mobad priests in the forefront, a ram was
sacrificed and heralds called on the Byzantines to abandon their
false beliefs and accept Ahura Mazda and the sacred fire. Heraclius
would have been astonished had he been able to understand the
words of encouragement that were being spread throughout the
Persian army by the junior officers. They were nothing less than the
same promises of rewards in this world and the next that were a
feature of his own appeals to his Christian troops and were to
characterize the Muslim jihad. Trumpets were heard and the Persian
army's drum-master began to sound the advance.

It is impossible to be certain what happened next as Theophanes was no strategist and gives us the briefest details. Almost certainly Heraclius successfully implemented a feigned flight. Initially organizing his army in three divisions, apparently matching the Persian host, and with the rising sun behind him and in the eyes of the enemy, the emperor advanced towards the enemy and made initial contact before wheeling away and fleeing into the sun. He was pursued by the apparently victorious Persians, who were dazzled by the bright sunlight and could not easily gauge the mood of the fleeing Christians. Practising something that he had rehearsed dozens of times on the plains of Bithynia only months before, Heraclius was aware that every man in his army knew the emperor's mind and would cease the flight once the Persians had overstretched themselves. Officers bearing flags at various points on a battlefield several miles wide took their lead from given signals and turned the Byzantines. The pursuing Persians were in disorder, some having ridden faster than others, some arrowless having used up their stock without realizing the enemy was out of range. The heavy cavalry was left far behind the lighter horsemen and was easily outflanked by the Byzantines, while the infantry no longer had any mounted support. The Persians suddenly found that the prey had become the predator. The Persian cataphracts, heavily armoured and dependent on the momentum of their charge, now found their horses blown and plodding. Without forward momentum these knights succumbed to the Byzantine horse archers or to the specially trained mounted infantry, who dismounted and rolled under the armoured horses, stabbing them in the body or hamstringing them. The agonized horses tipped the Persians onto the ground where their armour made them clumsy and they easily succumbed to Byzantine spears.

The Persians were routed in full view of Shahrvaraz and a panicky retreat back into the mountains took place. The dismounted Byzantine light cavalry pursued the fleeing enemy, toppling many into precipices and capturing the Persian camp. The contest cannot have lasted long although the rounding up of captives and pursuit of the Persian cavalry must have taken much of the day. Theophanes records some of the amazement felt by the Byzantines, who had not defeated the Persians for many years. He wrote: 'The Romans raised their arms aloft to give thanks to God and to praise earnestly their emperor who had led them well. For they, who previously had not dared to behold the Persians' dust, now found their tents undisturbed and looted them. Who had expected that the hard-fighting race of the Persians would ever show their backs to the Romans?'[57]

Having just achieved the first Byzantine victory over a Persian army in a generation, Heraclius had the firm ground cut from beneath his feet by disastrous news from the West. There the Avars, with whom he believed he had negotiated a treaty and bought their neutrality, had broken their pledge and invaded Byzantine territory, besieging the great city of Thessalonika. In August 622, therefore, Heraclius was forced to hurry back to Constantinople, leaving his army in Anatolia, probably under the command of his brother, the *curopalates* Theodore.

In their diplomacy the Avars were susceptible to treasure above all else and so we can guess where a good portion of Sergius's church loan to Heraclius ended up. The Avar khagan arranged to meet Heraclius at Heraclea to discuss a new treaty. The Byzantine emperor, bereft of any military backing and with his army hundreds of miles away in Anatolia, was eager to reach an agreement. When dealing with barbarian peoples the Romans had often tried to overawe the simple-minded tribesmen with a show of sophistication and even extravagance. With the Avars, however, such a tactic could not have been more inappropriate. They needed no reminders of just how rich the Byzantine lands were, particularly the capital city itself. One can only wonder at the vacuity of the advice Heraclius received from men with so much diplomatic experience.

The negotiations with the Avars continued through the winter of 622–3 and well into the spring. Eventually, it was decided to hold a meeting between the emperor and the khagan outside the Long Walls of Constantinople on 5 June 623. Heraclius, we are told, rode to meet the Avars armed with nothing more than a rich and ornate garment as a present for the khagan. Instead of guards he was accompanied by entertainers, acrobats, clowns and courtiers of all kinds in their most splendid apparel. The Avar khagan came fully armed with the simple intention of taking the emperor prisoner. Some Roman emperors – but no Byzantine ones to that date – had been taken prisoner in battle, notably at the hands of the Persians. In the end, Heraclius was saved neither by his guards, the

Excubitores, nor by his personal prowess in battle. His redemption came through the curiosity of some humble peasants who were suspicious of horsemen they saw hiding in bushes near the Long Walls of Anastasias. They turned out to be the Avars who were intending to kidnap the emperor. Once the news reached Heraclius he hastily changed from his imperial garb and, crown under his arm, rode at full speed back to Constantinople, surrounded by a few of his bodyguard and pursued by hundreds of Avar horsemen.[58]

Meanwhile, the khagan had unleashed his troops on the Byzantine officials and entertainers who preceded Heraclius to Heraclea. Hundreds of prominent Constantinopolitans were captured by the barbarians. However, fortunately for Heraclius, he won the race to reach the capital first. When the mass of the Avars arrived at the walls of the city and found them manned by soldiers they began looting the suburbs and burning churches and monasteries outside the main defences. It is said that they looted the great church of Cosmas and Damien at Blachernae and the Church of the Archangel at Promotos. The casket containing one of the most important of the city's holy relics, the Virgin's Robe, was rescued only just in time from Blachernae and taken into the city for safekeeping in Hagia Sophia. Only when the danger was past was the Virgin's Robe returned; in a ceremony on 2 July 623 emperor and patriarch headed a procession of tearful worshippers, carrying the relic back to Blachernae. From this point onwards, and vitally during the siege of 626, in the words of Averil Cameron it was the 'palladium for the city'.[59]

Heraclius's first response to his humiliation at the hands of the Avars must have been to send for his troops in Anatolia to defend the city. But, as wiser counsels prevailed, he must have realized that to withdraw his army to Constantinople would mean that the Avars and, through them, the Persians had forced him to surrender the – admittedly slight – gains of the year. He knew that he could no longer win the war by staying within his capital and allowing his enemies to fight in Byzantine territory. Only by driving the enemy back into their own homeland could he achieve the decisive blow that would lessen the stranglehold that the Persians had on the empire.

Nevertheless, while he had been in the capital his troops in Anatolia had sustained some setbacks, including the loss of Ancyra.

Moreover, an attack by Persian ships had resulted in the loss of Rhodes and several other Byzantine islands. In the winter of 623–4 Heraclius bought off the untrustworthy Avars at a cost of 200,000 gold pieces and six prominent hostages, including his own illegitimate son John Atalarichos. This settlement must have seemed sheer madness to many of his advisers. The Avars had never proved that they could be trusted. On the other hand, what options were left? Heraclius probably knew that it would only be a matter of time before the greed of the Avars overcame any sense of obligation they felt to abide by a treaty. But he knew that he must strike a decisive blow against the Persian homeland and bring the Persians to make peace before the Avars tired of waiting patiently for Constantinople to fall unplucked into their hands and tried to take it by force.

In 623 the Persian king had shown just how long his arm was. His clients, the Avars, had come within seconds of capturing Heraclius himself and without their charismatic leader it is doubtful that the Byzantines could have continued their resistance for much longer. However, for the moment, whoever it was that looked after Heraclius, and he believed it was the Virgin Mary, had given him a second chance. Any future dealings with the perfidious Avars would be with the sword rather than the purse or the tongue of diplomacy. Clearly, whatever the Byzantines could offer the Avars to depart, the Persian king could offer more for them to stay and harass Heraclius in his capital. Khusro II had made his intentions clear. He had pushed the Romans closer to total destruction than any previous Persian leader and, however much they might struggle, he had no intention of relaxing his grip.

Heraclius would still have preferred a peaceful solution and probably maintained diplomatic contacts with the Persians for as long as possible. However, the attitude of Khusro hardened at every Byzantine setback. Before beginning the campaign of 624 Heraclius and Sergius publicized a letter purportedly from the Persian king. A modern reader can detect the subtle hand of propaganda here as the style and content are altogether too convenient for the Byzantine cause. Had Khusro really sent this letter it would have been poor diplomacy and even worse strategy. The missive of 623–4 was apparently a response to one from Heraclius pleading for peace. In it Khusro said:

Hagia Sophia, exterior and interior. The significance of Justinian's great church can best be understood by the words he spoke at the consecration of the building: 'I have vanquished, thee, O Solomon!' For the Greeks Constantinople was the 'new Jerusalem' and Hagia Sophia the new Temple of a Chosen People. Until modern times no other building in the world contained so large a floor space under a single roof. Begun by the Emperor Justinian in 532 and completed three years later, this was the masterpiece of Byzantine architecture, its great soaring dome symbolizing the relationship between heaven and earth and between God and his chosen people. The medallions suspended from the ceiling bearing Koranic inscriptions were added after the Ottoman capture of the city in 1453. *(Turkish Tourist Office)*

This magnificent statue of a Persian knight, a *clibonarius*, depicts the Sasanian monarch Khusro II, equipped for war. It is twice life-size and is in the grotto of Khusro II at Taq-i Bustan, near Kirmanshah. Khusro wears an enclosed helmet, with an aventail of mail below and his shirt of mail conceals a breastplate. Significantly,

he has no stirrups, something the Persians did not adopt until after the Arab conquest. The Byzantine heavy cavalry of Heraclius had adopted stirrups by copying the Avars and it is likely that the Arabs learned the use of stirrups from their contact with the Byzantines. *(Michael Roaf)*

The ruins of Ganzak at Takht-i Sulaiman. The Persian town of Shiz (Arabic) or Ganzak was supposedly the birthplace of Zoroastra or Zarathustra. It also housed the most holy Fire Temple of the Zoroastrian religion, known as Atur Gushnasp – the Fire Temple of the King and of the Warriors. At the centre of the site was an apparently bottomless lake, whose waters were so rich in minerals that over thousands of years it had created a basin around itself some 40 metres deep. As well as the Zoroastrian Fire Temple, the Persian king Khusro II had a royal palace at Ganzak. In 624, the Byzantines under Heraclius destroyed the holy sites at Atur Gushnasp in retaliation for the Persian depradations in Jerusalem ten years earlier. For the remainder of the Persian campaign Heraclius used Ganzak as his military headquarters and it was here that he received the Persian surrender from Khusro's son Kavad in 627. *(Michael Roaf)*

Opposite: Jousting scene from Naqsh-i Rustam. Far from being a uniquely medieval activity, jousting by heavily armoured knights with lances originated among the Parthians and early Sasanians in the third century or even earlier. In this famous rock carving from Naqsh-i Rustam, the Sasanian king Bahram II is depicted fighting a foreign, probably Parthian, opponent. Significantly, Bahram is using the two-handed lance technique, making the use of a shield impossible. *(Warwick Ball)*

The most famous of all Sasanian Persian buildings was the palace at Ctesiphon, known as the Iwan-i Kisra. Even as late as 1888 the complete façade with its great central arch was still standing. The arch, which was built without centring, is the largest in any façade in the world. A flood in 1888 destroyed the right side of the façade, which is currently being rebuilt by the Iraqi Department of Antiquities. (*Warwick Ball*)

The River Yarmuk near the modern Jordanian village of al-Hamma. Somewhere near here, at the close of the decisive battle in 636, many escaping Byzantine soldiers fell to their deaths down the steep slopes and cliffs. *(David Nicolle)*

Petra, el Deir, Jordan. The Nabatean rock city of Petra was an important trading post on the route from Arabia to Syria. We know that as a young man Mohammed encountered many Jews and Christians on his numerous journeys from Mecca to Damascus and back. After the Persian invasion of Syria in the early years of the seventh century the desert regions east and south of Palestine teemed with Christian hermits and monks escaping from the invaders. Many monks reached far into Arabia, spreading their monotheistic beliefs at the same time that Mohammed was beginning his own mission. *(David Nicolle)*

Archangel Michael with military saints. This eleventh-century jewelled and enamelled icon from the Treasury of St Mark in Venice depicts the Archangel Michael surrounded by warrior saints of the kind that were invoked by the commanders of Byzantine armies of the tenth century during their most successful campaigns. *(Scala)*

Khusro, honoured among the Gods, lord and king of all the earth, and offspring of the great Armazd, to Heraclius our senseless and insignificant servant.

You have not wished to submit yourself to us, but you call yourself lord and king. My treasure which is with you, you spend; my servants you defraud; and having collected an army of brigands, you give me no rest. So did I not destroy the Greeks? But you claim to trust in your God? Why did he not save Caesarea and Jerusalem and the great Alexandria from my hands? Do you not know that I have subjected to myself the sea and the dry land? So is it only Constantinople that I shall not be able to erase? However, I shall forgive you all your trespasses. Arise, take your wife and children and come here. I shall give you estates, vineyards and olive trees whereby you may make a living.[60]

The Armenian historian Sebeos continues by relating how the Byzantines used this particular epistle:

When the emperor Heraclius received this epistle, he ordered it to be read before the patriarch and the magnates. Entering the house of God they spread the letter before the holy altar. They fell on their faces to the ground before the Lord and wept bitterly, so that he might see the insults which his enemies had inflicted upon him.[61]

In March 624, Heraclius left his capital once more to travel east and resume command of his armies there. As he left he knew that there could be no return without victory. His wife, Martina, travelled with him, along with his two children from his first marriage. The ruthless determination that Heraclius showed during the campaign that followed speaks of some major transformation. From the emperor down to his most humble soldier the Byzantines seemed inspired, as if driven by a new clarity in their cause.

Alert to the news that the Byzantines were at Caesarea in Cappadocia in considerable force, the Persians presumed that this presaged a major campaign by Heraclius to the south-east in an attempt to regain his recently lost lands in Syria. We are told by Theophanes that Khusro himself had assembled an army of 40,000 men and was camped at Ganzak, south of Lake Urmia, ready to rush reinforcements westwards if Heraclius should threaten the Persian conquests in Syria. But the Persians had once again misread the situation. This time Heraclius had made the Persian army his target not his lost lands. In a strategy that seems remarkably modern the emperor carried economic as well as holy war into the Persian heartland, forcing Khusro to pull back his troops from Byzantine territory in an effort to prevent the Byzantines from ravaging their homes. In a *Blitzkrieg* attack through Armenia Heraclius took the Persians by surprise, travelling at speed up the Euphrates valley past the fortified city of Theodosiopolis, ravaging the countryside as he passed. City after city was taken by surprise and left a smoking ruin by the relentless invaders. Next Heraclius turned south-west following the River Araxes, thereby splitting Persian Armenia virtually in two. The cities of Dvin and Naxcawan were taken and their populations put to the sword. Panic rode ahead of the Byzantine army, and the roads were filled with refugees fleeing from the anger of the Christian God and his warriors. Success bred success and gave credence to Heraclius's rousing words. The Persians had enjoyed easy victories over the Romans for so long that complacency had replaced watchfulness in the minds of their people in Armenia, who had not seen Roman armies for generations.

Heraclius now turned due south. He crashed through the Persian defences and into Atropatene, spreading destruction in the centre of the Zoroastrian faith. As the emperor approached the city of Ganzak or Shiz, where Khusro was waiting with the main Persian army, the king's nerves apparently gave way. After burning all the crops in the area, he fled into the Zagros mountains unable to face the imminent arrival of the Byzantine juggernaut. It was the defining moment of the entire war. Anticipating a much later code of chivalry, Heraclius was seeking out his opponent, apparently prepared to settle the war by single combat. A thousand years before, Alexander of Macedon had sought out his Persian opponent Darius at the battle of Gaugemala, only for the Persian to flee the field at the onset of his nemesis. Now history was repeating itself. In addition, the moral balance between Christian and Zoroastrian was shifting in favour of the former and Heraclius was determined to drive home his advantage.

Just as the terrible sack of Jerusalem ten years before and the loss of the True Cross had spread despondency through the Christian lands of the East now the situation was reversed and Heraclius was heading towards the target that clearly dominated his strategic planning for this campaign: the great Atur Gushnasp, Fire Temple of the King and of the Warriors at Shiz (modern-day Takht-i Sulaiman). This was the pre-eminent religious site of the Zoroastrian faith and Heraclius had called on his warriors to carry out holy war against the fire-worshippers, beginning here. Shiz was a city enclosed by a massive wall. At its focal point was a temple complex and a reputedly bottomless lake. In 624 Khusro had a palace there.

Emerging from the mountains onto a high plateau, the Byzantine scouts reported that ahead of the army lay the circular, walled city of Shiz, but that there was no sign of any Persian troops. Wasting no time the Byzantines devastated the city suburbs, driving the frightened inhabitants towards the nearby hills. Instead of having to break down the powerful city walls, the Romans were able to pass through the northern gate, entering like pilgrims. Ahead of them was a vast rectangular area which contained the sacred precinct. This was bisected by a processional way to the Fire Temple and then on to the lake. Systematically, for there must be no doubt about what was taking place, Heraclius ordered the destruction of this holy site. After carrying off all the treasures in the royal palace the Byzantines symbolically extinguished the holy fire as well as polluting the sacred waters of the temple lake with battlefield corpses. This was a holy war. Like the biblical prophet Elijah, Heraclius was overthrowing the statue of Baal. Constantine's great complex of buildings which had housed the Holy Sepulchre and which had succumbed to the flames of the Persians in 614 must be avenged! The psychological and political damage to the Persian leader would be far greater by this blow to the state religion than any defeat in battle could be. Like the rape of his queen, this event was a violation of everything that Khusro was committed to protect. If he could not defend the Holy Fire then his right to rule must be brought into question. The process of undermining the prestige of the Sasanian Shah had begun and Khusro, by fleeing rather than facing his enemy, had heaped humiliation upon himself.

The lowering of Persian morale that followed the destruction of the Fire Temple at Shiz cannot be underestimated. From this time onwards Heraclius seems to have been free to set the agenda while the Persians merely maintained a chase of this most elusive of

enemies. However, it was not just the destruction of the Fire Temple
that contributed to the erosion of Persian morale but also the
performance of the respective leaders. While Heraclius literally led
his troops, Khusro directed or latterly threatened from a safe
distance. In the Persian tradition, as Michael Whitby demonstrates,
it was the task of the Persian king to lead his troops in battle.[62] The
great rock carvings at Naqsh-i Rustam reveal earlier heroic rulers
like Shapur I, symbolizing manly, military qualities. Ironically, the
magnificent statue of Khusro II at Taq-i Bustan shows him as a
mighty knight in the tradition of his ancestors. However, after 603,
he never led his troops in battle and very much left the conduct of
the war against Heraclius to his senior commanders like Shahrvaraz.
The mounted statue, therefore, is merely symbolic and served no
purpose in inspiring his troops in battle. In contrast, Heraclius
inspired his troops not simply with words or with holy symbols but
with the sight of himself fighting in the forefront of the army and
challenging – and defeating – Persian champions. One event in 603
probably explains the unwillingness of Khusro II to lead his armies
into the fight. During a battle against the Byzantines, he was lassoed
– probably by a Hunnish mercenary – and dragged from his horse,
only being saved from death or capture by his bodyguards.[63]
Whether he exhibited personal fear or was prevented from exposing
himself by his advisers we cannot know. However, it was not in the
Persian tradition for a king to behave in this way and his flight from
Shiz in 624 when faced with the possibility of meeting the vengeful
Heraclius increased the likelihood that he would eventually be
overthrown by one of his generals, probably Shahrvaraz.

At a time when the military leadership of the Persian king was so
necessary, it is ironic that Persian art displayed Khusro II as the great
hunter. On the fine silverware and pottery of the period he is never
depicted fighting a human foe, merely killing deer, wild boar or lions
and leopards. It is certainly symbolic of the royal majesty but, as
Whitby points out: 'In the real world, however, Persian kings had to
win their victories, not just rely on the symbolism of the hunting
park and artistic allegorizations, and this was particularly true for
monarchs whose hold on the throne was not completely secure, or
had to be justified against the competing interests of nobility or
priesthood.'[64]

The symbolic importance of the Persian king for the Persian army was greater than the presence of the emperor for the Romans. Only Heraclius and John Tzimisces in Byzantine history seem to have approached the Persian rulers' level of military significance. In the case of Heraclius, his emphasis on holy war and the concept of martyrdom meant that he had a dual role in the eyes of the soldiers in his army. Not only was he a trusted military leader and a great general but he was also the 'chosen one' of God and as such was a direct link with the Almighty. In this latter context he was witness to the way every man had fought in battle. Thus when the angels recorded the names of the dead souls who qualified for a superior heavenly reward, the emperor, being in the forefront of the fighting, knew personally how each man had fought in defence of the faith. The motivational effect of having such a 'chosen one' in battle was equivalent to that of the warrior-saints who were believed on numerous occasions to have entered the fray on behalf of the Christian empire.

As the winter of 624–5 drew on and the Persians began to recover their nerve, Heraclius marched northwards into quarters in Albania's Kura valley. While his soldiers rested, Heraclius drove himself on relentlessly. Although he had enjoyed a campaign of unprecedented success he knew that most of his gains had been psychological and that he had secured no major victories over the Persian field armies, which still retained their hold on Byzantine territory. What he needed now was fresh troops inspired by the message that had driven his men to such feats of arms and this explains his choice of wintering in the north rather than returning westwards as the Persians had expected. The Armenian-born Heraclius was returning to a land where he felt his message of holy war would appeal to the Christian inhabitants. His call to the Christian princes of the Caucasus to come to the aid of the faith threatened by the hated fire-worshippers had just the result he had hoped for and troops flooded into his camp from throughout Georgia, Albania and northern Armenia. In addition to being the Christian Emperor appealing to his co-religionists, he was also a successful commander whose army was assured of loot. And so, whether through spiritual conviction or in the hope of rich booty at the expense of the Persians, the tribes of the Caucasus came to his aid. Finally, remembering all too clearly the way that Persian clients, the Avars, had almost captured him the previous year, Heraclius decided to seek an ally for himself in the shape of the Turks who dominated the lands to the north of the Caucasus mountains. He sent an ambassador named Andrew to visit the Yabghu Khagan, nephew and deputy to the khagan of the Turks, offering an opportunity to gain an 'immense and countless treasure' if the Turks would join with the Romans in invading Persia from the north. The Turks were apparently attracted by the idea because they responded immediately by sending an embassy to the Black Sea coast where they took ship for Constantinople. Heraclius was not there to receive them but oaths were taken and an alliance formed.

When despatches from the emperor reached Constantinople speaking of a campaign of unparalleled success they breathed fresh life into a people who now began to dare to hope. Yet Heraclius knew that during the next campaigning season he could not take the enemy by surprise again. News that three Persian armies would take the field against him in the spring told the emperor that he would have to exploit his greater mobility as never before. Yet he was confident in his troops who, with God's will, had achieved so much. And, what was more important, his troops were confident that their commander acted with the will of God and with the protection of the Holy Mother.

Khusro had suffered rare humiliation during 624 and his enemy had enjoyed the freedom to ravage the Persian heartland while the main Persian armies were away. But had Heraclius overstretched himself? The Persian king now summoned his troops and prepared to trap the Byzantines. Khusro recalled his best general, Shahrvaraz, from the west and the man who had sacked Jerusalem now moved to bar Heraclius's retreat through Iberia. Shahraplakan guarded against any renewed invasion of Atropatene while Shahen, with a freshly raised force of 30,000 men, guarded the Bitlis Pass to the south-west of Lake Van to prevent the Byzantines escaping south through Armenia. Heraclius therefore faced an enemy growing like Hydra's heads and yet, from a military standpoint, it was an enemy already divided and waiting to be defeated piece by piece.

While the Persians guarded possible Byzantine retreat routes, Heraclius was planning a renewed and this time decisive invasion of

Atropatene. Unfortunately, as he had added many Caucasian tribesmen to his army, he now began to suffer the stresses of coalition warfare. Many of his Georgian and Armenian contingents refused to
follow him so far from their homeland and while the Byzantines disputed over the campaign ahead, the Persian armies of Shahraplakan
and Shahrvaraz closed in, hoping to encircle them. It was at this
point that Heraclius's supreme generalship showed itself. In a series
of complicated marches and counter-marches he outmanoeuvred his
three opponents and was able to defeat them one after another.

Using tactics that were to become famous among Byzantine
generals of the following centuries Heraclius provoked his enemies
before apparently retreating in headlong flight just as he had in 622.
When the Persians pursued him he slowed up as if prepared to fight
them before marching off again and escaping during an all-night
march. These 'stop-go' tactics both confused the Persians and
encouraged their complacency against an enemy who seemed always
to flee at their approach. Finally, however, the Persians found that
Heraclius had taken up a strong position on a wooded hill – we do
not know its location – and was awaiting battle. The tables were
turned. Heraclius now defeated the separate armies of Shahrvaraz
and Shahraplakan and drove them northwards in genuine retreat.
But with the third Persian army, that of Shahen, still undefeated,
Heraclius needed to keep his men on a tight rein. As soon as Shahen
reached the proposed rendezvous with his fellow generals he found
Heraclius waiting for him instead. In a brief battle the Byzantines
put Shahen's army to flight as well.

Heraclius now turned south-west and moved towards Lake Van.
The implementation of his plan to invade Persia had been prevented
by the three Persian armies and the campaigning season had been
used up by his complicated manoeuvrings in first trying to avoid
encirclement by the Persians and finally in defeating them one after
another. Even so, with winter beginning early, he still found time for
a final attack on Shahrvaraz's camp in which the Royal Wild Boar of
the Persians barely escaped with his life. Theophanes gives an
unusually vivid account of Heraclius's final success of 625.

Assuming that the Byzantines had ended their campaigning, in
view of the onset of harsh conditions, Shahrvaraz's army took up
winter quarters at Salbanon, north of Lake Van. To reduce the

pressure on his commissariat, Shahrvaraz released many of the local troops, who returned to their homes. But he had underestimated Heraclius. Once the emperor heard news that the Persians had dispersed their troops he determined to attack them, in spite of the snowy conditions. Taking personal command of an elite squadron Heraclius travelled through the night to try to surprise Shahrvaraz in his camp. In the early hours of the morning, with the snow falling, Heraclius burst into the Persian camp, killing all the guards and heading straight for the general's tent. Shahrvaraz's personal body-guard died holding off the Byzantines, allowing the naked Shahrvaraz to leap onto his horse and ride away into the darkness. For the rest of his entourage there was no escape. His servants and wives huddled on the flat roofs of the village houses but were forced to the ground when the Byzantines burned the hovels from beneath their feet. Shahrvaraz's tent was looted and the riches of the conqueror of Jerusalem were laid at the feet of God's appointed champion. Heraclius took possession, like Alexander the Great before him, of a Persian commander's worldly wealth in the form of the general's golden shield, his sword, lance, golden belt set with precious jewels and even his boots. The Persian warriors in the camp were imprisoned or slain, while those who escaped returned in disgrace to a furious Khusro. Heraclius went back to his winter quarters to reflect on his *annus mirabilis*, during which the scales of victory were weighted ever more in his favour.

Heraclius had demonstrated his superiority over the Persian commanders and the morale of the still outnumbered Byzantine troops had risen so high that where once they had fought the Persians half-defeated by their own fears, they now fought in the name of God and expected victory. At this point Khusro extended the long arm of diplomacy as he had once before when he almost trapped Heraclius: he summoned help from his Avar clients in Europe. This decision was to bring on the greatest crisis of the period: the great Avar siege of Constantinople. But before that Heraclius faced another serious situation: Shahrvaraz and Shahen threatened Anatolia in an attempt to force Heraclius to release his relentless grip on Armenia and abandon plans to invade Persia.

Heraclius now found the tables turned. As he headed back towards Anatolia from his winter quarters around Lake Van he was pursued by the vengeful Shahrvaraz, who must have felt he had a personal score to settle with the emperor who had caught him literally with his trousers down. Shahrvaraz caught up with the Byzantines before they crossed the Sarus river and a battle took place at a strategic bridging point at Adana. According to Theophanes the outcome of the battle was determined by the personal courage of Heraclius, who secured the bridge for long enough to allow his army to cross the river and reached the Cilician Gates safely:

> When the emperor saw that the barbarians had broken ranks in pursuit and that many of the Romans who were standing on the bastions were being slain, he moved against them. A giant of a man confronted the emperor in the middle of the bridge and attacked him, but the emperor struck him and threw him into the river. When this man had fallen, the barbarians turned to flight and, because of the narrowness of the bridge, jumped into the river like frogs, while others were being killed by the sword. But the bulk of the barbarians poured over the river bank: they shot arrows and resisted the passage of the Romans. The emperor did cross to the other side with a few men of his guard. He fought in a superhuman manner so that even Sarbaros [Shahrvaraz] was astonished and said to one Cosmas who was standing close to him, 'Do you see, O Cosmas, how boldly the Caesar stands in battle, how he fights alone against such a multitude and wards off blows like an anvil?' For he was recognized by his purple boots, and received many blows, although none of a serious nature in this battle. And after they had fought this battle all day, when evening came, they drew apart.[65]

Nobody should question the personal courage of a warrior like Heraclius who had risen to prominence during the reign of the Emperor Maurice and was the son of a heroic father. However, it has always been the task of ancient and medieval chroniclers to attribute to their royal paymasters the kind of personal heroism which draws gasps of wonder from friend and foe alike. In this case it is left to Shahrvaraz to comment, though it must be doubted if an enemy commander could afford to be so generous and so chivalrous. One is reminded of the comments of Saladin's brother al-Adil about Richard the Lionheart at the battle of Jaffa in 1192.[66]

The Persians invaded Anatolia in 626 with two armies. In the south, Shahrvaraz had already pursued Heraclius but had – just – been given the slip in the battle described above. Meanwhile, Shahen's northern army was advancing from Armenia. Heraclius, free for a moment from Shahrvaraz's pursuit, suddenly headed north-east to take up a position at Sebastea, where he could keep watch on Shahen and still keep in contact with Constantinople. Aware that he could not prevent Shahrvaraz in the south from closing in on his capital, he detached a force of mounted troops – for propaganda purposes said to number 12,000 but in reality probably no more than 3-4,000 – who raced along the northern support road to reach the capital before the Wild Boar could get there and close the siege. It was strategic planning of the highest quality and this operation alone sets Heraclius among the great captains of history. Once again he had surprised the Persian planners by not withdrawing to defend his capital. Instead, he had kept his army active in the field, a constant threat to the Persians if they should overcommit themselves in Anatolia, leaving their homeland open to attack.

If Heraclius baffled the Persian generals he also bewildered the chroniclers who have left accounts of his manoeuvres. We do know that the reinforcements he sent from Sebastea reached Constantinople before Shahrvaraz arrived and set up his camp just across the Bosphorus on the Asian shore at Chalcedon. These troops, added to the fleet of small ships that Heraclius had built, proved invaluable to the Patrician Bonus and Patriarch Sergius, who were responsible for the defence of the capital during the Avar siege. Moreover, from Sebastea Heraclius maintained a line of communications to the capital, down which he was able to keep up a steady supply of military advice in the weeks ahead. We do not know exactly when he moved to intercept Shahen's northern Persian army. However, whenever the battle took place we do know that the Byzantines, led by the emperor's brother Theodore, won a decisive victory, shattering both Shahen's army and his reputation. Infuriated by more bad news, Khusro ordered his commander to return to Ctesiphon. Shahen, perhaps wounded in the fighting, died soon after. His body, packed in salt, was returned to the Persian capital where Khusro had it flayed and the skin, stuffed with straw, displayed in a gruesome example of royal pique.[67]

SIX

The Avar Siege

The Persians had been convinced that if they posed a threat to Constantinople then Heraclius would be forced to return to its defence, thereby relaxing his grip on the Persian lands. But they were wrong. Heraclius had considered the danger to his capital before he embarked on his counter-offensive. In a total war – and he knew that he was fighting such a conflict – he could not allow his grip to falter for a moment. The fate of Constantinople would be decided in Atropatene just as surely as on the shores of the Bosphorus. Any commander must be able to rely on his subordinates and, in Bonus and the Patriarch Sergius, he was fortunate. The emperor could not be everywhere at once and he must be able to rely on the men he had chosen to defend the capital, including his fourteen-year-old son Constantine. Heraclius refused to imprison himself in the city, assuming that he could do more damage with his main army. The destruction of Shahen's force had proved just that.

Shahrvaraz, meanwhile, camped at Chalcedon, awaiting the arrival of the Avar khagan. The approach of the Avars through Thrace was like the movement of peoples that had taken place during the fourth century. So vast and complex was the Avar horde, consisting as it did of a multiplicity of tribes and racial groups, that to the Byzantines it seemed as if the steppes of Asia were emptying themselves at the behest of a new Attila. At Adrianople the Avar khagan stopped for a month to prepare transport for his immense range of siege artillery but did not attempt to capture that city.

Figures for the size of ancient armies are impossible to verify. Nevertheless, we have no reason to doubt the statistics given to us by the numerous Byzantine eyewitnesses. Apparently, an advanced force of 30,000 Avars, Gepids and allied people, mainly Slavs, crossed the Long Wall and approached Constantinople on 29 June 626. This vanguard spent some time preparing for the siege ahead, choosing campsites, foraging for supplies and contacting the Persians across the Bosphorus by fire-signals. While this was going on Shahrvaraz at Chalcedon could do little more than watch. His role was entirely psychological. Occupying the Asiatic shore, his presence was a signal to the defenders of Constantinople that they could expect no help from their emperor in the east. Nevertheless, Shahrvaraz had no fleet and was unable to cross to the European side to join the Avars. The Avars had vessels of their own and it is conceivable that they might have been able to transport the Persians if they could gain naval supremacy, at least temporarily, over the Byzantine fleet.

Four weeks after the arrival of the Avar advanced guard the main body of the Avars, estimated at up to 80,000 warriors, arrived under the command of the khagan himself. As was the habit of the Avars before a siege, the khagan, spent some time gaining a psychological advantage over the defenders by parading the full strength of his army for all the inhabitants of Constantinople to see and fear. The lamellar armour of many of the Avar soldiers impressed the inhabitants of the city by reflecting the sun's rays in a dazzling way, seeming to increase their numbers tenfold according to some eye-witnesses. The khagan and other Avar champions indulged in the equestrian gymnastics typical of all the steppe-tribes,[68] demonstrating their riding skills and attempting to lower the morale of the defenders. The Byzantines retaliated with processions around the battlements by priests carrying holy icons and other Christian relics. It is doubtful if either side entirely understood the significance of their opponents' antics.

Two days of 'softening up' followed before the first general assault began on the Theodosian Walls on the last day of July. Fierce hand-to-hand fighting stretched the full four miles of the walls, though the main Avar threat was on the high ground between the Polyandrion and the Romanus Gates where the defenders were not able to directly overlook the assault troops. Unlike most of the steppe people, the Avars were masters of siege warfare, employing a wide range of instruments including Chinese lever-artillery, trebuchets and as many as a dozen siege-towers. They had learned a lot from the Chinese and combined the military skills of that civilization with the mounted tactics of the Hepthalite Huns and the Gök or Blue Turks. The Avars were far from being barbarians, particularly in a military sense. In some ways they were more advanced even than the Byzantines and the latter were able to learn much from them, including the use of stirrups, the wooden-framed saddle and the Avar bow. Constantinople, probably the most frequently besieged city in history, was about to undergo its baptism of fire, its first and probably most dangerous siege.

The khagan, a veteran of many sieges though hardly on this scale, gradually increased the pressure. After an attritional struggle on the walls he began to move his engineers into position to undermine the fortifications. Other craftsmen were deployed to fit together his siege engines which had been transported in pieces, including the dozen siege-towers high enough to overlook the city walls.

Inside Constantinople the two regents, lay and spiritual, played a waiting game. Aware that the Avars must eventually try to storm the walls, they had sought every advantage to delay that moment. In the meantime, they concentrated on strengthening the city's defences. They received a steady flow of advice from Heraclius, often arriving by water from the emperor's army on the Black Sea coast. From the writing of George of Pisidia we know that Heraclius had advised Bonus to strengthen the foundations of the city walls, erect barriers in front of them to prevent the Avar siege towers coming too close and to build walls projecting outwards from the city walls to hamper the besiegers. Aware that the Avars would try to make use of the naval strength of their Slav allies, Heraclius had also advised Bonus to concentrate much of his work on strengthening the city's sea walls, which were weaker than the land fortifications and which had never really been tested in battle. The emperor's forward planning had at least provided his capital with a substantial naval force, not of the great dromons that were a feature of Byzantine navies in the empire's prime, but of smaller, more manoeuvrable craft that were to be more than a match for the Slav canoes in the struggle ahead.

After the failure of the first all-out attack on 31 July the Avar khagan altered his tactics. The defenders had already demonstrated that the walls of Constantinople would not be crossed without an immense struggle, while at sea the Byzantine navy, assisted by all merchant ships in the harbour at that time, showed how difficult it would be for the Slav canoes to reach the sea walls. The khagan therefore reverted to psychological warfare, intending to show the Byzantines the hopelessness of their situation, with enemies controlling both the European and the Asian shores. Bonus, aware that time was on the side of the defenders rather than the Avars, was happy to prolong any negotiations. He sent word that the Avars could still withdraw from the city walls unhindered and take with them the tribute that had been agreed by Heraclius three years before. The khagan refused this suggestion, offering instead to spare the lives of the city folk provided that they withdrew and left him their property. After some initial negotiations of this sort the khagan asked Bonus to send envoys to further the discussions.

What was taking place was the kind of mind game that either preceded or even in some cases took the place of the physical phase of the medieval siege. The Avars were intent on lowering Byzantine morale so that the city would fall from within due to the collapse of its leaders' confidence. However, in Bonus and Sergius the Avars were to encounter men whose morale was unbreakable. Ten years earlier, perhaps, Constantinople would have fallen with the inevitability of so many Byzantine cities from Antioch to Alexandria. But the successes of Heraclius in Persia and the feeling that the empire was fighting with the blessing of God and the help of the Holy Virgin had made the Byzantines warriors of their faith and men who would not yield to pagan Avars and Persian fire-worshippers. The part played in the siege by Sergius and his monks cannot be overstated. It was the second half of the holy war that had begun in 622 when Heraclius undertook his crusade against the Persians. Now it was the turn of the ordinary citizens and soldiers of Constantinople to demonstrate their faith and if necessary to become martyrs for Christianity. George of Pisidia later referred to the Patriarch Sergius as 'the general of armed tears'; his tears were not those of fear or despair but of compassion and love for his people. During the siege Sergius kept up the spirits of the defenders with homilies and exhortations, and fixed icons of the Virgin over every gate into the city so that none should fall to the enemy. When he did this he challenged the Avars: 'The fighting is wholly against these pictures, you foreign and devilish troops. A woman, the Mother of God, will quell all your boldness and boasting with one command, for she is truly the Mother of Him who drowned Pharaoh with all his army in the Red Sea.'[69] From this moment onwards the Christians in the city firmly believed that they were under divine protection. Stories circulated both as rumours and as official propaganda that the Virgin Mother had been seen fighting to protect the city walls. As one commentator said: 'No city can be guarded unless it is guarded by God; our enemies attack us with cavalry and chariots and a great multitude, but we will be strengthened in the name of the Lord God. For the Lord himself will fight for us, and the Virgin Mother of God will be the defender of the city.'[70] Averil Cameron has shown the connection between the warrior-maiden image of the Virgin and the pagan figure of Victory. In some ways the Mother of God was viewed almost as a queen rather than a biblical figure.[71] In addition, Sergius and his senior clergy took part in processions bearing icons, exhorting the Virgin and the warrior-saints to come to the aid of God's chosen people.

Bonus sent a distinguished group of envoys from the city to meet the Avar khagan. They had twin purposes. Surviving the siege was the primary target but if relations with the Avars could be restored, even temporarily, then the outcome of the entire war with Persia might depend on it. As well as Anathasius, who was already known to the khagan, the envoys were the Patricians George, Theodore and Theodosius. But if they hoped to get the better of the Avars they were quickly disappointed. The khagan welcomed them to his tent where three ornate chairs had been set up. Bidding them stand facing him he then ordered his servants to escort three Persian emissaries, finely dressed in pure silk, to the chairs where they were seated in full view of the Byzantines. The Persians had brought the khagan news of the war in their homeland and had certainly put paid to any hope the Byzantines had of persuading the Avars to call off the siege. The khagan then reiterated his offer that the Byzantines could leave their city with their lives and a cloak and shirt, allowing him to take possession of Constantinople. The smiling faces of the three Persian envoys told the Byzantines everything they needed to know. They had won over the khagan with their lies.

The Avar khagan turned to the Byzantines and told them that the Persians had convinced him that Heraclius had not been victorious in Persia nor had he sent an army to save the capital. In frustration the Patrician George called out: 'These men are impostors and do not speak a word of truth, since our army is arrived here and our most pious lord is in their country, utterly destroying it.'

The atmosphere in the tent, clearly already tense, now boiled over into violence. One of the Persians jumped to his feet and threw insults at George. Only the absence of weapons prevented blood from being spilled. The khagan seemed almost amused to see the envoys of both sides spitting and fuming in his presence. The Patrician George, however, knew who was manipulating the situation. Ignoring the Persians and their insults he turned to face the khagan. All hope of a negotiated end to the siege was gone if the khagan had received a better offer than the Byzantines could give. While they had proposed money and tribute, the Persians had offered something beyond price – Constantinople itself. If the Persians had promised to keep the main Byzantine field army busy in the east while the Avars had a free hand to take Constantinople and keep it, there was nothing the Christian envoys could do. Before leaving George did score one diplomatic point. 'Although you have such great hordes, you still apparently need Persian help', he spat out as he departed the khagan's tent, leaving the Avars to question whether they had weakened the Byzantines at all by showing them the Persian envoys or whether they had merely stiffened the determination of the Christians to defend their city. In a matter of hours he was to have his answer.

That night the Persian envoys tried to cross the Bosphorus in disguise, hiding beneath the covers of a small skiff. The alertness of the Byzantine sailors prevented them reaching the Asian shore and provided the Christian authorities with a chance to issue a defiant reply to their enemies. One envoy was killed and decapitated in the skiff, while the other two were made prisoner. One of these unfortunates had his hands cut off and tied around his neck along with the head of the man slain in the skiff. In that condition he was returned to the khagan as a diplomatic answer to the Avar request for the city. The other man was sailed over to the Asian shore and paraded before the Persian troops at Chalcedon. Then he was decapitated and his head fired into the Persian camp. The Persians had their answer too.

The khagan's reaction was immediate if ill-advised. He decided to launch his sea canoes to fetch the 3,000 Persian veterans he had been promised by Shahrvaraz. An adverse head wind allowed the Slav canoes to evade the seventy Byzantine ships that were watching them and reach the Asian shore. Here they embarked the Persian force before attempting to run the gauntlet for a second time. This time their luck ran out and the Byzantine ships engaged them in a short but decisive naval engagement. For the Persians it was a massacre and casualty figures of as many as 3,000 or 4,000 drowned indicate that, however inflated these figures might be, the Christians won a total victory which they attributed to divine intervention.

Land operations reached a new intensity as the khagan, humiliated by the naval setback, prepared for a general assault to take the land walls. But the city's fortifications were too formidable an obstacle to be overcome in a quick operation and the huge Avar army was beginning to succumb to logistical deficiencies. Maintaining a vast army in the field was clearly beyond the strength of the Avar system. Soon so many men were away requisitioning food and other supplies that sorties from the city garrison were posing a real threat to the camp's security.

The khagan, by now as desperate as the city's defenders, began an all-out assault on the land walls. Throughout the day and night of 6–7 August the Avars threw all their strength into the attack. On the morning of the 7th a naval attack on the sea walls was coordinated with the land operations. The Slav fleet, following a pre-arranged signal from Blachernae, carried marines across the Golden Horn and against Constantinople's sea walls. But the Christian fleet, and we do not know how, had got advanced warning of the proposed attack and were waiting in ambush. In fact, they almost certainly made a false signal to the Slavs and drew them out to disaster. What followed was an even more dramatic version of the naval battle in which the Persians had been lost a few days before. The Slav ships were no match for the Byzantine fleet and most of them were destroyed. The fate of their crews was unenviable: many female bodies were later found among the dead and drowned; those who managed to swim ashore were either massacred by the Christians or by the furious Avars, who saw that with the defeat of their fleet there was no likelihood of forcing such a powerful city to surrender.

So sudden and so immense was the Christian victory off Blachernae that men sought an explanation in the divine intervention of the city's protector, the Holy Virgin. As so often in Byzantine history God's will was not merely manifest but visible. Many Christian warriors claim to have seen the holy mother of God with them in the combat, brandishing a sword and fighting as a warrior-maiden. It is said that the Avar khagan saw a veiled lady fighting in the Christian ranks and that this finally convinced him to call off the siege. The epic fight in front of the Virgin's own church at Blachernae was, in the words of Averil Cameron, 'one of the most complete moments of unity ever realized in Constantinople'.[72]

It required the strongest discipline for the Byzantine commanders to hold back their men, inspired by visions, from sallying forth and fighting the pagans beyond the walls. For men like Bonus, that way lay madness. It was not for the defenders of the city walls to throw away everything they had won and risk combat with a still powerful enemy. He would release the cavalry to harry the Avars once he had seen them disappearing over the horizon.

The Avar khagan had risked everything on a short, sharp operation and it had failed. His naval arm was lost and this meant that he could only succeed in capturing so great a city after a lengthy siege, for which he could not keep a sufficiently large force supplied. Moreover, there were rumours that all was not well within the polyglot Avar army. The khagan's treatment of the Slavs who survived the naval debacle hardly suggests that morale was very high within the Avar ranks. In view of the disintegration of the Avar polity that followed in the years ahead it is clear that the khagan's defeat at Constantinople had a decisive effect on his ability to command his subject races.

As night fell on 8 August, the khagan gave orders for his army to withdraw from the environs of Constantinople. Across the Bosphorus Shahrvaraz and his Persians watched the departure of their allies in silence. Flames on the European shore signalled the retreat of the Avars. The churches of SS Cosmas and Damien and of St Nicholas were torched. For a while the land walls of Constantinople were ringed by the burning siege towers that the Avars could not take with them.

Byzantine horsemen followed the retreating Avars, ensuring that this was no trick, but once it was obvious that there would be no attempt to renew the siege the two regents, Bonus and Sergius, rode out through the Golden Gate of the city to inspect the ruins of the Avar camp. All that was left was the flotsam of war: unburied corpses of men and animals, the charred ruins of once great siege engines, trebuchets and towers of the Chinese type that were to be studied by the eager engineers of Byzantium. The seashore was littered with the carcasses of the Slavs who had succumbed in the naval battle. The canoes and boats that had survived the fight to reach the shore were now burned by Christians eager to destroy every last trace of their enemy.

At Chalcedon Shahrvaraz had already begun marching his Persian troops eastwards. Stories that Theodore, Heraclius's brother, was approaching with an army may have hastened his departure. We cannot be certain whether the rumours were true or simply a further element in the disinformation campaign operated by the Byzantines.

The Byzantine victory at Constantinople was a turning point. Whatever now ensued in Persia, for Heraclius the empire was saved. The triumph of the Byzantine navy had demonstrated to the Persians that without a powerful fleet they had no chance of winning a decisive victory in the war.

Throughout the siege Shahrvaraz endured the frustration of military impotence. In spite of his strength he could offer little help to his allies or contribute much to the desperate struggle swaying back and forth on the European shore. Additionally, rumours continually reached him of developments in Persia where the Byzantines under their emperor were as yet undefeated. Moreover, news that the Turks had crossed the Caucasus and were invading Albania as allies of Heraclius proved to be accurate. The Turkish army was led by the Yabghu Khagan, the man who had made the original contract with the Byzantines, and his troops soon ravaged Albania. The Turkish commander sent an insulting ultimatum to Khusro, addressing him merely as 'governor of Mesopotamia'; the Turks, meanwhile, claimed their khagan as 'King of the North, Lord of the whole world, your king and the King of Kings'.[73] The Turks rampaged across Iberia and began besieging the provincial capital

Tiflis. With their homeland at the mercy of a pitiless enemy, the Persian soldiers pleaded with their officers to be able to return to protect their loved ones. Eventually, with the Avars clearly beaten, Shahrvaraz turned for home. There was nothing further that he could do for the moment and if he waited too long there was a danger that he could be trapped against the sea if the Byzantine army under the emperor's brother Theodore, which had already accounted for Shahen, should arrive at the capital.

SEVEN

Alexander Reborn

The defeat of the Avars at Constantinople was one of the most remarkable events in Byzantine history. Although the plaudits naturally went to the defenders of the city, the Patrician Bonus and the Patriarch Sergius, and even to the emperor's fourteen-year-old son Constantine, it was the careful defensive planning undertaken by Heraclius and his officers before they left for Persia that enabled the victory to be won. Above all, as was to be the case time after time in the future, it was the Byzantine fleet that saved the city by dominating the sea approaches. Future chronicles even equated the destruction of the Slavonic fleet in the Golden Horn with the drowning of the pharaoh's army in the Red Sea. With the Patriarch Sergius compared to a new Moses and the emperor to a new David, the biblical imagery played a decisive part in the successful propaganda war waged against the Persians by the Byzantines.

The chronicles are unclear about Heraclius's whereabouts in the winter of 626–7. The strategic situation suggests that he may have had an opportunity to spend some months in Constantinople. The Avars had withdrawn in the west and were beginning to experience the internal splits that were eventually to end in the their total disintegration, so Heraclius must have felt content to concentrate his attention on the defeat of the Persians. Shahrvaraz and his army had withdrawn from Chalcedon. The news that Heraclius's Turkish allies had invaded his homeland troubled the Persian general and resulted in his urgent withdrawal through Anatolia. For the moment, therefore, Heraclius must have been free to rest and plan his final campaign in the relative comfort of his capital.

Having sown the wind, Khusro now reaped the whirlwind. His diplomacy had inflicted the Avars on the Byzantine capital in 626. Now the Byzantines were retaliating by financing the Turkish invasion of the Persian province of Albania, which was situated between the Caucasus and the Caspian Sea. The Turks burst through the frontier defences and spread destruction throughout the Persian countryside, right up to the capital city of Partaw. It was an awful and unexpected disaster for Khusro, who had committed all his forces to fighting the Byzantines and now found himself bereft of troops to combat the Turks. Heraclius had made several attempts to reach a peaceful conclusion with the Sasanians but Khusro had refused. Having tasted great triumphs in the previous decade, he now found himself a victim of his own intransigence. Persian kings lived or died by the success of their armies. If he could not defeat the Byzantines during the coming campaign season he would be unlikely to escape an assassin or a palace coup.

In the spring of 627 Heraclius left Constantinople and travelled down the Black Sea coast to Lazica, where his main army had been wintering on the plains east of Trebizond. We are told that his small fleet carried much ceremonial equipment as well as the staff officers and military regalia that would be needed for the campaign ahead. The emperor was due to meet the leader of his new allies, the Yabghu Khagan Ziebel, nephew and deputy to the great Turkish khagan himself. The Byzantines were masters of such occasions, achieving diplomatic successes without speaking a word. All was done with a kind of ceremonial body language that transcended communication difficulties. Hundreds of Byzantine troops in their parade uniforms – presumably headed by the guards regiments with the Excubitores, acting as personal bodyguards to the emperor, in the forefront – were assembled for a great ceremony akin to a modern trooping of the colour. Heraclius, magnificently adorned in the mixture of religious and military garb that reflected the contrasting natures of his imperial power, rode on his favourite warhorse Dorkon surrounded by his senior officers and aides. On all sides there were priests holding aloft bejewelled crosses, and icons glittered in the bright sunlight. Hundreds of banners and holy standards fluttered in the wind, most bearing the holy cross in various forms. The nearby hillsides acted as an arena and were crowded with both Christian and Turkish troops. From the east the Turkish leader Ziebel rode towards Heraclius, surrounded in his turn by mounted horsemen bearing the banners and emblems of the Turkish people. Pre-eminent among these was the golden wolfhead banner of the khagan himself. Behind the mounted men there were many wagons fitted with masts from which hung yak tails and the black and white horsetails beloved of the steppe nomads. It seemed that the east was alive with horsemen darting in and out, racing up and down, showing off their gymnastics skills or whirling lassoes.

As the official parties from West and East drew closer the Turkish leader suddenly rode forward alone, vaulted from his horse and fell to his knees in front of Heraclius to do him obeisance. It was a tense and impressive moment. Heraclius, surprised at this spontaneity, smiled and leaned forward to gesture Ziebel to his feet. The two leaders embraced and volleys of cheers broke out from the hillsides, accompanied by the raucous sounds of the Turkish musicians. Once Heraclius had gestured Ziebel to remount his horse, he signalled to his servants to bring forward his own crown that he had brought with him from Constantinople and, in a ceremonial gesture, he called the Turk his brother, meaning his equal, and then crowned him. With the diplomatic ice broken, the two parties intermingled and Heraclius entertained the leading Turks to an immense banquet. When the feasting ended the emperor bestowed the rich plate they had used for the feast on his Turkish guests and then presented Ziebel with other rich gifts, including an imperial robe and pearl earrings. But Heraclius had been holding back his greatest present until last. To everyone's great surprise the emperor offered his guest the hand of his eldest daughter, the sixteen-year-old Epiphaneia-Eudokia, daughter of his first wife the beloved Empress Fabia-Eudokia. By such a marriage he hoped to seal his alliance with the Turks.[74]

His new Turkish allies were already besieging the Iberian capital Tiflis by the time Heraclius arrived. Unlike the Avars, the Turks were not renowned for their siegecraft and the Byzantines soon took over the bulk of the operation, deploying their heavy stone-throwers and siege engines. Heraclius even diverted a river to undermine the walls of the city but the defenders grimly held on until their leader, Stephen of Iberia, was killed in a skirmish. The allies managed to capture the outer parts of Tiflis but the garrison retreated into the citadel, from where it maintained a stout resistance. Heraclius had little interest in the capture of Tiflis and planned instead to head south, carrying his destructive campaign into the heart of the Persian state. He realized that the Turkish leader would be content to sack Tiflis and loot the wealthy city. Taking an elite force of some 40,000 Turkish horsemen with him, he separated from the Turkish khagan and marched south through the ancient Roman province of Transcaucasia, leaving his allies to starve Tiflis into surrender.

A Persian army under Shahraplakan had moved up from Ctesiphon but found it impossible to intervene because of the overwhelming strength of the Byzantine and Turkish force. Even a second Persian army, commanded by Rahzadh, confined itself to a watching brief. Yet again the Persians mistook Byzantine intentions. Expecting the Byzantine army to pass westwards through Armenia and return to Anatolia they were outmanoeuvred by Heraclius, who once again turned south and this time invaded Atropatene, determined to deliver a decisive blow to the Sasanids. With his Turkish allies Heraclius spread destruction far and wide through the Persian province. But as he moved south he was taking his steppe-born allies further and further from their natural habitat and into desert regions where they were ill at ease. Moreover, with winter approaching the Turks called an end to their campaigning season, withdrawing to the north, loaded with booty and carrying the thanks of a Christian emperor. For Heraclius, however, there could be no easy withdrawal. Having reached the Zagros mountains he was now closer than ever to the capital of his enemy the Sasanian shah.

The Persian commander, Rahzadh, had been following Heraclius, unable to intervene to put an end to his devastation of Atropatene because of the Turkish presence. But once he heard that the Turks had withdrawn he prepared for a decisive battle to end the Byzantine invasion. Meanwhile, Heraclius was off again on a lightning march, this time across the Zagros mountains and into Mesopotamia. All the Persians could do was follow in the Byzantines' wake and hope to bring them to battle before they reached Ctesiphon, which was clearly now Heraclius's target. Khusro, whose nerve seems to have cracked by this point, called on Rahzadh to bring Heraclius to battle come what may. He must be prepared to fight even if it cost him his life and the lives of his men – hardly the instructions of a well-balanced strategist who could still call on Shahrvaraz's unbroken army.

When Heraclius heard from his scouts that Rahzadh and his men had crossed the Great Zab river, he sent out an elite reconnaissance force under a commander named Baanes. Baanes ambushed a company of Persian soldiers, killing their captain and bringing his head back to the emperor on a pike. He also brought back captives, including an important man who was the sword-bearer to the Persian general himself. This young man, probably a squire, told Heraclius – either from fear or bravado – that his master was under instructions from Khusro to fight the Christians as soon as he met them and to fight them to a finish. Furthermore, Rahzadh was expecting reinforcements from Ctesiphon in the shape of 3,000 men, including some heavy cavalry. Heraclius was determined to exploit this news and to force Rahzadh to give battle before his reinforcements arrived. He therefore sent out scouts to find a suitable place where he could draw Rahzadh into a fight. Once a location was identified he formed up his army into the traditional three divisions. Rahzadh, eager to fight, had clouds of scouts of his own and as soon as he knew that Heraclius was preparing for battle he hurried forward, having formed his own troops into three dense formations.

Heraclius knew that the decisive battle had been forced on him and must now be fought. His usual advantage in manoeuvring was denied him because the enemy scouts were aware of all of his preparations and Rahzadh was not himself seeking any tactical advantages. The Persian commander, leading a mixture, one suspects, of inexperienced recruits and older soldiers, possibly even garrison troops from Ctesiphon, knew that his best chance against Heraclius, a brilliant strategist, was to grapple with him and to fight an attritional battle in which the Byzantines would be seriously weakened if not defeated. Such a bloodbath would force the Christian emperor to call off his campaign and withdraw to his own territory. Heraclius may well have understood that these would be the Persian tactics but he had no opportunity to avoid battle with Rahzadh and had to take the consequences. If he wished to capture the Persian capital Ctesiphon, he must expect to suffer heavy losses in doing so.

The decisive battle of Nineveh was fought on 12 December 627.[75] The sources are not entirely reliable in their accounts of the size of the forces, though it seems likely that the two armies were equally balanced. The Byzantines, though exhausted after such a long campaign, were thoroughly battle-hardened by now and, moreover, were veterans of many victories over the same enemy. The battle itself took on a legendary importance for later crusaders because of the exploits of Heraclius himself. Theophanes describes the sort of combat in which Richard the Lionheart would have excelled but we cannot be certain that the emperor's guards would have allowed him to expose himself so willingly. At the age of fifty-one Heraclius was approaching late middle age and might easily have succumbed to a powerful opponent. Nevertheless, it was the task of chroniclers to maximize the achievements of a leader so clearly selected by God to lead his chosen people in battle. Moreover, Theophanes, writing a century after the events, was basing his account on contemporary eyewitness reports or documents produced by the emperor's staff officers. With this in mind we must give some credence to the chronicler's account of Heraclius's success in individual struggles against three Persian knights – one of them wounded him in the lip and another injured the face of the emperor's famous horse, Dorkon. Fortunately, the heads of Byzantine cavalry horses were protected by lamellar armour and in this instance Dorkon came to no great harm. Theophanes described how it happened: 'The emperor's tawny horse called Dorkon [meaning 'the Gazelle']⁷⁶ was wounded in the thigh by some infantryman who struck it with a spear. It also received several blows of the sword on the face, but, wearing as it did a cataphract made of sinew, it was not hurt, nor were the blows effective.'

According to Theophanes, at Nineveh Heraclius led by example, riding out to the front of his army and responding to a challenge by one of the Persian champions.⁷⁷ This kind of chivalric behaviour has parallels in medieval history. Even King Robert the Bruce responded to the challenge of Sir Henry de Bohun at Bannockburn in 1314. We know that the Persian commander Rahzadh died at Nineveh but there is no evidence to suggest that he was the first man killed by Heraclius. Nevertheless, as a demonstration of God's will and protection, the emperor's successes must have inspired his soldiers with the feeling that they could not lose.

Once the preliminaries were over the trumpets sounded and the two armies rushed at each other. Normally, the Sasanian archers began by showering their enemies with arrows but the foggy conditions that prevailed on the morning of the battle meant that they were unusually ineffective. In any case, Sasanid bows did not have the power of the Hunnish or the Byzantine bow and the heavily protected Byzantine troops did not suffer heavy casualties in this stage of the battle. The mass of troops on both sides were light cavalry armed with bows or lances, and the Byzantine horse archer was a more effective soldier by now than he had been at the start of the war. Horse archers outnumbered the heavy cavalry in each army by as many as ten to one. The Byzantine infantry, however, was of a much better quality than the Persian. The Armenian infantrymen fighting with the Byzantine army were well equipped, heavily armoured and well motivated. The Persian levies were, by contrast, very poor in quality and fought under compulsion. It is recorded that on occasion they were chained together to prevent them fleeing from the first onset of battle. Their leather-covered cane shields were in marked contrast to Byzantine ones made of wood, leather or iron. The contempt shown by the aristocratic horsemen in the Persian armies for their own infantry echoes similar attitudes held by the Parthians and even the Achaemenid Persians who had succumbed to Alexander's elite Macedonian phalangists 1,000 years before the battle of Nineveh.

Both Roman and Sasanian cavalrymen rode full-sized horses, rather than the Asiatic ponies used by the Huns or Turks. As such they had enormous momentum in a charge and expected to over-throw their enemies by weight alone. The Byzantine cataphracts had been modelled on Parthian forces and thus in action there was little to choose between the effectiveness of individual warriors. The Sasanians also had an elite reserve cavalry nicknamed 'the 10,000 Immortals' in memory of the famous Achaemenid infantry unit of that name. However, as a cavalry force, it must have been far smaller in number than the Achaemenid infantry and by the time of Nineveh its morale must have sunk to a low ebb after heavy losses suffered in covering many Persian retreats.

Most fearful of all the weapons fielded by the Persians at Nineveh, as elsewhere, were the elephants which added stability to the reserve. Although these huge pachyderms often terrified and disordered the Byzantine cavalry they were as immobile as stone block-houses and could easily be evaded. Their effectiveness in battle was often related to the overall morale of the force and they only contributed chaos and terror to a beaten and fleeing army.

We know that Nineveh was an extraordinarily hard-fought battle which is said to have lasted from dawn to late in the evening. This suggests that an air of desperate defiance, perhaps even suicidal resistance, inspired the Persians, so near to their capital. For both sides the consequences of defeat were unthinkable. For the Byzantines retreat from the centre of Persia was impossible: slavery and death must be the price of military defeat. For the Persians, however, defeat would mean national disaster. The enemy was within a short distance of their capital and if the battle was lost Ctesiphon must fall. These considerations undoubtedly underpinned the struggle that now took place. Casualties on both sides are impossible to quantify although losses among the senior commanders were particularly heavy. It is reported that all the senior Persian commanders died, leaving their troops leaderless. Eventually, the Persians pulled back from the battlefield to their camp and afterwards into the hills north of Nineveh. Before they did so, however, the chroniclers tell us that they maintained a 'death-watching honour guard' by one of the streams on the edge of the battlefield. The fact that they were able to do this unhindered indicates that the struggle had exhausted the Byzantines and they did not pursue their beaten foe.

Heraclius, lightly wounded, needed treatment and for once he did not display his usual lightning tactics. The booty the Persians left behind was immense and the Byzantines devoted their efforts to pillaging the enemy camp. Twenty-eight Persian banners had been taken in the fighting and although many thousands of Persians lay dead on the battlefield, some 6,000 prisoners were taken whose lives were spared on the orders of the emperor himself. According to Theophanes, the Byzantines: 'took many gold swords and gold belts set with pearls, and the shield of Rahzadh, which was all of gold and had 120 laminae, and his gold breastplate; and they brought in his caftan together with his head, and his bracelets and his gold saddle.'[78]

Heraclius was now able to turn south, unfettered by any immediate threat from Persian forces, and advance upon Ctesiphon. After resting his army for a few days he commenced his march towards the Persian capital but found himself hampered by the complex of canals and tributaries of the great River Tigris. Each river crossing delayed him because the closer he got to Ctesiphon, the more fanatical was the resistance he encountered from disorganized Persian troops. He crossed the Little Zab and spent Christmas of 627 with a Christian family. Then on 26 December the Byzantines began capturing the palaces and castles on the outskirts of Ctesiphon. All the time the remnants of the Persian army defeated at Nineveh shadowed the Byzantine forces, fearful of battle yet seemingly determined to harass the invaders. An unopposed crossing of the River Diyala brought Heraclius the prize of the magnificent palace known as the 'Paradise of Beklal'. Deserters from the Persian court brought the emperor news that Khusro was torn between a last stand with his guards or flight from his palace at Dastagerd. Apparently, self-preservation prevailed and the Persian shah fled rather than face the relentless Christian emperor.

There is an almost surreal quality to accounts of this period which is probably the result of the confused information that can be gleaned from the chronicles. We are left with an image of Heraclius, so rapid in many of his military manoeuvres that he leaves his opponent virtually gasping, now settling down with the fruits of his conquests and holding horse races and games in the hippodrome which lay alongside the palace at Beklal. The Byzantines sauntered at liberty in a vast menagerie of ostriches, deer and zebra. Yet while they rested or behaved like tourists the Persian shah was only a few miles away and still organizing resistance. On waking from this apparent dream the emperor gave over the herds of animals to his troops and everyone ate well for the first time in months.

The Byzantines now pushed on towards the fortified royal city of Dastagerd, which the Sasanian kings had used as their capital for the previous 100 years. Here the vast wealth of the kingdom was stored and its capture by Heraclius was the final episode in the great 1,000-year struggle between the Greco-Romans and the Persians. In the royal palace at Dastagerd the victorious Byzantines felt the pressure of history as nowhere else. Here they found more than 300 Roman standards, relics of Roman defeats stretching back to Crassus at Carrhae nearly 600 years before. The triumph of the great Shapur over the Emperor Valerian at Edessa in 260 resulted in the capture of many of these standards, for an immense Roman army was defeated and enslaved on this occasion. It is said that as many as 70,000 Romans were taken prisoner, that they took Persian wives and that their descendants formed the backbone of the population of Khuzistan by the seventh century.[79]

Although Khusro, in his flight, had taken much of the royal treasury, piled up on the backs of elephants, camels and mules, enough had been left behind to astonish the Byzantines, no strangers themselves to such luxuries. Theophanes has left us a lengthy account of the wonders that met the eyes of soldiers, some of whom had been campaigning with Heraclius for six years and who were now to be rewarded for their efforts:

> They also found the goods that had been left behind, namely a great quantity of aloes and big pieces of aloe wood, each weighing 70 or 80lb, much silk and pepper, more linen shirts than one could count, sugar, ginger and many other goods. Others found silver, silken garments, woollen rugs and woven carpets – a great quantity of them and very beautiful, but on account of their weight they burnt them all. They also burnt the tents of Khusro and the porticoes he set up whenever he camped in a plain, and many of his statues. They also found in this palace an infinite number of ostriches, gazelles, wild asses, peacocks and pheasant, and in the hunting park huge live lions and tigers.[80]

In addition to the wealth of the Sasanian state, Heraclius also found in Dastagerd many Christian slaves who had been brought to Persia over the previous two decades from the cities of Syria and Egypt. Captives from Edessa, Alexandria, Damascus and most of all Jerusalem flooded to the emperor in pure joy at the great Christian victory. Few Roman generals and still fewer emperors had presided over so great a liberation of Roman citizens from the oppression of a pagan regime. The name of Moses was on everyone's lips as Heraclius set his people free. The emperor himself was constantly aware that this was God's fight and that he came to avenge the depredations of pagan fire-worshippers in Christian lands. While he rewarded his soldiers with the loot of the defeated Persians he destroyed the palaces of Khusro as punishment for the violations of Jerusalem. Just as Alexander the Great burned Persepolis a thousand years before, so Heraclius torched Dastagerd, with the cold eye of God's avenging minister.

Thousands of palace servants and eunuchs were brought before Heraclius for judgement but he was not at war with such people. He questioned many to find news of Khusro and learned that the shah had fled by escaping through a hole in the wall. For a Persian ruler it was an abject and humiliating retreat, costing him what was left of his already tarnished reputation. Khusro fled with his wives and servants in a tumult of screaming women and wailing children, eventually sheltering for the night in a farmer's tiny hovel with enough room for just himself inside. His dependants spent the night at the mercy of the elements and presumably the pursuing Byzantines. He would have felt chagrined if he had known that while he crouched on the dung-covered floor of a farmer's hut the Christian emperor was drinking his best wine and Byzantine troops were dining on his ostriches and zebra.

Before abandoning Dastagerd, Khusro had set about ensuring that if he should fall, Persia would fall with him. Shahrvaraz was the only Persian commander still in the field with an organized army. Jealous of his general, Khusro sent a message to Kardarigas, Shahrvaraz's lieutenant, calling on him to murder the general and take command himself. By chance, the messenger was captured by the Byzantines and this meant they now possessed a powerful weapon with which to divide the Persians.

The last days of Khusro II were almost as humiliating as those that his conqueror was to suffer thirteen years later. Having escaped from Dastagerd, Khusro fled to Seleucia, where he stayed with Shirin and three of his daughters. All his other wives and children were sent to the east. He was apparently so terrified of the approaching Byzantine army that he cut the bridges across the canals surrounding his palace so that nobody, friend or foe, could approach. When senior Persian officials and soldiers tried to contact Khusro he accused them of being traitors and told them they were responsible for the catastrophe that had struck the kingdom. He was on the verge of insanity and his satraps concluded that their lives would never be safe while he lived. Shirin, Khusro's Christian wife, persuaded him to crown her son Merdanshah immediately but when the news became public, conspirators released Khusro's eldest son, Kavad, who had been imprisoned by his father. Once free, Kavad called a meeting of twenty-two Persian generals and told them what Khusro had done. Accompanied by the sons of Shahrvaraz, Kavad staged a coup, liberating 20,000 prisoners from the cells in Ctesiphon. The news pushed Khusro over the edge and he took off his royal robes and hid in a thick clump of bushes in the palace garden. He was found and dragged off to the cells, bound hand and foot. With his father ruined, Kavad was crowned king on 25 February 628.

The last days of Khusro's life were wretched. First he was starved and when he asked for food he was told by his jailers that he who had amassed so much wealth in his lifetime could eat gold. His satraps and generals came to visit him and insult him one by one. Then, like the Emperor Maurice who had once placed him on the peacock throne, he had to watch while his jailers killed Merdanshah and all his male children before his eyes. Finally, his own son Kavad ordered his execution and he was slowly shot to death with arrows.

For Heraclius the war was won but as yet he had not taken the main part of Ctesiphon itself and the complicated canal system surrounding the city made this task enormously difficult. Lacking a leader, the surviving Persian troops from several beaten armies could not take the field again against the Byzantines. However, they were capable of maintaining a guerrilla war, blocking fords and crossing points and making it likely that the conquest of Ctesiphon would only be achieved at an exorbitant cost. Heraclius knew that he was thousands of miles from Constantinople and still deep within a densely populated if temporarily defeated state. A minor military setback or indeed the arrival of Shahrvaraz's army might still turn the tables on him and rob him of his great conquests. Great warrior that he was, Heraclius still had a predisposition towards peace and conciliation. To Khusro he had stressed, 'The fire must be put out before it burns up everything.' Heraclius's letter breathed the spirit of reason. All he asked was a return to the frontiers that had existed in 602 when the war had begun, and for the release of all prisoners taken since that time.

With his father dead, Kavad now assembled his satraps and told them that he was determined to make peace with the Byzantines.

Everyone agreed there was no reason for the war to continue and so a letter was composed to Heraclius. The ambassadors who were chosen to deliver the virtual surrender had a hard journey from Ctesiphon to reach the Byzantine headquarters at Ganzak. The grimness of the journey must have weighed heavily on the minds of these men as they rode through the snow-covered countryside. Wherever they looked were the ruins of a great civilization, burned and destroyed either by the retreating Khusro or by the triumphant Byzantines. It was reported that between Ctesiphon and the Zagros Mountains they counted the corpses of over 3,000 Persian soldiers killed by Byzantine and Turkish patrols. Eventually, their hearts virtually broken by the sights they were forced to endure, they passed on their letter to an Armenian with orders to take it to Heraclius. He and a companion were captured by a Byzantine patrol and taken to the emperor so that they could deliver their letter, and so the last great war of antiquity came to a curiously undramatic end.

On receiving the letter Heraclius sent out officers to bring the Persian ambassadors to him but the heavy snowfall blocked the passes and there was some delay before Kavad's peace negotiators could reach the Byzantine camp. Kavad's letter, in which he addressed Heraclius as his brother, was a relatively humble one by Persian standards. It announced his accession, the death of his father and the general desire for peace. It acknowledged the right of the Byzantine Empire to exist as a state and recognized its equality of status with Persia. It also announced that Kavad was prepared to release all Roman prisoners of war immediately and that Persia would return Roman territory conquered in the war. Heraclius, it seemed, was to get all that he required. Although Heraclius replied that he would also release his prisoners, he addressed Kavad as 'his son' which, in the language of diplomacy, implied his superiority over the Persians, something that could hardly be denied in view of the military situation. Heraclius's tough stance was partly brought about by the knowledge that the Persians had dismissed all of his previous peace offerings with contumely, and that the three ambassadors he had sent to Khusro in 615 had never been seen again. (Kavad was eventually forced to admit that one of the men had died of illness and the other two had been executed by Khusro.)

In Ctesiphon, Kavad was unaware of the difficulties his ambassadors had encountered. Hearing no news of them, he sent out his
secretary Phaiak with another party of emissaries and this group
arrived at Ganzak a week before the original ambassadors were able
to force their way through the snowdrifts. Heraclius, ever the
peacemaker at heart, told Phaiak that he had never wanted war with
Persia and had no designs on Persian territory. He had not even
hated Khusro and would have maintained peace with him had he
survived. As the weather improved he sent Phaiak along with his
own secretary, the tabularius Eusthathius, back to Kavad, piled high
with gifts for himself and his master. When Eusthathius reached
Ctesiphon and presented the gifts, Kavad made the gesture of
signing an order for Shahrvaraz to begin the evacuation of Byzantine
soil. This, of course, was easier to order than to achieve: by this
stage, Shahrvaraz was in Syria and inclined to follow his own path.

The terms of the agreement between Heraclius and Kavad have
not been accurately preserved by the Greek chroniclers. One of the
main demands from Heraclius, for example, was for the return of
the True Cross. Kavad was apparently entirely happy to restore this
relic. However, he did not know where it was. Khusro might have
had the answer but his lips were now sealed. In fact, it was
Shahrvaraz who knew where the relic was and as yet he was not a
party to the peace negotiations.

From his camp at Ganzak, Heraclius sent his victory despatch to
Constantinople, where it was read aloud in Hagia Sophia on 15 May
628:

> Let all the earth raise a cry to God; serve the Lord in gladness,
> enter into his presence in exultation, and recognize that God is
> Lord indeed. It is he who has made us and not we ourselves. We
> are his people and sheep of his pasture. Enter into his courts with
> hymns and give thanks to him. Praise his name because Christ is
> Lord, his mercy is unto eternity, his truth for generation upon
> generation. Let the heavens be joyful and the earth exult and the
> sea be glad, and all that is in them.
>
> And let all we Christians, praising and glorifying, give thanks to
> the one God, rejoicing with great joy in his holy name. For fallen
> is the arrogant Khusro, opponent of God. He is fallen and cast

down to the depths of the earth, and his memory is utterly exterminated from earth; he who was exalted and spoke injustice in arrogance and contempt against our Lord, Jesus Christ, the true God and his undefiled Mother, our blessed Lady, Mother of God and ever-Virgin Mary, perished is the profaner with a resounding noise. His labour has turned back upon his head, and upon his brow has his injustice descended. For on the 24th of the past month February . . .disturbance came to him at the hands of Seiroe [Kavad], his firstborn son, just as we signified to you in our other missive. And all the Persian officials and troops who were there, along with all the army that had been amassed from diverse places by the cursed Khusro, gathered to the side of Seiroe together also with Gurdanaspa, the former commander of the Persian army. That God-abhorred Khusro proposed to resort to flight and, being arrested, was cast in bonds into the new fort which had been built by him for protecting the wealth amassed by him.

And on the 25th of the same month, February, Seiroe was crowned and proclaimed Persian king, and on the 28th of the same month, after keeping the God-abhorred Khusro bound in irons for four days in utter agony, he killed the same ingrate, arrogant, blaspheming opponent of God by a most cruel death, so that he might know that Jesus who was born of Mary, who was crucified by the Jews (as he himself had written) against whom he blasphemed, is God almighty; and he requited him in accordance with what we had written to him. And thus perished in this life that opponent of God, but he departed on the path of Judas Iscariot, the man who heard from Our Almighty God, 'It were good for that man not to have been born'; he departed to the unquenchable fire which had been prepared for Satan and his peers.[81]

It would have been easy for Heraclius to have lost a sense of perspective after such a change of fortune. Six years had seen him lifted from the depths to the heights in a way given to few men. Total victory over Rome's oldest enemy was now in his hands. But Heraclius saw hubris for what it was and showed that he was no conqueror by nature. His father's holy wisdom and love of his country had set him on the road to greatness. If he could have spoken to the older man now, he would have heard the word that he now spoke of his own volition: peace. God and the Virgin Mary had watched over him as he freed his chosen people from the assaults of their enemies. He had no intention now of going one step further than was necessary to restore the empire to what it had been under the murdered Maurice. When the new Persian ruler offered terms of peace, Heraclius was only too happy to accept them. George of Pisidia wrote in his *Heraclead*:

> The source of the moonless night was gone,
> The light shone forth and dark was banished,
> A new and better life was born,
> Another world and way of life.

Heraclius left his younger brother Theodore in charge of his armies in the field. The emperor never again led his army in action, preferring to leave the fighting to a younger commander. This was inevitable but the absence of their inspirational general cannot have failed to lower the troops' morale. Continuous victories under Heraclius must have inspired the confidence of the Byzantine forces but perhaps under lesser generals there may have been complacency on their part. This goes far towards explaining the lacklustre performance of the empire's troops during the following decade.

Before leaving Persian territory Heraclius freed all his prisoners and sent orders that all Persians held in Byzantine territory should be released also. However, disengaging the warring forces after so long a struggle was very difficult. When Theodore tried to occupy Edessa he found that the Persian and Jewish garrison there resisted him, insisting that they were acting on orders from Shahrvaraz, who had not accepted the new Persian king's peace terms. He immediately besieged Edessa, forcing the Persians to surrender and granting them their lives, but killing the Jews who refused to submit. When news reached Heraclius, who was now in Armenia, he realized that he needed to return to Constantinople with some speed so that he could get a general settlement in place and put an end to the fighting.

The emperor's triumphant journey through Anatolia with just his elite bodyguard for company must have been one of the supreme moments of his life. Everywhere he was cheered by crowds of his people, praising him as their saviour. Yet as he travelled along the imperial road from Amida to Tomisa, on to Melitene, then from Tarantos to Tsamandou and finally on to Caesarea, he saw ruined homesteads, burned fields and signs of the devastation brought by war. After resting briefly at Caesarea, he travelled the 600 miles that still remained to bring him to the coast of the Bosphorus, opposite the capital and in earlier years often the campsite for his Persian enemies. He took ship for the short journey into Constantinople and arrived at the Hiereia Palace, on the Asian shore, in September 628.

Few returning Roman emperors – perhaps no others at all – had ever combined the ecstasy of victory with the relief of survival in quite the same way. Julius Caesar and Scipio Africanus may have returned to Rome with victories almost as great, and Hadrian and Trajan among others had earned the plaudits of the Roman masses, but none of them had carried the fate of the empire in their hands so completely.

On his short trip across the Bosphorus Heraclius was met by a flotilla of craft from the city, manned by rich and poor alike. With sails painted in hastily applied colours and with flags, pennants and flowers flapping from their masts in the brisk wind, they comprised a scene of unequalled splendour for a city that had known only the grim colours of war for so long. On the quay the emperor could see thronging crowds waving olive branches and carrying large candles. Rank upon rank of the officials of the city were arrayed in their finest robes of office. With them stood one young man, his heart pounding even faster than all the others – Constantine, son of Heraclius. Now sixteen, he had rarely seen his father in the previous four years. How had the exuberance of youth allowed him to remain at home during that time, fed only on the reports that travel-stained riders brought into the city periodically, speaking of triumphs and setbacks, joy in victory and grief in loss? He had longed to be at his father's side instead of waiting restlessly under the stern looks of his tutors. Now their separation was at an end. Attempting not to betray the impatience of youth, he stood waiting for the imperial bodyguard to disembark from their transports and march towards him, with his father concealed somewhere within their ranks. Then the soldiers parted and Heraclius was revealed. Constantine, throwing aside all inhibitions, sprinted towards his father, tears pouring down his face. He threw himself down before his father. Heraclius, as tearful as his son, bent down and lifted Constantine to his feet, hugging him in a tight embrace which hid for the moment the tears both men shed. The crowd's cheers at the sight of the emperor reached a crescendo, almost drowning the hymns of joy that burst forth from the lips of thousands of priests who had flocked to the harbour to witness the return of God's chosen one.

Adrenaline alone must have been driving Heraclius by the end of 628, but some observers noticed the price he had paid for victory in the epic struggle. The new David, once golden haired, had become grey, 'dyed with the snow of care'. He was now in his mid-fifties and it was difficult to believe that this man had led by example, fighting in the front line and killing a Persian commander in single combat before the battle of Nineveh even began. During his absences from his capital four of his children had died, two sons and two daughters, succumbing to the ailments of childhood. Although his wife Martina had accompanied him on most of his campaigns, he had enjoyed none of the pleasures of family life that comprised the benefits of peace. Once he was able to detach himself from the crowds at the harbour he retired to the Hiereia Palace where he enjoyed a few days with his family and friends.

In the meantime, preparations were made for one of the greatest of all imperial triumphs.[82] Since the time of the Roman republic, generals returning home with the booty and prisoners that victory accorded had been welcomed into the capital by a mighty demonstration of public acclamation. Yet, in the whole history of Constantinople the city never experienced a day to match the triumphal entry that was being arranged for Heraclius. Not since Theodosius the Great had a Roman emperor led the army in the field. Moreover, none had enjoyed a greater triumph; the overthrow of Sasanid Persia, the eastern colossus, was something even Belisarius, Justinian's great general, had failed to do. The Sasanids who had imprisoned Roman emperors, who had dared to invade their lands, had now, in their turn, been overthrown by Heraclius.

It was a happy eparch who undertook the preparations for the glorious day. As governor of the city his work had been mainly concerned with its defence against Persians and Avars. Now he could literally let joy be the motivating factor. Extravagance and excess was now the order of the day in war-weary Constantinople.

The triumphal procession was to proceed down the main highway of the city, the Mese, which since dawn had been swept and cleaned with sawdust. The whole route was decorated with flowers and rich hangings made of silk, embroidered with gold and silver thread. The numerous statues were crowned with flowers and the overhanging arches and upper storey of buildings were a blaze of colourful blooms. The greatest citizens, competing to outdo each other, loaned the eparch the finest carpets and candelabra that their own palaces boasted so that at least part of the route was decorated with their own personal thanks to their emperor who had saved their wealth from the Persian and Avar soldiery and kept the seas clear for merchants and businessmen like themselves. The various quarters of the city through which the procession was to pass were the jealously guarded territories of the guilds and these proud citizens spared no expense in advertising their presence to the returning hero. The largest guilds were those of the potters and leather-makers, though there were perhaps as many as twenty-three at the time of Heraclius, from gold and silversmiths, to parfumiers and grocers, pork butchers and cobblers. However humble their callings, the guild members knew no modesty when it came to such an occasion and all went out of their way to proclaim their joy at the emperor's victory and a hoped-for return to normality and good trade. From the Golden Gate to the Chalce, the entry to the palace, the roads were ankle-deep in rose petals, and the aromas of rosemary, myrtle and bayleaves contributed to a riot of sweet smells.

The whole city wore a festive air, with every house covered in flags and carpets and flowers. It was as if a whole community had driven the shadows of defeat and despondency away. Crowds had flocked in from the countryside of both the European and the Asian shores, to join in the celebrations. The members of the two factions proudly flaunted their colours, blue and green, and occupied different parts of the routes in force. The faction members all held lighted candles and burning torches aloft, though in the bright sunlight of the day these were symbolic rather than practical. The chronicles relate the excitement, almost hysteria, that flickered through the crowds when four magnificent white Persian elephants appeared in the streets. They had been captured at Dastagerd and brought back to Europe as a symbol of the wild, strange lands which the local warriors had visited and still returned victorious.

The official procession began at the Golden Gate, the main entrance to the city through the Wall of Theodosius. Here the streets were thronging with officials, guardsmen and every kind of vehicle filled with Persian booty and driven by men bearing the flammula, the purple flags of the emperor. Here the elephants waited to take their place behind the emperor, his son Constantine and the rest of the imperial party which arrived at the Pegae Pier, having come by boat to avoid the crush. The master of ceremonies known as the praepositus, presented Heraclius with the royal crown and, thus apparelled, he moved off to join the throng assembled at the Golden Gate. Here he met the eparch, the guards commanders and the demarchs, leaders of the Blue and Green factions. As tradition dictated, he first presented the eparch with a large reward, then accepted homage from the two demarchs, both magnificently dressed in the colours of their factions, embroidered in the finest gold and silver thread. From each demarch Heraclius accepted a wreath of roses before ascending a chariot drawn by four white horses.

On such an occasion the chroniclers, notably George of Pisidia in his *Heraclead*, revealed unexpected skills as fashion correspondents. They described Heraclius's costume in great detail. The emperor was wearing a chiton or long tunic made of multi-coloured scaramangion embroidered in gold and silver, with a cloak of imperial purple over his shoulders and purple sandals. The bright sunlight was juggled by the prisms of his diamond-encrusted crown. In his left hand he held a cross and in the right a golden lance. If every inch of his outward appearance seemed designed to illustrate his God-chosen status, his long white beard – how changed from the golden one his people remembered – was the closest reminder of his mortality. He had no fear of hubris when he glanced down at the white hair that covered his human heart under all the trappings of earthly majesty. Yet this was no time for such thoughts. His victory transcended human fragility. Ahead of him were hundreds of riders and in their hands were the battle flags of over 300 Roman military units, legions, cohorts, regiments, taken during 500 years of war with the Persians, now liberated by Heraclius and brought home at

last. Greatest of all in Roman eyes were the legionary standards of
Crassus taken by the Parthians at Carrhae, one of the empire's
greatest defeats. After his victory at Nineveh, Heraclius had
liberated not only the ghosts of previous disasters but the living
remnants of more recent defeats. With the procession marched many
Roman soldiers freed by Heraclius and brought home at last to live
on pensions in their own homeland.

At the head of the column where it had been throughout
his campaigns was the icon of the Saviour, the famous icon 'not
made by human hands', the miracle-working symbol of God's
presence. When he had undertaken holy war in 622, Heraclius had
fought for his faith and now God was rewarding him with the fruits
of victory.

At a signal from the praepositus the Golden Gate was swung open
and Heraclius was able to see his capital laid out before him as never
before, thronged with cheering people celebrating peace, safety and
the blessing of God. It would have been a hard heart that did not
melt at that moment. We know that Heraclius was a very emotional
man and it is difficult not to feel the elation welling up inside him or
to imagine that the man inside the purple cloak looked around to see
where his loved ones were in the procession, his son Constantine
nearby and his beloved Martina, further back with his younger
children, his sons in miniature armour to imitate their father, his
daughters in garlands of flowers. The factions were chanting his
name: 'Welcome, Heraclius, Emperor of the Romans! Welcome,
Heraclius, who has routed the enemy phalanxes! Welcome, most
valiant conqueror!' It was one of the most glorious pages of
Byzantium's history written by Heraclius.[83]

Slowly the procession moved along the Triumphal Way until it
joined the Mese boulevard, passing under the arch of the gate in the
walls built by Heraclius's famous predecessor, Constantine, before
moving through the Forum of Arcadius and then on to the Forum of
the Ox, where the corpses of Phocas and his friends had been
burned eighteen years earlier when Heraclius won the throne. The
official events of the day might have seemed tedious to anyone less
in love with his city and its people. Ceremony after ceremony
attended each stop as they passed through the quarters of the city,
each proud to welcome their chosen one. Officials, great and small,

dressed in their ceremonial best, welcomed their emperor with preplanned speeches, tedious and otherwise.

Heraclius dismounted from his chariot at the Arch of Milion and walked to the Augusteum where he came in sight of the entrance to Hagia Sophia. The church steps were lined with senators, all holding lighted candles and behind them stood the clergy, resplendent in robes of many colours and chanting hymns. Heraclius walked towards Patriarch Sergius, the man who had stood by him in the darkest moments and had lifted him to this great triumph. No emperor had ever found a truer friend. The two men – one representing the spirtual world, the other the temporal – exchanged kisses at the doorway of the great church and then they entered together, exchanging the bright sunlight for the deepest shadow of that immense building, the heat of the day for the cold of the voluminous church. Above them, apparently unsupported by earthly means, was the stupendous dome, source of all light in the church and other-worldly in its symbolism. They both knelt before the icon of the Theotokos, Mother of God and guardian of the city in its darkest hour. For Heraclius, the Virgin had been the ever-present force with him since he sailed into harbour on the day he took the throne. God's glorious will had been done at last in Constantinople. After the darkness had come the light. As Heraclius and Sergius looked up into the dome they could be excused for seeing only God's will for a peaceful future.

After the church service came the games. The emperor's people had suffered much and now came the time to play. Heraclius mounted a white horse and rode into the Hippodrome where elephants and the horsemen carrying the banners again paraded before him. Then, once the crowd's appetite for processions was sated, everyone settled down to enjoy the horse-racing and the chariot events in which the usual blue and green rivalry had the added spice of the emperor's presence. In the days ahead Heraclius enjoyed both a family event and a great state occasion with the marriage of Constantine, his eldest son and heir, to Gregoria, eldest daughter of his beloved cousin Nicetas, who sadly did not live long enough to witness the young couple's happiness.

Heraclius's triumph was in the tradition of the Roman emperors and generals of old but it also contained marked differences. The religious symbolism of the occasion was very clear. Theophanes even likens the six years of the emperor's crusade to the six days of the Creation with Heraclius returning on the seventh to rest as God had done. Most significant of all, however, was the change that took place in the imperial titulature. From 629 onwards Heraclius, and all subsequent emperors, dropped the title Augustus, with its traditional Roman provenance, and chose instead to be called Basileus, the Greek word for emperor. However, the simple change from Latin to Greek was only part of the transition, for the new title Heraclius adopted was *pistos en Christo basileus* ('the believing emperor'). This emphasized the dual role of emperor, as both the earthly ruler and as the living embodiment on earth of Christ in heaven. From this time onwards the emperor's throne room in his palace in Constantinople became a microcosm of God in heaven. The room itself was modelled not on previous palace architecture, but on ecclesiastical buildings; its closest architectural parallels are churches and its pictorial decoration consisted of scenes from the life of Christ.'[84]

If anything blighted the emperor's happiness at this time, it was the fact that he had not yet recovered the True Cross from Persia. The chaos into which this crumbling realm fell on the death of Khusro II meant that nobody seemed to have the authority to carry out a proper search for the holy relic. The real power in Persia was not the series of impotent kings who ascended the throne and fell just as quickly. Heraclius's doughtiest rival, Shahrvaraz, still had an unbroken army and probably knew where the Christian relic was concealed. It was too important a bargaining piece for him to surrender it to Heraclius without securing his own position, probably as ruler of Persia himself.

The new king of Persia, Kavad, died almost immediately after succeeding, passing the throne to his helpless son, the seven-year-old Ardashir, a situation a great leader like Shahrvaraz could not accept. He called on Heraclius to negotiate with him for the Persian evacuation of the Byzantine provinces of Syria, Palestine and Egypt which he had conquered himself. Heraclius, realizing the delicacy of the negotiations ahead, agreed to talk with his mighty adversary. He met Shahrvaraz at Arabyssos in Cappadocia in July 629 and an agreement was reached by which Shahrvaraz would take his people out of the captured Byzantine provinces and give back the True

Cross in return for which Heraclius promised to support Shahrvaraz's claim to the Persian throne. Heraclius was prepared to make
compromises now to guarantee peace. He had achieved what he had
set out to do and he realized that the Persian king was unable to
guarantee any agreement in which Shahrvaraz and his army were
not involved.

By June 629 the Persians were already leaving Egypt and as a
pragmatic gesture Heraclius tied the 'strong man' of Iran by
arranging to make him a member of the family. The emperor's son
Theodosius, his second by Martina, was married to Shahrvaraz's
daughter Nike. Straight from Arabyssos, Shahrvaraz advanced on
Ctesiphon and seized power, imprisoning the child-king and having
him murdered within the year. Shahrvaraz then attempted to drive
the Turks out of Armenia but suffered a defeat and had to rely on a
political crisis deep inside Central Asia to persuade the Turks to
withdraw their troops. True to his word, Shahrvaraz located the
fragments of the True Cross and arranged for them to be returned to
the emperor.

Heraclius's pilgrimage to restore the True Cross to Jerusalem
is commemorated in the Christian calendar on Holy Cross Day,
14 September. Its significance was so great throughout the Christian
world that the historical events have become shrouded in legend, so
much so that it is difficult to reconstruct the details. The return of
the relic was clearly of great importance to the emperor who had
made it the most important of all Byzantine war aims. For
Heraclius, as for all Christians, the Cross was itself the symbol of
victory in a war which had been conducted as a crusade. In contrast
to the flamboyant earthly triumph he had been awarded on his entry
to Constantinople, the return of the True Cross to Jerusalem was
conducted as a pilgrimage by a penitent emperor.

Heraclius left Edessa in the early months of 630, accompanied by
his wife and family and set out for the city of Hierapolis, where he
met the Byzantine general David, who had been negotiating with
Shahrvaraz for the return of the Cross and had it in his possession.
Taking the holy relic Heraclius then travelled to Tiberias on the Sea
of Galilee, where he stayed the night before going to Jerusalem. The
story of his entry into the city has become deeply entrenched in
miraculous happenings which mirror the times.[85] The historical

event, however, needed no such ornamentation, being one of the most memorable in the history of the Christian Church.

Arriving as a pilgrim, rather than as an emperor, it is likely that Heraclius entered Jerusalem as a barefoot penitent, wearing a white chiton and carrying the precious relics in their casket, not shouldering a lifesize cross as has been depicted by some artists and claimed by some chroniclers. The streets of the holy city were thronged with people and hundreds of monks had come in from the Syrian monasteries that would have been rebuilt after the Persian holocaust of 614. The splendours of the Byzantine centuries in Syria and Palestine had been seriously damaged during the Persian occupation, with the churches and buildings of the city and its environs bearing the signs of the effects of a terrible war. The whole area seemed to have declined from a rich, imperial province with the villas of the wealthy everywhere apparent, to the aftermath of a great human tragedy.

Yet on that early spring day everyone's eyes were on a better future. Monophysites and Jews were, presumably, not present in large numbers and the Orthodox faithful enjoyed the moment of triumph as Christendom's holiest relic was restored by their emperor. The onlookers, we are told, all carried torches, as well as candles and bayleaves. They sang at the top of their voices and wept with joy as the penitent emperor, the first Christian ruler ever to enter the city of Jerusalem, walked slowly over the cobbles towards the Church of the Holy Sepulchre, no longer the pristine building it had been when Constantine built it 300 years before. We know that repairs had been carried out to the complex during the Persian occupation, but the dome of the Anastasis had been severely damaged and the Martyrion, Constantine's great basilica, had been burned to the ground. Yet whatever damage had been caused to the exterior of the church had in no way altered the fact that here was the centre of the Christian religion and God's deputy on earth was returning the symbol of Christ's death to the place of his Resurrection.

After Heraclius had returned the wood from the True Cross, contained as it was in an ornate box (presumably the same one for which Shahrvaraz had killed and tortured priests in the kitchen garden in 614), he turned his attention to appointing a new patriarch to the city, the heroic Zacharias having died in captivity in Persia.

His choice fell on Modestus, Bishop of Joppa, who had administered the city during the Persian occupation. Heraclius had been pleased by the way in which Modestus had maintained church morale during this difficult time. Yet Modestus was not to enjoy his promotion for very long. Having followed the emperor to Damascus to arrange the funding of further restoration work in Jerusalem, he died on his return to the holy city and was succeeded by Sophronius.

The emperor's humility on entering the holy city was made more real by the sight that met his eyes. Neither he nor the Constantinopolitan church leaders had seen the city during the sixteen years of Persian and Jewish occupation. With its wealth completely stripped away it was a shadow of the splendidly rich centre of population that it had become under the Byzantines. And yet this stark and grim city, wearing its suffering on its scorched walls and in its empty markets, was a more real symbol of the fight that Heraclius had been involved in for the last twenty years of his life than the golden interior of Hagia Sophia. Here he was no emperor, merely a humble Christian warrior who had fought for his faith whatever the cost to himself and his family.

Had he died in Jerusalem, his task completed and at fifty-five years no young man, Heraclius would have joined the pantheon of the great leaders of history, matching Julius Caesar and Alexander of Macedon, and exceeding by far his great predecessor Constantine. Heraclius the Great would have been one of Christianity's greatest temporal figures, forever associated with the liberation of the True Cross and the survival of Christianity against the threat from the East. Instead, he lived to see much of his work undone. He enjoyed no comfortable old-age, no golden autumn, no satisfaction in a task well completed. Exhausted and prematurely aged, he was called upon to face a trial even greater than the one had just endured. It was more than he could bear. In 630, however, all this lay in the future. Once he had restored the True Cross to the Church of the Holy Sepulchre, Heraclius moved on to Damascus to reconstruct the administration of Syria after exempting the survivors of the Persian conquest from taxation. It was time to turn the swords into ploughshares and to rebuild the Christian empire in the Holy Land, where it had been born.

EIGHT

The Prophet

Heraclius's victory over Persia was achieved at a very high cost. In economic terms his empire was close to ruin, with much of the Balkans a wilderness in contrast to the thriving economic unit it had been less than a century before. In the East whole provinces, including Syria and Egypt, had suffered devastation and foreign occupation. To sustain the struggle in the East Heraclius had mortgaged the state to the church, borrowing the immense sums needed to rebuild his armies. Only time could redress the balance and with the Avar and Persian empires overthrown, Heraclius had good reason to believe that his victories had earned him that time. Modern historians, however, have pointed out that Heraclius faced an internal foe almost as implacable as the Muslim Arabs in the shape of the Orthodox Church, which had funded his crusade and now wanted its money back, without delay.

For a seventh-century economy, dependent on tax revenue, the two decades of continuous war had been almost fatal. Although figures from so far back are scarcely reliable, it has been estimated that perhaps 200,000 Byzantine soldiers died in the wars and many civilians.[86] The loss of population inevitably led to reduced revenue, as did the destruction of livestock, urban businesses and normal trade on land and at sea. The great port of Alexandria had been in foreign hands for much of the conflict, while cities like Damascus, Jerusalem, Antioch and Caesarea had also been under Persian control throughout the 620s. In addition to suffering loss of tax revenue, Heraclius had been forced to use vast sums of money to bribe his Avar enemies and his Turkish allies, as well as to recruit troops in Lazica and Iberia. But the greatest problem was the

Church; once the True Cross had been regained and the threat of total defeat removed, crusaders, having done their job, became expensive luxuries.

The Patriarch Sergius had always been both statesman and churchman. The support he showed to Heraclius in his darkest hours was absolutely vital. But, powerful as he was, Sergius was not the only voice that counted in the Church. The chronicles suggest that Sergius came in for much criticism for his decision to use Church funds to support the army. Many of his more conservative colleagues would have claimed that the affairs of Church and state were separate and that it was fundamentally wrong for the Christian Church to support war, even so-called 'holy war'. Centuries later Sergius was still being criticized for his decision. One can almost hear the indignation of the ninth-century chronicler Nicephorus as he condemns the sale of Church property to pay for the services of pagan Turks!

Under immense pressure from within the Church, Sergius called on Heraclius to repay the loan that had saved the empire. History records few examples of restraint such as Heraclius showed in attempting to comply. The emperor was a deeply religious man and it would never have occurred to him to try to explain his sense of priorities to the churchman: the empire could be lost not just by foreign conquest but by economic collapse and that was a very real danger in the 630s. The more the Church pressurized him to repay the loan, the more he needed to make cutbacks in the army. But Sergius must have felt justified in pointing to a clear horizon – the enemies of the empire had been defeated to the west, the east and to the north. A period of peace was assured,

Heraclius made haste to repay the Church loan. Instead of being allowed to filter through the system from hand to hand, revitalizing the economy, all the booty taken in Persia was instead stored in Church coffers, mouldering away in catacombs of gold and silver. In addition to cutting back on army reforms, Heraclius found himself having to reduce the subsidies paid to minor princelings throughout the empire, which had been a fundamental part of Roman strategy in the East for centuries. Christian Arabs, like the Ghassanids, found that their services were no longer considered vital and so their subsidy was reduced. Whereas common sense must have told Heraclius that the people of the devastated provinces needed a period of financial calm to reconstruct their lives and to build up their businesses again, he felt obliged to press them to fund the cost of a war from which it is doubtful that they felt they had benefited. The Monophysites of Syria and Egypt, having exchanged the tolerant Persian invaders for the tax collectors from Constantinople, were clear that there had been no gain, and, having had a glimpse of freedom, they were not willing to place their necks in the halter again.

As well as being a man of action Heraclius was also a deep thinker on matters of philosophy and theology. Twenty years on the throne had revealed to him dangers from internal disunity as great as those from external foes. The Persian conquest of Syria and Egypt had been made easier by the profound religious split within Christianity itself between Greek Orthodoxy or Chalcedonism and the Monophysitism of the eastern lands. With his physical enemies subdued, the crusading emperor now turned his attention to repairing the spiritual schism within the Church which, linked to nationalist and separatist sentiments in the provinces, threatened to undermine his great military achievements. The issues are almost impossible for the modern reader to appreciate. The discussions of the 'single' or 'dual' nature of Jesus, and of the 'will', 'energy' or 'acting force' bring to mind the obsession of medieval theologians with how many angels could stand on the head of a pin or whether Jesus ever laughed. However, the Christians of the Byzantine Empire took these matters so seriously that they were willing to die for their own interpretation of their faith. In a society where hermits and ascetics could stand naked on a column for thirty years until maggots ate their flesh away, or could chain themselves in a cage so that they could not stand up or lie down, it was not surprising that true believers would agonize over the smallest detail of their faith, let alone the true nature of Jesus himself.

Monophysitism was strongest in Syria, where its followers were known as Jacobites and in Egypt, where they were part of the Coptic Church. The fundamental difference between Monophysitism and Chalcedonism, as represented by the Constantinople Church, was on the nature of Christ. At the Council of Chalcedon in 451 a split had occurred between the supporters of the majority or

Orthodox view of Christ's nature, which said that it was a dual
nature within a single person, and those who insisted on merging the
human and divine natures into a single nature. Believers in the
second theory became known as Monophysites. Both Chalcedonians
and Monophysites believed that they were Orthodox and that the
rival view was heretical. Of the five patriarchates of the Church,
Rome, in the west, was least troubled by the dispute, which formed
part of the struggle for control of the Eastern Church by the
patriarchs of Constantinople, Alexandria, Antioch and Jerusalem.
Constantinople assumed the role of protector of Orthodoxy or
Chalcedonism and it was in the other three patriarchates that
Monophysitism was strongest, notably in Egypt and northern and
eastern Syria. Heraclius and Sergius produced an idea that they
hoped might heal the rift between Orthodoxy and Monophysitism.
It was called Monoenergism and it accepted the Orthodox view that
Christ had two natures (Dyophysitism) – human and divine – but
asserted that he had only one 'energy'. This was a very fine point
that theologians might spend lifetimes debating. However, the true
believer might be content to accept this blurring of differences as a
way of healing the damaging rift. It was a political solution rather
than a religious one and it was hoped that if the higher clergy could
be persuaded to forget their differences then their followers would
do likewise. Monoenergism started strongly with Patriarch Sergius,
himself a Syrian from a Monophysite background, encouraging
Christians everywhere to give the new interpretation a chance. Pope
Honorius in Rome lent his support to Monoenergism, while
Patriarch Athanasius, the Monophysite leader of the Antioch
Church, accepted it, as did most of his bishops.

With the need for a new patriarch in Alexandria, Heraclius
naturally chose a man – Cyrus of Phasis – who could be relied upon
to favour Monoenergism, particularly when the emperor offered
him a substantial additional carrot in the shape of the rank of
prefect of Egypt. At a council held at Alexandria in 633 Cyrus
managed to 'sell' the emperor's new package to the Egyptian
bishops. When the Armenian Church fell into line on Monoenergism
it seemed as if Heraclius was not just a great general, he was a
magician too. The schism in eastern Christianity had been healed.
But appearances were deceptive.

In higher Church circles there was euphoria in the immediate aftermath of the Persian war. In 626 Christianity had faced oblivion with the great siege of the capital and now that Byzantine authority had been restored throughout the east Heraclius was held in very high esteem. For a few years he was able to bask in the credit he had earned through his victory. However, as reality reasserted itself, and taxes were reimposed on the devastated areas of Syria and Egypt, the old bitterness against rule from Constantinople began to reappear. That this renewed hostility to Byzantine Orthodoxy coincided with the appearance of unusually assertive Arab raiders on the old frontier with Roman Palestine was one of history's more mysterious examples of cause and effect.

Both the Byzantines and the Sasanian Persians had relied on client Arab tribes to patrol their frontiers with the desert Arab peoples and limit incursions. The Byzantines, as we have seen, looked to the Ghassanids, a Christian Arab tribe whose territory included parts of Syria and Roman Palestine and who thus had a vested interest in keeping the tribes to the south quiet. In assessing the reasons for the collapse of Byzantine power in the Arab lands the search for a military solution can often be misleading. The political failures of generations of administrators in Constantinople contributed to a collapse which could not be rectified on the battlefield. The Christian Ghassanids were not seen by the Byzantines in the same light as they saw themselves. The Ghassanids were judged by their paymasters as little more than mercenaries, like the thousands of paid professionals who had made up Byzantine armies for centuries. They were auxiliary soldiers, little better, except for their loyalty to the empire, than the primitive tribesmen they were keeping in order. They were the hired policemen of the desert. This was a fundamental political blunder. The Ghassanid leaders saw themselves – and were so regarded by many of the desert tribes – as great kings. They may have been big fish in a little pool, but nevertheless they were people who could have been used to create a strong buffer state. While the Byzantines accorded the Ghassanid king the title Strategos Parembolon, meaning 'commander of nomad auxiliaries', he would more wisely have been called shaykh.

In the early 630s the Ghassanids were slowly recovering, like much of the Eastern Empire, from two decades of Persian rule.

Thousands of Christian Arabs had accompanied Heraclius and other Byzantine generals on their far-flung campaigns and many had paid with their lives. In return the Ghassanids now needed peace and time for recuperation. Instead, they were hit by three unexpected blows: the restoration of heavy taxation on those parts of their lands that lay within the empire; the challenge of Monoenergism to their Christian faith; and the increased pressure from the Arabs to the south.

Whereas they had always seen themselves as the natural leaders of the many thousands of Christian Arabs who occupied the Semitic regions, they found this leadership challenged and swept away by the Islamic movement during the 620s. Before the rise of Mohammed, Arabia had experienced a period of intense Christianization. The imperial authorities in Constantinople had made conversion to Christianity a condition for Arab tribes who wished to receive subsidies in return for military service. In addition, monks and wandering ascetics carried the Christian message from tribe to tribe and Christian monasteries were set up in wild regions where they became the centre of monotheist studies, even influencing the development of Islamic ideas. The biggest influx of Christian monks into Arabia coincided with Mohammed's own mission. The conquest of Syria and Palestine by the Persians in the period 610–14 had seen thousands of Christians fleeing into the deserts to take refuge with Arab tribes and escape the relentless pursuit of the Zoroastrians and their Jewish allies. These refugees eventually reached all parts of Arabia, even as far south as Yemen.

The social and religious revolution in Arabia that was kick-started by the Romano-Persian Wars occurred while the great powers of the East were too preoccupied fighting each other to notice the transition taking place on their southern borders. It seemed as if each development on the Greek-Sasanian front brought direct benefit to the Arabs, not least in the military advantage that came from the Arab tribes inheriting vast stockpiles of Sasanian weaponry from the shattered Lakhmids and from defeated Persian garrisons in Egypt and Palestine. Moreover, the Christian Syrian trading centres like Damascus and Emesa had been damaged by the Persian occupation; Mecca and Medina began to take over trading routes and grew even richer on their rivals' misfortunes.

Yet it is wrong to exaggerate the causal chain linking the rise of Islam to the religious schism in the Byzantine Empire between Metropolitan Orthodoxy and Monophysitism in the Christian Arab lands. To do this is to minimize the role of the Prophet Mohammed and reduce the importance of the individual historical figure to simply a single factor in a multi-faceted movement.

Mohammed was born in Mecca, the son of Abdulla and his wife Amina, just four months after his father's death in what, by common consent, was the year 570 of the Christian calendar. (Five years later the future Christian emperor, Heraclius, was born in Armenia or Cappadocia.) Mohammed belonged to the Hashim clan of the Korayshi tribe. In early childhood Mohammed was nursed by Umm Ayman, a young Christian woman from Abyssinia, and later by a bedouin woman named Halima, so that he might benefit from the healthier desert climate instead of the stifling oppressiveness of Mecca itself. Significantly, Halima eventually returned the five-year-old infant to his mother because it seemed that he suffered from the falling sickness or epilepsy. Naturally, no evidence of fits associated with this ailment has been recorded.

Mohammed was apparently only six years old when his mother died and he was taken into the care of his grandfather, Abdul Muttalib. When he too died just two years later the child was passed on to his uncle, a man of some reputation and influence named Abu Talib. The experience of frequent bereavement must have made Mohammed an independent, self-reliant boy, who spent much of his time tending the flocks of the city along with boys of his own age. By the time he was twelve his uncle felt that he was ready to move into the world of men and so he was taken by Abu Talib on a business trip to Syria. Travelling as part of a camel train, Mohammed passed through Byzantine territory, visiting the important Nabatean city of Petra, much declined by this date, as well as Jerash and Amman. While he was in the Syrian city of Bostra, an important Christian site of ancient origin with a fine cathedral, an incident occurred which has become so much part of legend that discovering the truth behind it is impossible. On seeing the young Mohammed a Christian monk named Bahira was apparently struck with wonder by the aura that surrounded the boy. He claimed that the boy had a mark between his shoulder blades which confirmed the greatness that was to come. Bahira spoke to the lad and then declared that he was the prophet sent by God to the Arab people, who would destroy idolatry and cleanse the temple of the Kaaba in Mecca.

It is not appropriate for modern scholars to comment on what has become a matter of faith. Suffice it to say that any twelve-year-old told that he had been chosen for greatness would have found it difficult to suppress such thoughts during his adolescent years. In other respects, however, Mohammed's experiences were like those of any Arab boy. He played a part in the regular skirmishing that took place between the various Arab tribes, though at first this was confined to gathering up the enemy's arrows so that his own side could fire them back. Most of his time, however, was spent travelling with the camel trains between Mecca and Christian Syria, mixing with people of all races and religions, discussing monotheism with the Christian and Jewish Arabs with whom he frequently travelled, and occasionally even meeting the Arabs from the region of the Persian Gulf who, while still themselves pagan, were increasingly experiencing the ideas of Zoroastrianism. For a young, impressionable young man it was a veritable melting-pot of ideas, increasingly centred on the model of 'one god' as against the polytheism of the Arabs of the peninsula. Mohammed even had some experience of trading with the Christians of Abyssinia, who until recently had exerted a strong influence on the people of southern Arabia and the Yemen.

The year 610 was as decisive for Mohammed as it was for Heraclius. By his mid-thirties Mohammed was a man of very serious nature, very inward-looking and apparently tormented by doubts over the pagan beliefs of his people. Since childhood he had exchanged ideas with the monotheistic Christians and Jews and was convinced that the one god must have a message for the Arab people similar to, but distinct from, the one he had sent through Moses and Jesus to the Jews and the Christians. Increasingly Mohammed spent time alone in the hills around Mecca, subsisting on minimal food in the manner of the hanifs or ascetics who had been finding their own faith for centuries in Arabia. In 610 on the twenty-seventh day of Ramadan, known to the Muslims as the 'Day of Power', Mohammed found himself near a cave at the base of Mount Hira, a few miles outside Mecca. It was a cave that had often been used by the hanif Zayid ibn Amr, but on this night Mohammed was alone. As he meditated in the cave he heard a commanding voice. It told him to read and when the frightened Mohammed enquired what he should read, he felt himself squeezed by a great force and the voice spoke these words: 'Read in the name of Allah who created man from a clot of blood. Read, for the Lord is beneficent and has taught man the use of the pen.' Mohammed remembered the words; they became the first chapter of the Koran.

He hurried homewards, frightened that he was possessed by demons, but his wife Khadija reassured him and helped him to come to terms with the revelation. She convinced her husband that God had chosen him to lead his people away from idolatry. Traditional stories assert that Mohammed learned from a Christian living in Mecca that the voice he had heard was that of the Angel Gabriel and from that time onwards the angel became the particular guardian of the Muslim people.

Mohammed's wife played an important part in the development of the future prophet's views. Convinced by what her husband had told her she took him to meet a kinsman of hers, a Christian named Waraka, who was learned in Hebrew and in the monotheistic scriptures. Waraka pronounced that Mohammed was a prophet in the same line as Moses. He warned Khadija to tell him that his people would vilify him and reject him, but that if it was God's will, then he would succeed. Mohammed heard no more voices for up to three years and must have feared that he had been mistaken in the first place. During this time he spent much time exchanging ideas with Christian Arabs around Mecca until, in 613, he began to receive many more messages which he remembered and incorporated in the Koran.

When Mohammed began to talk openly about the messages, he won over some people but alienated many more. The hostility that he eventually faced in his home city of Mecca became so severe that by 621 he was already making preparations to move to Medina. To that purpose he arranged to meet secretly with twelve notable figures from that city. The twelve agreed to become followers of Mohammed, obeying him in everything, and no longer worshipping idols. They swore an oath to him, known as the First Oath of

Akaba, and returned to Medina to spread his teaching amongst the people there. Within a year a second meeting took place where seventy-three Medinans confirmed the first oath and agreed to protect any of Mohammed's followers who came to Medina, even at the cost of their lives. Still following the examples of Christianity and Judaism, Mohammed chose from amongst this group twelve disciples, telling them 'Moses chose from among the people twelve leaders, and Jesus twelve apostles. You twelve shall be my sureties for the rest.'[87]

The drama of the Hegira – Mohammed's departure from Mecca in 622 – may seem greater now than it did at the time. Mohammed had prepared the ground carefully and was sure of a good reception at Medina. Moreover, most of his followers had already departed from Mecca, leaving their leader with just Abu Bakr and a mere handful of supporters. Nevertheless, such an important event has become surrounded with drama, just like Constantine's conversion. Leaving Mecca at night, Mohammed and his men rode for nine days with a Bedouin guide who helped them move in darkness. Eventually, on 28 June 622, the fugitives arrived at Medina, where they received a great welcome. The Hegira was complete and the first date in the Muslim calendar was taken from this event.

The description of the event as Mohammed's 'flight' from Mecca implies that he was pursued and was in danger of capture, a view that was supported by the story of the Muslims' taking shelter in a cave and being hidden from their pursuers by a spider weaving a web across the entrance and convincing the Meccans that nobody had entered. The nature of the the Hegira can be interpreted in another way, and one more in tune with Mohammed's intentions – 'expulsion'. Mohammed had been driven out by those who had rejected him in his own city. From that moment onwards his aim was to return to Mecca, once he had been accepted everywhere else as the 'Chosen One'. For Mohammed, the successful return to Mecca would be the defining moment in his mission to bring monotheism to the Arab people and to overthrow the idols in the Kaaba. But he knew that much blood would be shed before victory could be achieved.

Within a few months of arriving in Medina Mohammed was organizing raids on Meccan property as the only certain way of forcing the occupants of that city to acknowledge him as a problem that would have to be addressed. The targets of these *razzias* were the camel caravans that left Mecca to begin the journey he knew so well to Damascus. Many ascetics and hanifs had carried the wisdom of the 'One God' in the past but their beliefs had been of interest mainly to the poor and the downtrodden. Mohammed's argument was with the wealthy and influential of Mecca, and he would hit them in their pockets by striking at their trade and redirecting it towards the people of Medina. What followed was therefore a typical Arab trade war, carried out by raid and counter-raid, until the Meccans were prepared to listen to what Mohammed had to say. But if the Meccans thought such a war would be conducted by the comfortable rules that had grown up over centuries they were wrong. Mohammed intended to set the agenda. First he broke the age-old rule that forbade fighting during the Arabian sacred months: he was not prepared to be bound by decisions made in an idolatrous past. In January 624 he ordered his men to raid a Meccan caravan, during which several on each side died. The booty taken salved the wounds and bereavement as it always had in Arab history but even his own supporters were shocked at Mohammed's breach of the rules of warfare. Mohammed's response was to claim that he was doing God's will and men's petty rules could not apply in the case of the will of the Almighty. However, Mohammed soon recognized that, outnumbered as he was bound to be in his struggle against the Meccans, he needed something that would inspire his own followers to fight with the courage of two men. And so the jihad was born – at the very moment that Heraclius and his Byzantine commanders were reaching the same conclusion in their epic struggle against a stronger foe, the Sasanian Persians.

Jihad is much misunderstood among non-Muslims, particularly in the western world.[88] Modern usage has equated it with terrorism, largely as a result of the misguided efforts of the western media. Educated Muslims have always been aware of the full implications of jihad, recognizing the difference between the 'Greater Jihad', which was an internal, moral, spiritual concept, concerned with the individual struggle against evil, and the 'Lesser Jihad', which was an external concept, taking the form of a political, often military, struggle. It is with this latter idea that the critics of jihad have generally been concerned. In the seventh century the word was used by the followers of Mohammed in a highly specific way. The fear of death is such a fundamental human emotion that anything which lessens or even removes it for the soldier, who faces death every time he meets the enemy, must have a major effect on morale. Heraclius certainly preached the idea of a martyr's crown and a guarantee of heaven to his Christian troops. Mohammed presented an even more attractive picture of sensual delights to his followers. Any Muslim who died in battle did not, like the rest of the dead, have to wait until the Day of Judgement for resurrection, but would instantly be transported to Paradise. There, according to the Koran, the fallen warriors would enjoy sensual delights they could never afford on earth. They would be attended by beautiful young boys 'in whom you will find delights and a great kingdom'. Doubling as catamites, these boys would serve the faithful the best wines and the purest water. In addition, the fallen warriors of Islam would lie on couches with dark-eyed damsels of 'stainless purity' and 'swelling breasts'. These paragons would combine everlasting virginity with everlasting sexual readiness.[89] The pleasures in Paradise, the warriors were told before each battle, would be infinitely greater than anything one could achieve on Earth, however wealthy one might be. The formula was clear: fight the good fight but do not value your earthly life so highly that the danger of its loss should inhibit your fighting spirit. (The Vikings and Germans of western Europe had a rather more 'rough-hewn' version of the after-life in Valhalla.)

The troops who won the initial victories for Mohammed un-doubtedly benefited from very high morale so, in that sense, Jihad must be considered to have worked. On the other hand, it could lead to fanaticism against a more highly trained and intelligent foe. There are numerous examples of early Mohammedan warriors driven by a virtual death-wish so that they sought martyrdom in a way that hardly reflected high morale. It was recorded that the first Muslim martyr was a boy of sixteen named Omayr ibn Hubab. At the battle of Badr in 624 he was eating grapes while listening to Mohammed haranguing his troops. As soon as he heard the Prophet promise the wonders of Paradise to anyone who fell in the battle ahead, he threw down the grapes, seized his sword and rushed to his death on the enemy's spears. Contemporary poetry records that at the battle of

Siffin in 657 an elderly Muslim saw a soldier killed in the fighting and then, with the clouds parting above him, he saw the body taken up by 'gazelle-eyed women, scantily attired'. The old man, impatient to enjoy Paradise, armed himself and sought out a foeman who duly killed him.[90] The similarities between these 'gazelle-eyed' houris and the Germanic warrior-maidens, the Valkyries, who carried dead heroes from the battlefield cannot be overlooked and indicate a cross-cultural mixture, perhaps produced by the widespread movements of mercenary soldiers. Even the Byzantines had transformed the Virgin Mary, Mother of God, into a warrior-queen by the time of the Avar siege of Constantinople in 626.

The effectiveness of Mohammed as a guerrilla leader and as a motivator of men was clearly demonstrated in the early victories. However, it was not until after the decisive battle of Badr in 624 that the true political significance of the Islamic revolution became clear. The brief campaign leading up to the battle began like so many others. Scouts brought in word that a very large and rich Meccan caravan was approaching the city from Syria under heavy escort. Mohammed decided to ambush it when it reached a place named Badr, about twenty miles from its destination. Ironically, the caravan was led by one of the Prophet's fiercest enemies, Abu Sofyan, of the Omayyad tribe. Mohammed once again decided to break all the rules of Arab warfare by filling in the wells – a great crime against traditional Arab culture – to deprive the enemy of water. Unknown to the Prophet, however, the Meccans had learned of the planned ambush and sent out a large relieving force. Abu Sofyan, meanwhile, outmanoeuvred Mohammed, and brought his caravan down the coast and into Mecca from the west. The Meccan relieving force now attacked Mohammed and a fierce battle took place.

Robbed of the chance of booty by the escape of the caravan, Mohammed had to motivate his followers with the arguments of the jihad: the Medinans were doing God's will in fighting the idolators from Mecca. Mohammed took no actual part in the fighting but rested under a shelter made from palm leaves, constantly praying to Allah for victory. This irritated Abu Bakr, who reminded him that if he was doing God's will then God would defeat the Meccans as he had promised. Mohammed, however, knew that the battle would be a close one and that his whole future and that of his movement rested on its outcome. At one point he became so nervous that he fainted and had to be revived by his servants.

A sandstorm apparently came to the aid of the Muslims, blinding the Meccans and representing, as Mohammed claimed, 'A thousand angels falling upon the enemy.' Many of the fighters on both sides, no doubt overstressed by the pressures of battle, later claimed to have seen angels fighting on the side of the Muslims and it is said that one of the Meccan leaders, Joal ibn Soraka, eventually fled saying, 'I see that which you cannot see.' There is a marked parallel here with the appearance of warrior-saints and even the Virgin Mary herself at decisive moments in Byzantine battles, notably during the great Avar siege of Constantinople in 626 when the Avar khagan is reputed to have withdrawn, speaking almost the same words as the Meccan leader quoted above.[91]

Badr was not a big battle by world standards but its consequences were enormous. Mohammed's 350 fighters had defeated 700 Meccans, killing fifty of them for fifteen of the Prophet's own men. But mere statistics tell us little of the effect this battle had in the Arab world. For generations Arabs had fought skirmishing actions, with light casualties. Their camels and horses gave them the mobility to escape decisive defeat and so the balance of power between tribes changed only slowly. At Badr, however, Mohammed exploited his victory in a decisive way. Although only fifty of the enemy had died in the fighting, many captive Meccans were executed – a course of action previously unknown to the Arabs. These men had merely been protecting their property from the marauding Muslims and had expected to be granted their lives by surrendering to the victors. The ruthlessness of Mohammed after his victory at Badr brought a chilling new element into the conflict.

Abu Sofyan, who had manoeuvred his caravan to safety but had missed the battle of Badr, now decided to take the initiative against Mohammed by invading Medinan territory. With an army that was enormous by desert Arab standards – 3,000 men – he challenged Mohammed to battle at Ohod in 625, putting the Medinans to flight in spite of every exhortation by the Prophet, who was actually wounded in the fighting. The battle was a triumph for one particular soldier, the Meccan general Khalid ibn al-Walid, and Mohammed decided to win the general to his cause. Khalid, the 'Sword of God' as he was later to be known, was to prove the greatest of all Arab generals and more than a match for his Christian opponents in the years to come.

Convinced that Mohammed's cause was in terminal decline, the Meccans attacked Medina with an army of 7,000 men, made up of many Bedouin tribesmen and idolators from throughout the Hijaz who were determined to put an end to Mohammed's campaigns against them. At this vital moment Mohammed found that one of his faithful followers, known as Salman the Persian, had unexpected skills. Salman, though a Christian, had come from a Zoroastrian family, and in his long conversations with Mohammed this learned man was able to draw on material from a mixture of religions. But it was not as a theologian that Mohammed needed him in 625. The Meccan army had surrounded the city walls of Medina and was only held back by the fortified trench that Salman, drawing on his Persian experience, directed the Medinans to dig. Unable to breach the ditch or indeed to come up against the walls, the Meccans faltered against the determined defenders and were eventually forced to retire.

By 628 Mohammed's teaching had spread far and wide throughout the Arabian peninsula. It had even reached the Christian areas of the Byzantine Empire, which had been under Persian control for the previous decade, and Mohammed decided to publicize his movement on an international scale. He therefore had letters written to the rulers of the neighbouring states. The most astonishing of all was the missive sent to Heraclius shortly after his decisive victory over the Persians at Nineveh. Addressing the Byzantine emperor as the 'Emperor of Rum' (indicating the ancient use of Rome for describing the Eastern Empire), Mohammed called on him to abandon the idolatrous worship of Jesus and Mary and told him to acknowledge the mission of Mohammed as God's Prophet. Heraclius, himself an educated man and a philosopher of note, took a tolerant view of the letter, assuming its was from some harmless lunatic.[92] The irony of this historical moment was not lost on later chroniclers. As modern readers we can only wonder at the fate that granted both men a great cause in 610, a holy war in 622, and for Mohammed a death at the height of his powers in 632 but for Heraclius a final decade of ignominious failure.

While the struggle between Medina and Mecca occupied most of the 620s, Mohammed also campaigned against neighbouring tribes, notably Jewish Arab and Christian Arab ones. In September 629 he sent an emissary to one of the princes of the Ghassanids. Mohammed had naturally called on the Ghassanids to reject Christianity and accept him as the Prophet of Allah. When they rejected his letter and killed the emissary, the Prophet sent a military force against them under his own adopted son Zayid and Khalid ibn al-Walid, who had by now come over to Islam. Overconfident as a result of their frequent victories over untrained Arab tribesmen, they encountered a Christian force near Mota and were heavily defeated. Mohammed's son Zayid was killed in the fighting and it was a further three years before Zayid's son Osama took his revenge on the Ghassanids in July 632, shortly after Mohammed's death.

Sustaining a decade of continuous fighting was not the Arab way. The men who had joined Mohammed in search of loot either satisfied their greed or became tired and bored and wanted to return to their homes. Only the devout followers of his teachings were willing to use their swords to spread the Prophet's words. Mohammed found it hard to lead the military campaigns himself. Aged sixty or more his health was not good and during 630 his troops grew rebellious, on one expedition actually jostling him, tearing his clothes and forcing him to take shelter under a tree. It was even said that some of his followers planned to murder him on the road back to Medina by forcing him over a cliff.[93]

Mohammed had made the capture of Mecca his prime aim and as his influence spread throughout the Arab tribes fewer and fewer men were prepared to oppose him. His most relentless foe, Abu Sofyan of Mecca, was old and longed for peace. Mohammed had married Abu Sofyan's daughter many years before, and between father and daughter there was consequently much bad feeling. Nevertheless, Abu Sofyan tried to approach the Prophet by enjoining the help of his daughter. She, however, would not even let him sit down in her room and rolled up the carpet to make her point. Abu Sofyan commented in disappointment, 'My dear daughter, either I am too good for the carpet or the carpet is too good for me.' She replied, 'It is the Prophet's carpet and you are an unbeliever.' Abu Sofyan ruefully reflected, 'Truly, you have changed for the worse since you left me.'[94]

On 11 January 630 Mohammed rode into Mecca at the head of an army of 10,000 believers. Abu Sofyan tried to arrange a meeting with the Prophet but when the seventy-year-old encountered Mohammed he was asked if he now believed that there was only one God and that Mohammed was his prophet. Abu Sofyan hesitated until Mohammed's ally, Omar, drew his sword and threatened to kill him on the spot. This settled his mind and all further resistance to Mohammed collapsed.

The Prophet next visited the Kaaba where he ordered all 360 idols to be destroyed and the paintings on the walls of the temple to be erased. In Mecca only one person dared to outface the Prophet and that was a woman. Hind, wife of Abu Sofyan, repeatedly heckled him and when the Prophet asked who was making the noise and interrupting him she declared herself openly.[95] Mohammed took no action against her, aware that to make a martyr of her might reunite his enemies in Mecca. Hind had fought successfully against Mohammed with other Meccan women at the battle of Ohod. Ironically, this fierce woman was to fight as heroically for the Muslims against the Byzantines at the battle of Yarmuk, where her personal intervention saved the Arab camp after the Byzantines had broken through.

Meanwhile, Khalid ibn al-Walid was carrying terror into the regions, tearing down tribal idols and massacring any people who refused to cooperate, for example, the Jazima tribe. The whole pace of the Islamic conquest of Arabia was increasing and Mohammed was able to muster quite formidable armies. At Honyan in 630 12,000 Muslims won a bloody and hard-fought battle against the Hawazin tribe.

When Mohammed died in 632 and was buried in Medina, his followers faced the problem of how the Islamic movement should proceed. Mohammed had once said: 'Two religions cannot exist in Arabia. Let there not remain throughout this land any faith except Islam.' With many areas of the Arabian peninsula still dominated by pagans, Christians and Jews, the message was clear enough. In his final years, Mohammed had pursued a policy of eliminating pockets of resistance to Islam wherever he found them. This policy of

religious 'cleansing' had seen the eradication, even the extermination, of tribes who tried to cling to their traditional beliefs. For
Mohammed's successors – the four caliphs Abu Bakr, Omar,
Othman and Ali – the next question was how far to extend the
frontiers of Islam. If Mohammed had been sent by God as the
Prophet of the Arab people, did that mean that his message was
intended for areas which were not within the peninsula, like Syria or
Egypt? At the moment that a triumphant Heraclius, still fresh from
his victories in Persia, was struggling to heal the rifts in Christianity,
a people united by Mohammed was about to take the Prophet's
words to an unsuspecting world.

NINE

Islam Rampant

Mohammed's successor Abu Bakr faced the immediate difficulty that many Arabs had only accepted Islam out of fear of the Prophet himself and now that he was dead, they fell back into their old ways. What followed was known as the 'Wars of the Apostasy' with Abu Bakr implementing a severe policy of reconversion in which virtually the whole of the peninsula was purged of dissidents and apostates. Faced with the collapse of everything he and Mohammed had worked to create, Abu Bakr was forced to follow cruel and repressive policies. He survived his friend by just two years and was buried alongside him in Mecca. However, in those two years Abu Bakr made a decision that was going to change the world: he decided to push back the frontiers of Christianity by sending Arab armies to convert Syrian and Palestinian Arabs to Islam. This would inevitably lead to war with the forces of the Christian empire but Abu Bakr never hesitated for a moment.

Heraclius can be excused his failure to keep abreast of developments in distant Arabia while he was involved in his life and death struggle against Sasanian Persia. Only the most acute observer could have correctly predicted the rise of Islam. For those Byzantines who did take an interest in Arabian affairs it seemed as if Mohammed represented a successful and new Christian sect which had splintered from Monophysitism. As such, Islam was limited in its aims and carried no military or political threat to the security of the empire as a whole.

In 633 Abu Bakr ordered four Arab armies into southern Palestine. It was less an invasion than an armed raid, different in style from anything the Roman inhabitants had experienced from that direction before. Previous tribal raids had resembled desert storms – wild, violent but soon gone – whereas these Arab forces had a discipline that suggested a more coherent purpose. Moreover, even if these were merely raids, they were very large ones and could not be ignored. The local Byzantine commander, Sergius, the Duke of Palestine, assembled what troops were available and brought one of the Arab forces to battle near Gaza. To his surprise he found a far more professional enemy, better armed and better disciplined than he had expected. The conglomerate Byzantine force might have expected the Arabs to break and flee at the sight of a disciplined, imperial army. They were wrong. The Arabs fought with an unexpected determination and defeated the Byzantines, killing Sergius in the process.

When news of these events reached Heraclius at Edessa he was alarmed. Perhaps he felt the cold shadow of doubt suddenly pass across his mind. The south was the one direction that he had not brought under his control; Avars, Turks, Persians were no longer a threat, but the Arabs? Everything hinged on peace in the south: an end to religious schism with the Monophysites; the opportunity for cost-cutting exercises in the army and reduced subsidies to the Christian Arabs who guarded the frontier; the peaceful re-establishment of Byzantine rule in Egypt. There must be no war there. Heraclius needed to rebuild an empire shattered by three decades of constant war. Surely this threat from the Arabs could be quelled by the troops and the commanders who had achieved success in the past? He summoned his brother Theodore, who had been one of his stoutest commanders in the wars against Persia, to take the Army of the East into Palestine.

Heraclius has been accused of under-reacting to the Arab threat. Yet these troops and this commander had fought so well in the last years of the Persian wars that they had established a psychological superiority over the previously invincible Persian armies of Shahen and Shahrvaraz. However, in the Arabs Heraclius was facing a more formidable enemy than he, or indeed anyone else, expected. When studying the early Islamic conquests historians have tended to describe the Muslim armies as fanatical rather than well-led and efficient. This does scant justice to the superb qualities of a number of individual Arab commanders, in addition to the justly famous Khalid ibn al-Walid. According to one historian, the early Islamic generals made up one of the finest 'teams' of military commanders in the history of warfare.[96] If Theodore judged the Arabs according to what he, and Byzantines for centuries before him, understood to be the traditional Arab mode of warfare, he was bound to fail.

When news reached Abu Bakr that a Byzantine army under the emperor's brother was threatening his forces in Palestine he might have been expected to order his commanders to separate their troops to avoid being forced into a pitched battle, or at least to withdraw into the desert to entice Theodore's troops into an unwise pursuit. Flexibility had always been the Arab way of warfare; it was virtually unknown for them to concentrate in the face of a professional army and face a clash of arms. But that is precisely what they did, combining their forces and meeting Theodore in battle at Ajnadin, between Jerusalem and Gaza. Details of this vital encounter are scarce although the outcome was clear: Theodore's army suffered a complete disaster.

An epic incident of early Islamic history occurred before the battle of Ajnadin and contributed to the Arab victory. Once the Byzantine army had begun to arrive in Palestine by sea, disembarking at the port of Jaffa, it was obvious to the Muslim commanders that they would be heavily outnumbered in the campaign ahead and so they appealed to Abu Bakr for reinforcements. The caliph contacted Khalid ibn al-Walid, who was at that time campaigning in Iraq with a small, elite force of about 500–800 infantry equipped with camels for mobility. Alerted to the threat to the Arab forces in Palestine, Khalid led his troops across nearly 400 miles of mainly desert terrain in temperatures that would have killed most soldiers. Unable to carry enough water for the journey and having no time to find water holes, Khalid's men used their camels as living water-carriers. Before beginning the march the camels had been deliberately deprived of water to make them more thirsty than usual. As a result, when they did drink, they filled their stomachs to bursting point. When water was desperately short, in the cauldron heat of the Iraqi desert, the Arabs slaughtered the camels one by one and cut open their stomachs to fill their water bottles.

The arrival of Khalid in Palestine meant that command of the combined Arab armies devolved to him and it was he whose reputation gained most from the victory at Ajnadin. After the battle he was accorded the title 'Sword of God', though it would be wrong to attribute Islamic military success to him alone. Several other able commanders, notably the great Amr ibn al-As, later conqueror of Egypt, fought at Ajnadin. In fact, in some ways, the victory at Ajnadin was harder fought and more decisive even than the more famous battle at Yarmuk two years later. Certainly, Arab losses at Ajnadin were very heavy, particularly among the leadership of the army – the 'Companions' – who had been closest to the Prophet himself. Nevertheless, the psychological advantage that the Arab warriors established at Ajnadin ensured that when they met Christian forces in the future their morale was already very high.

The Byzantine commander, Theodore, carried news of his own defeat back to his brother, at Emesa. Heraclius was furious. Apparently he felt that Theodore had disobeyed his orders and we can only conclude that Heraclius had instructed him to avoid a full-scale battle. The usual Byzantine tactic would have been to wait for nomadic warriors like the Arabs to lose interest in a lengthy campaign and withdraw to their homes with their loot, often without the need for a battle. Whether such fabian tactics would have worked with Muslims of the Jihad is open to doubt, but it may have been what Heraclius had in mind. To add to the seriousness of the military defeat Theodore had suffered, personal recriminations now broke out between the brothers, undermining Byzantine resistance to the Muslim invaders. We can never know how the argument developed but we know the subject of their dispute. Theodore, like the other members of the emperor's family, had long resented the influence that the Empress Martina exerted on Heraclius. Theodore had always regarded his brother's marriage to his niece as incestuous. Furthermore, he regarded Martina as a threat to his nephew Constantine's orderly succession to the throne. He feared that Martina might try to turn Heraclius against his eldest son in favour of her own son, Heraclonas; this, Theodore and the bulk of the Byzantine army were determined to resist. With the bitterness of defeat already poisoning the atmosphere Theodore apparently insulted Martina telling his brother that 'his sin is continually before him'. Heraclius ordered him to return to Constantinople and stripped him of his command. This was an unexpected victory for the Arabs because Theodore was a formidable commander with a proven record against the Persians. With Theodore gone, Heraclius had no obvious commander to replace him.

Khalid's victory at Ajnadin established Arab rule in the whole of Palestine and opened the floodgates to thousands of immigrants from Arabia. Yet Khalid knew that he had won just the first battle in a war; the Byzantines would not abandon these lands without a far greater effort. He pushed his forces northwards into Syria, defeating the Armenian general Vahan in battles at Fihl and Marj as-Suffar early in 635. His target was Damascus, which he reached in March and which surrendered to him after a six-month blockade. By the end of 635 most of Syria and Palestine, apart from the small Christian enclaves of Jerusalem, Caesarea and some coastal cities, were in Arab hands.

To add to this military setback the worst possible news reached Heraclius from Jerusalem. The new Patriarch, Sophronius, supposedly a firm supporter of Orthodoxy, had in fact brought his people out against Monoenergism. The emperor had expected difficulties with the Monophysites of Egypt and Syria, but on hearing of Sophronius's defection he must have felt that God himself was abandoning him. And when the Patriarch Sergius himself, co-author of the concept, began to express doubts Heraclius felt finally abandoned. As a result, during 634 Heraclius abandoned Monoenergism and turned his attention to the deteriorating military situation in Syria and Palestine.

What seems to have been entirely lacking in the struggle against the Muslims was any kind of strong motivation on the part of either Byzantine commanders or troops. This may be accounted for in a number of ways, not least the perception that the Byzantines had of the Arab invaders. Here the dangers of hindsight for the historian are very clearly illustrated. Writing 1,300 years after an event provides us with perspective but also the distortion that comes with the knowledge of how everything turned out and therefore how significant each event was. Heraclius, for example, has been as roundly criticized for his failure to combat the Arabs as he has been praised for his triumph in Persia. Yet he was the same man, with the same troops in both situations. What was missing in the 630s was not only ten years of a man's vital energy but also an understanding of the nature of the enemy. In the 620s Heraclius knew that the empire was on the brink of extinction at the hands of Avar and Persian barbarians. One mistake in 626 could have seen the end of eastern Christianity. These mighty issues, symbolized by the loss of the True Cross, served to concentrate everyone's mind to the point where even the Church was prepared to throw its not inconsiderable wealth into the earthly struggle for survival. It was as clear as that. The Arab invasion, however large and well-organized, did not seem so dangerous. The Arabs were a known quantity, having been restless raiders for a thousand years. The Byzantines described them in insulting terms like 'wild, untamed beasts' or 'beastly and barbarous enemies'. It was known that they had been pagan worshippers of a piece of black rock in Mecca but in recent years it was believed that many of the tribesmen had adopted monotheism, becoming either Jews or Christians. The letter that Heraclius had received from an Arab named Mohammed indicated that some kind of new, semi-Christian heresy had emerged in the last few years and perhaps it was this that was inciting the frontier tribes to try to take advantage of the breakdown of Byzantine authority on the Palestine frontier. However Heraclius and his advisers viewed the situation, the Muslims did not compare with the Sasanian Persians as a threat to the survival of the empire.

Thus while many of the Arabs who fought during the campaign to capture Syria were convinced that they were fighting a holy war, none of their Byzantine opponents felt that religion was an issue in what began as little more than frontier skirmishing and territorial conquest on a local scale. In neither case was it possible for Byzantine leaders to appreciate the spiritual inspiration with which the Muslim warriors were filled. Many of the frontier Arab tribes, for example, had soldiers in both Christian and Muslim armies and at this stage it was hardly apparent that there were substantial differences between their respective monotheistic beliefs.

The defeat of Theodore at Ajnadin marked a watershed for Heraclius. Although serious cracks had already appeared in the imperial edifice they had passed unnoticed. After 634, however, these cracks grew so wide they could never be repaired. While the military situation worsened, unity in the Church proved elusive. The damage, ironically, was caused not by the emperor's spiritual enemies but by those friends on whom he had most relied, the Orthodox bishops. Heraclius, feeling the pressures of his increasing age once more shuffled the pack and replaced the concept of 'single energy' with that of 'single will'. Still supported by his loyal friend, Sergius, the emperor produced the *Ekthesis* in 638, forbidding further discussion of the energy question and introducing instead monotheletism. The doctrine was displayed for all to read in the narthex of Hagia Sophia. Unfortunately, the emperor's opponents, having tasted blood, rejected monotheletism out of hand. Monophysites and Chalcedonians for once saw eye to eye in rejecting the aged emperor's last attempt to achieve spiritual unity. The death of Sergius and the defection of Pope Honorius to the ranks of the opposition condemned Heraclius to spiritual defeat to match the military disasters that rent the empire between 636 and 638.

The approaching loss of Syria to the Arabs clouded the last years of Heraclius's life. His reputation as one of the greatest of all emperors has been tarnished not so much by his own failings as by the extraordinary accomplishments of others. In preparing for his great counter-offensive against the Persians between 620 and 622 Heraclius had used two special weapons: religious propaganda and Turkish allies. In 635 and 636 there is no evidence to suggest that either of these weapons was deployed against the Arabs. In the first place, the religious threat from the Persians in the 620s seemed very real to Christianity as a whole, whereas the new faith of the Arabs, if known at all by the Byzantines, was not understood. As a result neither Heraclius nor Sergius saw the religious argument as necessary to inspire their soldiers. Furthermore, with the war being conducted in the southern provinces, almost entirely Monophysite in outlook, it was probably felt that appeals from the Orthodox Church would be counter-productive. The other weapons that Heraclius had used against the Persians, namely appeals to the Christian tribes of Transcaucasia and the decisive alliance with the Turks, were geographically inappropriate and apparently militarily unnecessary. Heraclius must have believed that he could raise and equip an army large enough and good enough to defeat any invasion from the south. As the problem was mostly psychological, he cannot have found it easy to identify the immense chasm that separated the morale of the two armies. He may have believed that the sheer professionalism of his own troops could match the military potential of the Arabs, without being aware that their morale was high as a result of religious elation and the spirit of jihad. Ironically, neither of the two dominant figures were present on the battlefield at Yarmuk. Mohammed, exponent of the Muslim jihad, had already been dead for four years; Heraclius, the first Christian crusader, was enduring a living death in Antioch.

History is written by the winners and the Muslim accounts of the conquest of Syria are more flamboyant, if not always more coherent, than those of the Byzantine chronicles. So central was the campaign and the victory at Yarmuk to the history of the Arab people that legend has frequently taken over from hard facts in glorifying the achievements of both commanders and warriors. Forcing their way into the pages of history beside Khalid ibn al-Walid, are Hind, ferocious wife of Mohammed's old enemy Abu Sofyan, Zarrar ibn al-Azwar, Arab hero, and his equally heroic sister, Khaula Bint al-Azwar. Although Khalid ibn al-Walid had been recognized by this stage as the most able of the Muslim commanders he was not highly regarded in religious terms and this latter factor still meant that overall command would rest with Abu 'Ubaida, 'the faithful guardian of the people'. More political commissar than general, Abu 'Ubaida was a skilful diplomat and far more conciliatory with a beaten enemy than the ferocious Khalid. Alongside Abu 'Ubaida in command of the Muslim forces was 'Amr ibn al As, a subtle politician and later conqueror of Egypt.

If the Byzantine commanders had the strength of professionals, they also had the weaknesses that sometimes went with the task of command: rigidity and lack of imagination. Against this the Arabs had the advantages of the skilled amateur, a willingness to try the untried that had no justification in military terms, and a higher level of motivation. The Byzantines thought that they understood the desert Arabs. They were wrong. Twenty years had changed the Arab warrior out of all recognition. The Byzantine troops fought for their pay and for little else: at best it took them to the ale house, at worst to the grave. The Arabs fought for their faith and willingly accepted martyrdom because as it took them to Paradise. Leadership and morale were the main factors behind in the Arab victory at Yarmuk and the Christian loss of Syria.

The size of the Byzantine army that Heraclius eventually sent south from Antioch will never be known for certain. All we can say is that it was very large for action in Syria or Palestine, as such a threat had never previously appeared from that direction. Figures as large as 40,000 are given by chroniclers but these are probably too high. Nevertheless, there is little doubt that the Byzantines would have outnumbered the Arab forces, large though these were by Arab standards. On receiving news that the expected Byzantine counter-attack was under way Khalid ibn al-Walid persuaded his colleagues to fall back, abandoning captured Syrian cities including Emesa and Damascus and concentrating the various Arab contingents at Jabiya, near the River Yarmuk. Here the Arab forces enjoyed ample water and pasture for their animals. However, within days the Muslim army was dislodged from Jabiya by an army of Christian Ghass-anids. Khalid once again advised retreat to a position he had studied between Dara'ah and Dayr Ayyub. In this area much of the terrain was very difficult, consisting as it did of a lava plain. With the steep cliffs of the Yarmuk river gorges covering one flank and lava the other, the Arabs were in a strong defensive position. The Byzantines had also taken up a strong defensive position south of Damascus and were in no hurry to advance and give battle.

The commanders who led the Byzantine army at the battle of Yarmuk were an ill-assorted group, revealing perhaps that at the end of an exhausting war Heraclius was scraping the barrel. The emperor's appointment to replace his brother may have been a civil servant as he was known by his title, Sekellarios or Treasurer. His name was Theodore Trithourios and his real role with the army could have been administrative, notably financial. Lack of pay was the quickest way to break up any army, particularly one based on a mercenary system like the Byzantine force at Yarmuk, and so the presence of an imperial paymaster was reassuring to the troops. Probably the military command rested with the Armenian general Vahan, who had recently been with Heraclius and probably knew his intentions. The troops under his command were a mixture of fresh Armenian soldiers, Arab tribesmen, local Syrian Greeks and even Greek troops from Constantinople and Anatolia. In addition, there was also Nicetas, Christian son of Heraclius's old Sasanian opponent Shahrvaraz, who may have commanded mercenary Sasanian units left behind in Syria and Egypt when those provinces were evacuated by his father. Most significant of all, however, in the Byzantine command structure was Jabala, last king of the Ghassanids. He was truly loyal to Heraclius, unlike Vahan and Nicetas, and had fought through the Persian campaigns with his Christian Arab troops. He was to survive the defeat at Yarmuk and, unable to accept Islam, settled with many of his tribesmen in Cappadocia, becoming so much part of the Byzantine world that a later emperor of the ninth century, Nicephorus I, claimed descent from Jabala the Ghassanid.[97]

It has been suggested that the Byzantine commander, and here we are forced to assume that Vahan was making most of the decisions, was hoping to allow his troops to acclimatize. His army was a mixture of units, some of whom had only just arrived in the desert heat from the northern uplands of Armenia or Anatolia. They would have been quite unaccustomed to the tough conditions in southern Syria. In addition to the hostile terrain they must have found the local populace very hostile, consisting as it did of Monophysite Christians and Jews, who were eager to see the Orthodox Byzantines beaten.

The two armies, both strongly entrenched, spent the next three months hoping to see the other make a mistake or withdraw. Time favoured the Arabs, who were more able to receive reinforcements and supplies from the south, while the Byzantines were constantly subjected to the hostility of the local tribes. The Byzantines fought the war in the manner they knew best – by attempting to dismantle the opposition through bribery and trickery. They tried to detach individual Arab leaders from their colleagues. Negotiations went on day after day, with Byzantine money attempting to break the Muslim resolve as Byzantine weapons could not. The Arabs were content to wait and to negotiate. When the moment was ripe they would strike. And, suddenly, detecting that the Byzantine hold on Jabiya had slipped, a quick Arab raid secured the town.

The harsh terrain that lay between the two armies was favourable to neither but the Byzantines were worst affected. They relied on cavalry and were less flexible than their opponents. But it was in the minds that the waiting battle was being fought and won by the Arabs. The Byzantine army, essentially a coalition force rather than a national one, was subject to endless disputes between the various parts. Orthodox Greeks and Monophysite Ghassanids were likely to be at odds with each other, and frequent brawls involving bloodshed lowered morale. Even the commanders could not abstain from quarrelling. In the large Armenian contingent, it is reported, one of the senior officers refused to obey the orders of his commander, a general named George. Among the Christian Arabs there was the inevitable uncertainty they felt at facing fellow Arabs and, in many cases, members of their own tribe who were fighting with the Muslim army.

While the Byzantine army was succumbing to its own fears the Arabs were becoming stronger as reinforcements joined them from outlying areas. Many experienced Yemeni archers arrived – they would never have reached the battlefield had the Byzantines taken the initiative and attacked the Arabs while they were at their weakest. Eventually, realizing that as time passed the Arabs grew ever stronger while their own morale dropped, the Byzantines decided to attack. It is reported that before he gave the order Vahan arranged to meet Khalid to offer an immense fortune to the Arabs if they withdrew from Palestine. It was the same error that Maurice had made with the Avars less than fifty years before.

David Nicolle estimates that the battle front may have been as long as 13 kilometres and that by the time the fighting began the Byzantines had been reduced, by desertion and other factors, to not much more than 20,000 men.[98] Nevertheless, they still enjoyed a comfortable numerical superiority. The Byzantine right was made up of infantry, armed with large, heavy shields which could be virtually locked together to form a wall or 'tortoise'. Vahan commanded mainly Armenian troops in the centre. We do not know the name of the Armenian officer who was in charge of the left, though he was apparently the insubordinate officer who would not take orders from George. The Ghassanids under their King Jabala operated as a mobile reserve of light cavalry, similar in style to many of the Muslim units. We know that the Byzantines had left a force of soldiers to guard the bridge over the Wadi Ruqqad, several miles behind the front line.

Overall command of the Arab army had been given – at last – to their most capable general, Khalid ibn al-Walid. It was probably realized by the more political or religious officers that this was one battle which needed unity of command. Understanding the Arab formation is difficult but one account gives it as consisting of four large divisions of infantry, each comprising nine separate units. The cavalry formed up into four squadrons with one held in reserve and the others supporting the flank and centre infantry. The Yemeni archers, of whose numbers we are unsure, were spread thinly across the battlefield and cannot have concentrated their fire at any one point. The Muslim camps were situated behind the tribal warriors and contained not just the transport camels but the women who had accompanied the army, some of whom had come to fight.

The battle of Yarmuk was not decided in a single day, nor by a decisive charge nor even by incompetence on the part of one of the commanders. It was an attritional struggle which took a full six days to reach a resolution. As usual the battle began with skirmishing and duels between champions, but it is reported that a number of Christian Arabs changed sides, which can have done little for Byzantine morale. Nevertheless, around midday Vahan ordered his infantry to advance and a hand-to-hand struggle took place for much of the afternoon until the sun set. On the second day, the Byzantines attacked early and caught the Arabs at their morning prayers. It was at this time that the Byzantines broke the Muslim left flank which fell back on its camp only for the Arab women to turn the tide of battle. Ululating and singing songs to encourage the warriors, the Arab women rushed into the fight wielding spears and even tent poles. Led by the ferocious Hind, who in earlier battles had apparently cut out and chewed the livers of her victims, they drove their men back into the fight, shouting to them to cut off the arms of the uncircumcised.

The veteran Abu Sofyan, concluding that death at the hands of the Christians was preferable to a beating with a tent pole from his wife, turned his horse and rallied his men, leading them back into the fray. Behind him, Hind had taken up the refrain of the song she had sung at the battle of Ohod when the Meccans had defeated the Prophet himself. Her singing and that of her fellow viragos settled the matter and the Arabs held their camp, driving the Byzantines back. A younger hero, Zarrar, accustomed to the more mellifluous voice of his sister, Khaula Bint al-Azwar, charged the retreating Byzantine horsemen and won a respite for the Muslim army and for Arab husbands in general. However, by the third day Byzantine numerical superiority was having an effect. Arab casualties were growing and it seemed only a matter of time before the Muslim camps succumbed to the Byzantine cavalry attacks.

The fourth day was decisive. Vahan, almost successful with his flank attacks on the two previous days, continued to grind the Arabs with his superior numbers. As a change of tactics Khalid made a flanking manoeuvre which won the battle, although two further days were needed to convince the Byzantines to retreat. The decisive moment followed an apparent Byzantine breakthrough by Armenian infantry and Ghassanid mounted troops. As they pushed through the Arab centre-right division they found themselves hit on both flanks simultaneously by the Arab cavalry under Khalid himself. The heaviest fighting of the entire battle now followed until the Armenians gave way and fell back, leaving the Ghassanids to be decimated. The absence of the Byzantine cavalry, who were looting one of the Muslim camps, exposed the Armenian infantry to the full force of Khalid's horsemen. Separated from their infantry, some of the Byzantine cavalry now fled the battlefield.

To compound this disaster, the ebullient Zarrar, commanding the Arab reserve cavalry, saw the Byzantine horsemen fleeing and pursued them back towards the bridge over the Wadi Ruqqad that the Byzantines had been holding since the start of the battle. The garrison was swept away by the retreating horsemen and Zarrar, coming up behind, was able to capture the bridge and cut off the retreat of the entire Byzantine army.

However, this epic battle had many twists and turns. While Khalid and Zarrar were making decisive tactical gains, a general problem was undermining the Arab forces in other parts of the field. The widely spread Yemeni archers could not match the concentrated effects of the Byzantine bowmen and this fourth day of fighting became known to the Arabs as 'The Day of the Lost Eyes'. Without cavalry support some Arab infantry units succumbed to the Byzantine horse archers who were unchallenged and therefore found it easy to shoot down footsoldiers. It is said that one Muslim infantry unit was totally annihilated by cavalry. At this stage it seems two of the heroines of the battle, Hind and Khaula Bint al-Azwar, were in the forefront of the fighting. Khaula was severely wounded by a sword cut to the head, while Hind, leading a charmed if not a charming life, continued to exhort the men to redouble their efforts.

The likely outcome of the battle was still not clear except to the Byzantine commander who, with the loss of the bridge, knew that escape was impossible. Unprepared to fight to the last man, an approach which would probably have brought him victory, the chroniclers claim that he tried to negotiate a withdrawal with the Muslims, but without success. The Byzantines had been out-manoeuvred by Khalid and were badly placed strategically, separated from their camp and with their backs to the gorges of the Yarmuk river. There was little fighting on the fifth day, though the Muslims consolidated their position and Khalid concentrated his cavalry for a last, decisive charge should it became possible.

At the start of the sixth and final day of the battle the Armenian general George was killed and his troops were thrown into disorder by his loss. Byzantine chroniclers claim that a sandstorm coincided with this setback and struck the Byzantines, blinding them. This is probably untrue, it being a common feature of many Arab victories for the losing side to attribute defeat to the intervention of the elements which were always believed to favour the men of the desert. Whatever the explanation, this seemed to be the moment when morale collapsed and the Byzantine army began to disintegrate. Individually and then in larger numbers men began to surrender, first throwing down their arms and then riding towards the enemy. The Arabs, perhaps unused to the customs and practices of such encounters, were not prepared to take prisoners and killed their enemies, both armed and unarmed. Once the Arabs' actions became apparent, the Byzantines simply fled the field, heading towards the steep gorges of the Yarmuk river. Here hundreds fell to their deaths or tried to leap into the water only to be smashed on the rocks below. Others fled back to the bridge which was now in Arab hands and tried to force their way through. Clearly some succeeded for thousands of the Byzantine army made their escape, some north to Emesa and others south to Egypt. However, 20,000 men, Byzantines and Arabs, were lost in the long drawn-out battle.

The Armenian commanders on the Byzantine side were all killed on the battlefield, as was the slightly mysterious Theodore Trithourius, whose role in the whole campaign never became clear. The Ghassanid ruler Jabala escaped and survived to live out his life in Cappadocia. On the Arab side, the elderly Abu Sofyan lost an eye but survived the battle, as did his wife Hind.

The Byzantine high command had not countenanced the possibility of defeat and had no plans for an organized retreat. Heraclius had put his all into assembling this, his last, army and news of its defeat seems to have broken his will to fight on. With Khalid now taking a step back so that political generals like Abu 'Ubaida could take over once again, the Arabs began mopping up the pockets of resistance in southern Syria, of which there were very few. The invaders were welcomed by the population as liberators and the fleeing Byzantine troops found little help as they travelled north until they reached Anatolia.

Heraclius summoned a meeting of his advisers at a church in Antioch and scrutinized the situation. He was told and willingly accepted the fact that this defeat was God's decision and was a result of the sins and disobedience of his people. The accusation that had earned his brother Theodore's dismissal must have resurfaced at this stage. Even though the emperor's incestuous marriage to his niece Martina had taken place more than twenty years before, there was no way that people would allow him to forget it. High churchmen encouraged Heraclius not to despair of the lost land but to seek divine repentance. Once God had forgiven him then Syria would be regained just as it had been from the Persians. Heraclius retired to his capital, possibly making the famous observation, 'Peace be with you, Syria – what a beautiful land you will be for the enemy.'[99]

Heraclius must have wondered at the divine symbolism that had seen him return the True Cross to Jerusalem in 630, entering by the Golden Gate, only to have to go back again like a thief in the night just six years later to take away the holy relic so that it did not fall into the hands of the all-conquering Arabs. The relic was taken to Constantinople where it was kept in Hagia Sophia. This was the beginning of a period lasting hundreds of years when only the mighty walls of Constantinople stood between militant Islam and the True Cross, the overthrow of the empire and of eastern Christianity.

Like so many of the events in this most dramatic and decisive period of history the Muslim occupation of Jerusalem in February 638 is shrouded in legend. All accounts report that it took place as peacefully as the city's loss to the Persians in 614 had been violent. Furthermore, most reports say that the inhabitants refused to surrender except to Caliph Omar in person and that it was his arrival that saved the city from a bloodbath wrought by fanatics on both sides. Omar's entry into Jerusalem, riding a white camel and dressed in rags, marked him out as the most unusual conqueror of the holy city. The event was witnessed by the new Patriarch Sophronius, who conducted Omar to the site of the Temple of Solomon. Here Omar stood alone for a while, gazing outwards and upwards. It was believed that Omar's friend Mohammed had ascended into heaven from here, and this spot would become one of the holiest places in all Islam – the site of the future Dome of the Rock. As the caliph stood, bareheaded and in a tattered robe, the patriarch's resolution left him and in despair he said, 'Behold, the abomination of desolation, spoken of by the Prophet Daniel, that standeth in the Holy Place.' Some Arab sources, however, record that the city was surrendered like so many other Christian cities, without violence and without special dispensation. They say the caliph did not take the surrender himself but arrived later to see the city that had been so important to his friend Mohammed.

During the later stages of the Arab conquest of Syria Heraclius suffered from the onset of a disease which, although referred to in the chronicles by the archaic medical term dropsy, was almost certainly an insidious cancer. Nicephorus informs his readers that 'every time that he voided water, he was obliged to lay a board across his stomach to prevent its spurting into his face'.[100] When the nature of his affliction became known it was widely believed that this was God's punishment on the emperor's reproductive organs for his incestuous marriage to his niece. The description of the disease as 'dropsy' indicates swelling, possibly from a tumour that interfered with the normal processes of the body. We cannot be sure whether the cancer contributed to the mental problems that Heraclius suffered at this stage. However, the chroniclers report that when he returned from Antioch following the collapse of the Byzantine defences there in 638, he insisted on staying at the Hiereia Palace on the Asian shore rather than crossing the Bosphorus to Constantinople. In modern parlance he suffered a nervous breakdown though, in view of the onset of his cancer, the nervous collapse might well have been an early symptom of the underlying malady.

At this crucial time when the emperor's presence in the capital was essential, the officials who visited him at Hiereia found a trembling figure, holding on to the frame of the door as he spoke to them. When official or ceremonial occasions demanded his presence, he sent his sons instead – to the Hippodrome, to Hagia Sophia or even to the Senate. The phobia from which he was suffering meant that he could not look at water without suffering unbearable panic. Saddest of all the emperor's afflictions, perhaps, was the onset of mood swings and uncharacteristic brutality. Paranoia drove this gentle warrior and model parent to suspect some of his closest friends and relatives of plotting to overthrow him. His savage suppression of one 'revolt' by his illegitimate son Atalarichos and his nephew Theodore saw both men banished after having their hands and noses cut off. When Theodore arrived at the island of Gaudomelete, where he was to spend the rest of his days, it was to find that an imperial order had come ordering the governor to cut off one foot as well.

In his final madness only his wife Martina – mother of ten of his children and yet in the eyes of the Orthodox Church and most of the inhabitants of Constantinople the cause of both his personal afflictions and those of the empire – could cope with the shattered emperor. It was she, indeed, who devised the idea for a means of moving Heraclius across the sea to his capital. Nicephorus suggests a pontoon bridge was the means put forward to circumvent Heraclius's water phobia.[101]

A thousand years before, Darius and his Persians might have managed it but in view of the distance and the current it would have been virtually impossible to build a bridge of boats across the Bosphorus. It would have required between 500 and 1,000 ships of the largest kind, chained or tied together, with a road built across each of the decks and a hedge of bushes and trees running alongside it so that the eyes of the emperor could never for a moment glimpse the waters of the Bosphorus. The task of constructing this bridge would have imposed too great a burden upon the Byzantine economy. Maritime trade would have come to a halt and the Byzantine navy would have been out of action for the weeks or even months necessary to build such a bridge. Nicephorus and his fellow chroniclers were almost certainly mistaken in their belief that such a project was planned. Something simpler but equally effective could have been constructed using just a single boat in such a way as to conceal the water from the emperor's eyes. However it was done, the 'First Crusader' returned to his capital, no longer the triumphant conqueror of 628, nor the humble penitent who had returned the True Cross to Jerusalem in 630, but simply a man coming home to die – *Vanitas vanitatum, Omnia vanitas.*

Once Jerusalem had surrendered, the Caliph Omar decided to turn his attention to Egypt. There were good strategic reasons for doing so, both military and economic. As the Arabs moved further along the Syrian coast they were constantly aware that behind them in Egypt lay a large Byzantine garrison as well as the major naval base for the imperial navy. Furthermore, Egypt, with its rich, grain-producing soil, was the main food supplier for Constantinople. Finally, it was the hinge between the Near East and Africa. If Islam was to spread along the North African coast, Egypt would have to be taken.

However, the Arabs faced more than merely a second-rate Byzantine garrison in Egypt. The land of the pharaohs had legendary status within Arab culture, as it did with peoples throughout the region. In Egypt the new conquerors felt like pygmies in a world of giants. Not only the vast edifices of the pyramids, the Sphinx and the numerous temples towered over them but also historical figures like Rameses II, Alexander the Great, Cleopatra, Julius Caesar and Mark Antony. When, later, they stood and gazed at the skyline of Alexandria, they felt like tourists rather than conquerors.

The eventual conqueror of Egypt, the Muslim general Amr ibn al-As, was convinced that the task ahead would be easy as long as he did not try to chase shadows. He took a matter-of-fact view of the operation. After all, he reasoned, if the Byzantines could not hold Syria with their best troops and their best generals, how would they hold Egypt with their worst? As he said, 'There is no country in the world at once so wealthy and so defenceless.'[102] The Caliph Omar was uneasy, however. Everything had proceeded so smoothly that he could not believe it could continue. Might an invasion of Egypt without adequate troops end in disaster and put an end to the good fortune that had hitherto accompanied Arab arms? Amr seemed too confident, offering to conquer the whole, vast country as far as Libya with an army of just 4,000 men or fewer.

We have a good description of Amr as he set out to conquer Egypt. ibn Hajar describes this 45-year-old as 'warlike, fiery, eloquent and shrewd'. He adds that Amr was 'one of the four Arabian political geniuses of Islam'.[103] Short in stature but broad-shouldered, Amr was a great horseman and swordsman. He had dark, piercing eyes, heavy eyebrows and a large mouth, and he used a black cosmetic on his full beard. He was noted for his fiery temperament but was as quick to laugh as to express anger, and his eloquence and wit made him a popular companion. Of all Muslim commanders Amr held the honour of being appointed directly by the Prophet himself. Mohammed told him, 'I am sending you forth as commander of a troop. May God keep you safe and give you much booty.' When Amr questioned the need for booty, saying, 'I did not become a Muslim for the sake of wealth, but for the sake of submission to God', Mohammed replied, 'Honest wealth is good for an honest man.'[104]

Eventually Omar was won over by Amr's enthusiasm for an attack on Egypt but told him to keep the project secret until he was actually in Egyptian territory. Amr set off and had reached Rafah, near the Egyptian border but still in Palestine, when messengers from Omar rode up with a letter. Amr suspected that Omar might lose his nerve and had been half-expecting to be recalled. The letter ordered him to retreat if he was still in Palestine and only to go ahead if he was already in Egypt. Amr, keeping his own counsel, crossed into Egypt and then called a meeting of his senior officers to read the caliph's words. Amr, pretending to follow his orders, asked his officers to identify their current location. When told that he and his men were actually in Egypt, he ordered the expedition to continue.

The Muslim army was a composite force made up of Persian and Byzantine converts as well as members of the Akk and Ghafik tribes. The Persians were the remnants of the armies of Shahen and Shahrvaraz that had conquered Palestine and Syria nearly twenty years previously. When the Persian armies withdrew in 628 and 629 they had stayed behind, either offering their service as mercenaries or drifting into areas where they came under the influence of Islamic teaching. The Byzantines were mainly soldiers, probably Syrians who had survived the conquest of their province and had, like the Persians, seen the Arabs as their most likely future paymasters.

In January 640, with Heraclius in Constantinople and now a bloated caricature of the glorious figure who had come ashore to rescue his people thirty years before, Amr's small column of Arab troops arrived before Pelusium, gateway to Egypt, a city full of ancient monuments. The accuracy of Amr's assessment of Egypt's defences was immediately apparent. When the Persians besieged Pelusium in 616 they had found the city well fortified with strong ancient walls, but their powerful siege engines had wrecked the stonework defences and nobody had repaired them since. As a result, although Amr had no siege engines with him and had to depend on the two reliable but slow weapons at his disposal – starvation and treachery – the outcome was never in doubt. After a matter of weeks the Arabs succeeded in taking the city. However, the siege brought home to Amr the impossibility of his small force conquering a country that contained so many fortified centres, including Alexandria, a city whose defences were inferior only to Constantinople in the whole world. Without substantial reinforcement in men and equipment Amr's expedition must fail.

The feeble defence of Pelusium was a strategic blunder by the Byzantine high command and may well reflect the fact that at the heart of the empire was a dying man. A pre-emptive strike against the small Arab army by the garrison of Pelusium itself or by some of the large garrison at Babylon would surely have overwhelmed Amr's forces before they received reinforcements. But the opportunity was missed and many Bedouin, scenting rich pickings and identifying Amr as a likely winner in the forthcoming struggle, flocked to join him. By the time Amr reached Babylon his campaign was gathering momentum. It was clear that both sides were expecting a decisive struggle: Cyrus, the Patriarch of Alexandria, joined Theodore, the overall Byzantine commander in Egypt, inside the fortress of Babylon, while Amr set up camp nearby, waiting for the help he had asked the caliph to send.

Amr quickly realized that it would take many months to capture the city and so he left half his force to maintain the siege while with the others he struck south at the rich city of Fayum. In order to seize Fayum he needed to cross the Nile, which he did by seizing boats and transferring his troops and their horses and camels to the other bank.

The military commander at Fayum was named John and his presence in Egypt gives the lie to the contention that neither Heraclius nor any of the authorities in Constantinople gave much attention to the defence of the province during the Arab invasion. John, we surmise, was both a young and a brilliant general, who had been sent to Egypt by Heraclius on a special mission, thus indicating his seniority and the trust the emperor had in his ability. When Heraclius and the Patriarch Sergius had completed their *Ekthesis* they sent it via John to Cyrus, Patriarch of Alexandria.[105] In addition, John brought with him to Egypt a holy cross, possibly one containing a fragment of the True Cross.

For the first time in the narrative of Amr's conquest of Egypt we detect some professionalism from the Byzantine leadership. During Amr's Nile crossing and his approach to Fayum we are told that that the Arabs were harassed by Byzantine archers and light horsemen. John, apparently with a force of fifty scouts, had been following the Arab army and setting up cordons of troops to hinder its advance. When Muslim scouts told Amr that he was being followed by an enemy force, he turned on John's squadron and pursued them. John tried to regain his main camp but was cut off by the Arabs and forced to take cover by day in palm groves and thickets. However, a Bedouin reported to Amr where he had seen the Byzantines take cover and the Arabs overran John's position, killing him and all his men. This was just one in a series of disasters that struck the Byzantines in Egypt, though possibly one of the worst. John had displayed qualities in command that might have proved important in the battles ahead.

Heraclius was certainly shocked when he heard of John's death. John must have been a person of some importance because of the steps that were taken to recover his body. The commander-in-chief Theodore was immensely distressed at the news that John had been killed and ordered an extensive search for his body which, incidentally, the Arabs had thrown in the Nile. The remains were eventually brought ashore in a net and taken to be embalmed. Then, with all the trappings of ceremonial mourning, John's body was taken down river to Babylon before being shipped to Constantinople.[106]

Amr's advance on Fayum had been slowed by John's strategy and he decided to head back towards Babylon. However, he did not regard his failure to capture Fayum as a serious setback. After all, he had killed the best Byzantine general and he had won time for more reinforcements to join him from Arabia and Syria. And when help came it was decisive. Omar sent a new army of 4,000 high-quality troops, a powerful force of zealots under one of Mohammed's original companions, al-Zubayr. Furthermore, the caliph promised to raise two additional columns of the same strength, boosting Amr's strength to 20,000 men.

Following John's death, Byzantine strategy became atrophied. With the Arabs split on either side of the Nile, this was a prime opportunity for the Christian commanders to destroy them. Incredibly, however, they stood by while Amr recrossed the Nile with his entire force and rejoined the troops he had left before Babylon. It was a dereliction of command by Theodore and it would have broken Heraclius's heart to see it.

Amr now commanded a powerful and united army at his camp at Heliopolis, the city of the sun – but no longer the unconquerable sun of the pagan Romans. Ironically, after their victory, the Arabs renamed the city Ain Shams, meaning 'Fountain of the Sun', supposedly the fountain alongside which Joseph, Mary and the baby Jesus sheltered during their flight to Egypt.[107]

With the kind of military imagination that believes only in frontal assaults, Theodore had been assembling garrison troops from throughout the Delta so that his full strength could be brought to bear on the enemy. He strove for no advantage and received none from the Arabs, whose reinforcements had arrived from Arabia, among them the cream of Islamic soldiers. More of the 'Companions' and 'Helpers' of Mohammed himself had arrived by now than had even taken part in the Syrian campaign. In terms of quality, the Arab army was far superior to the Byzantine force and this seemed to be acknowledged by some of the empire's officers who reflected that these were the same men who had defeated the best imperial troops at Yarmuk and the Persians at Qadisyah in 637. Nevertheless, the Byzantines had a numerical advantage and Theodore seems to have been convinced that this would be enough. He never considered that by stripping his garrisons and by bringing the troops into the open for a single battle he was doing the Arabs' job for them. If the Christians were defeated, many now undefended cities and towns would have to surrender immediately.

Amr was determined to draw the Byzantines as far away from Babylon as possible so that there could be no retreat and the city would be left defenceless. Moreover, a high proportion of Theodore's army was made up of infantry who would suffer on a long march in the desert heat. Amr had already positioned two large units of cavalry – in fact, the entire Muslim army was mounted – along the line of advance of the Christian army so that they could fall upon the flanks and rear of Theodore's force after it passed.

The Byzantine army left Babylon in the half-light before dawn, hoping to avoid the heat of the sun on the early part of their march. The air in the gardens through which the sleepy soldiers trudged felt cool, while their ears picked up the sounds of prayers from the numerous monasteries in the city. Soon they were marching out into the desert in the growing heat, while in the distance they could see clouds of Arab scouts studying their formation and riding into the rising sun to take the news to Amr at Heliopolis. In fact, Amr had already left camp and was slowly advancing towards the Byzantines, keen to encourage the Christian scouts to believe he was eager for a frontal engagement. The two armies eventually came within sight of each other near Abbasiah. When the Byzantine columns failed to detect the Arab ambushes the outcome of the battle was certain. As soon as Amr was able to fix the enemy to the ground, they were an easy target for the cavalry, led by Kharijah, whom he had left behind to attack their rear.

Few details of this decisive encounter have survived. Battles never quite follow the pattern the opposing commanders would like but this one held few surprises. Once the Byzantine cavalry was defeated by the Muslim mounted arm, the Christian infantry was trapped in a position from which escape was almost impossible. The Arabs, participating in a jihad, did not take prisoners and so Christian casualty figures must have been enormous. Once Theodore's army lost cohesion it was massacred. Those who did escape reached the Nile and made their way back to Babylon by boat, but when news of the full extent of the disaster reached the city many of the Babylonians simply took the easy way out and fled downstream to Nikiou. The garrison troops at Fayum abandoned the city and also went down river to Nikiou, abandoning the inhabitants to a dreadful massacre once the Muslims arrived.

Virtually all of Egypt upstream of Babylon was now in Muslim hands, but Amr faced the problems of his own success. He would eventually need to take Alexandria itself but as he captured more and more cities to the south, survivors and refugees, many of them soldiers, headed for the great city, making the task of besieging it even more difficult. However, before he could move northwards he decided that he must capture Babylon, now stripped of much of its garrison, lost on the bloody sands of Heliopolis.

In spite of the confidence that he must have felt in view of his unbroken successes, Amr was daunted by the massive walls and towers of Babylon, particularly in view of his acknowledged deficiencies in siege warfare. Nevertheless, his own faith and that of his men had triumphed over every adversity so far. The defence of Babylon was in the hands of the Patriarch Cyrus, for the commander-in-chief Theodore had continued downstream to the coast after his defeat at Heliopolis and soon arrived at Alexandria. The Babylon garrison consisted of some 5,000 men under the command of a general named George, but the civilian population had been swollen by refugees from outlying areas that had fallen to the Arabs. Amr was facing an impasse. In the open the Arab had proved a far superior warrior to the Byzantine, but behind stone walls the Greek defenders had all the advantages. Moreover, the Arab was a desert fighter and had no skill on the waters of the Nile, which gave the Christians superiority there. Amr would either have to force the Byzantines to give battle in the open as they had, rashly, at Heliopolis or he would have to try to negotiate their surrender. Ironically, the Patriarch Cyrus was thinking along the same lines. He held a meeting of his senior advisers within Babylon and told them that he would try to buy off the Arabs with tribute. He cautioned them all, however, not to allow any word of this to reach the men of the garrison or any of the religious zealots in the city, of whom there were many. News that he was seeking a way out short of victory in battle would damage morale and would also be widely seen as treachery. He therefore plotted with the military commander for some of his confederates, including the Bishop of Babylon, to secretly cross the Nile and approach Amr in his camp.

Amr must have been surprised to find a Christian bishop in his camp, yet he welcomed him and the other emissaries with courtesy and listened to what they had come to say. At first the Christians told him that they had come to warn the Arabs that they were facing disaster – a huge Christian army was due at any time from Constantinople. They said he would do well to accept the tribute offered and withdraw just as so many barbarians had accepted money from the Byzantines in the past. Amr simply said that he needed two days to consider the proposition, during which time the Christian emissaries had the freedom of his camp. Amr's aim was obvious: the Byzantines had totally misjudged the Muslims if they believed that they could be bribed into giving up the siege. Amr believed that once the Christians realized the Muslims did not value material things and that death held no fear for them because it brought them closer to Paradise, then they would give up the struggle and surrender Babylon. When the two days were past Amr summoned the emissaries and sent them back to Cyrus with the traditional Muslim offer: 'Only one of three courses is open to you: Islam with brotherhood and equality; payment of tribute and protection with an inferior status; war till God decides between us.'

Cyrus had failed to buy off the Muslims, whom he, like so many Byzantines of the time, regarded as little better than Bedouin raiders. He now recognized that once the waters of the Nile fell the Arabs would be able to tighten the siege. As a result, it was wiser to get the best terms he could to surrender the city. He sent messengers to tell Amr that he was prepared to negotiate. A curiously revealing incident occurred when Amr sent his delegation headed by a huge black man named Ubadah ibn as Samit. Cyrus recoiled from

Ubadah saying, 'Take away that black man: I can have no discussion with him.' Ubadah then explained that he was the chief negotiator and so Cyril was forced to continue. Typically, the patriarch resorted to threats, trying to overawe the Muslim by saying that huge armies were preparing to come to relieve Babylon. Ubadah was unimpressed, stressing that neither he nor any of the other Muslims was afraid of death in battle: 'Our prayer is for martyrdom in the cause of Islam, not for safe return to wife and children.'[108] He then told Cyrus that he must accept one of the three conditions set by Amr. Much as Cyrus wriggled, Ubadah remained intransigent. Eventually the patriarch realized that he had no option but to accept subjection to the Muslims and the payment of tribute. But first he asked Amr for permission to present these conditions to the emperor himself. Surprisingly, Amr allowed Cyrus to do so. The patriarch travelled down river to the coast and then took ship to Constantinople.

Cyrus's mission to Constantinople was doomed from the start. The terms of his treaty with Amr were so unclear that Heraclius, in his fragile health, was hardly likely to commit himself and his people to them. Was Cyrus negotiating for the surrender of just Babylon or, as began to seem likely, for the whole of Egypt? Heraclius had been furious at the inadequate performance of the Byzantine government in Egypt, both military and political. How could Cyrus believe that the emperor would allow him to bribe the desert barbarians to retire when his generals had failed to drive them out of the province? As the emperor's representative in Egypt, Cyrus was asked to explain himself. The patriarch tried, telling Heraclius that the Arabs were like no other people he had ever met, having no fear of death nor greed for treasure. Their fighting powers were such that they were invincible in battle.

Heraclius was in the last days of an agonizing illness and must have believed that God had forsaken him completely. A warrior all his life, he knew that men were no different the world over. If the Arabs were as Cyrus described them it was because somebody had made them so, not with lies and cruelty but with the promise of something that transcended the normal run of a soldier's life. Had he not trained his own men with care in 620 and turned a defeated rabble into proud warriors who fought for a cause for which they were prepared to die? Now he was having to listen to the reports of rogues and cowards. These Muslims were fighting for their faith just as he had called on his own soldiers to in 622 and afterwards. He had promised a martyr's reward to his men should they fall in battle fighting the Persians. Now, it was reported, these Muslims believed in the same fate and fought with the zeal of martyrs. In Egypt his forces were involved in a holy war against the Muslims but only one side seemed to realize it. Before him stood the patriarch, not full of the spiritual leadership that the soldiers needed, but seeking the coward's way out, through bribery. In despair as much as in anger Heraclius rejected Cyrus's mission and sent the patriarch into exile. He then sent orders to his troops in Egypt to do what they were paid to do: fight the Muslims.

With the emperor dying in Constantinople the Byzantine cause in Egypt was dying too. There was no longer any leadership and the troops merely awaited the inevitable. Then one day in March 641 a great cheer arose from the Muslim camp at Babylon, temporarily alarming the defenders but otherwise fading away like the life of the emperor whose death it commemorated.[109] Heraclius had died in Constantinople, nearly a decade after the Prophet Mohammed. Yet while Mohammed's words still lived in the hearts of the desert people who ringed the fortress of Babylon, Heraclius's had died the moment the final breath passed out of his body. It was as a relic that he was remembered by his people, an effigy redolent of other, more memorable times in their lives. Some of those who filed past the body, grotesquely swollen and misshapen by the emperor's cancer, could reflect on the golden-haired hero in his white armour coming ashore from his flagship under the icon of the Virgin. Others had witnessed his return in glory from Persia, surrounded by his Excubitore guards, with banners fluttering in the breeze and with the image of the Virgin carried ahead. Some had even watched the barefoot penitent returning to Jerusalem with the Holy Cross in his arms. Now, stripped of human affectation, the man himself went to meet the God he had served so well all his life. For three days his body was left on an open bier while his wife Martina and his sons squabbled over the succession. With Egypt slipping into the hands of the enemy the body of Heraclius was taken to the Church of the

Holy Apostles where it was laid close to that of the first Christian emperor, Constantine. Even here Heraclius was not allowed to rest for long. Within three months his sarcophagus was opened on the orders of his son and successor, Constantine, and the golden crown in which he had been buried was wrenched from his head, breaking off, it is said, part of his skull in the process. *Sic transit gloria!*

News of the death of Heraclius inspired the Arabs outside the walls of Babylon. As one wrote, 'God broke down the power of the Romans by his death.'[110] Redoubling their efforts the Muslim commanders vowed to take the city or die in the attempt. Al-Zubayr, Companion of the Prophet himself during Mohammed's lifetime, took a solemn oath that he would lead a storming party onto the ramparts. Under the cover of darkness he and his men set up a solitary scaling ladder and trusted to Allah to conceal them from the eyes of the watchers above. Al-Zubayr himself led the warriors up the ladder and, sword in hand and with the great cry 'Allahu Akbar', he leaped out of the darkness onto the battlements. The Byzantine defenders were exhausted after months of siege and responded slowly. In contrast, al-Zubayr's storming party poured out onto the top of the walls and swept away the desultory resistance. Expecting to have to face a powerful counter-attack, al-Zubayr was astonished when the defenders suddenly stopped fighting and the Christian commander offered to surrender the city to save it from a sack. Al-Zubayr, his blood thoroughly up, wanted to refuse the surrender and massacre the garrison but Amr, watching from a distance, intervened. He gave the Byzantines three days to leave the city and took Babylon with all its treasure without striking a further blow.

The siege of Babylon had lasted for seven months and the day the Byzantines left with just their lives was Easter Sunday, the day of Christ's resurrection. It is doubtful, however, that even in this spiritual age anyone cared to draw any conclusions from this coincidence.

The fall of this powerful fortress to a desert people without siege weapons says everything about this stage of the campaign. Amr now held the entire eastern side of the Delta and, with Babylon secured, he could control traffic on the Nile. The conquest was all but achieved, except for Nikiou and Alexandria, and Nikiou was next on the list. Not since the dark days under the Emperor Phocas had the Byzantines suffered so humiliating a loss as the strongly fortified city of Nikiou, where cowardice – pure and simple – saved the chroniclers the search for a more subtle explanation of its fall. The Christian commander, hearing that the Muslim army was approaching, commandeered a boat and escaped down river to the coast. When this news spread around the city the rest of the garrison, abandoning hope, simply tried to follow him, fighting to gain possession of the fleet of boats moored along the banks of the Nile. Panic broke out as Muslim troops reached the city and the boatmen, abandoning their human cargo, cast off and headed downstream. The garrison was caught on the banks of the river, some floundering in the water, others eaten by crocodiles; virtually every man died in the quite unnecessary chaos. Amr was able to occupy Nikiou unopposed. What followed, however, was an inexplicable massacre of the inhabitants, unjustified even by the savage usages of holy war.

It was only now – with the war already lost – that the Byzantines began to stiffen their resistance. The new emperor, Constantine, rushed in reinforcements by sea from the capital. The new arrivals were better soldiers than the essentially second-rate Egyptian garrison but by now the Arabs had a powerful grip on the strategic points in the country and with the iron leadership of Amr they were not easily going to relinquish their hold. As Heraclius had showed in 622, leadership and morale in warfare made the average soldier into a good one, and that is what Amr had done. On the other hand, the example set by the Byzantine commander, Theodore, was weak. He was so tainted by defeat that only a dynamic replacement might have effected a change. In the event, no such officer was forthcoming. Instead, it was more of the same.

When the Arabs finally arrived at Alexandria they were halted in their tracks for the first time since they entered Egypt. The sheer beauty and grandeur of the sight that met their eyes was stunning. The historian Alfred Butler describes what met their eyes:

Far as the eye could reach ran that matchless line of walls and towers which for centuries later excited the enthusiasm of travellers. Beyond and above them gleamed domes and pediments, columns and obelisks, statues, temples, and palaces. To the left the view was bounded by the lofty Serapeum with its gilded roofs,

and by the citadel on which Diocletian's Column stood con-
spicuous: to the right the great cathedral of St Mark was seen, and
further west those obelisks called Cleopatra's Needles, which even
then were over 2,000 years old, or twice as old as the city's
foundation. The space between was filled with with outlines of
brilliant architecture: and in the background, towering from the
sea, stood that stupendous monument known as the Pharos,
which rightly ranked as one of the wonders of the world. Even
these half-barbarian warriors from the desert must have been
strangely moved by the stateliness and grandeur as well as by the
size and strength of the city they had come to conquer.[111]

Perhaps Amr was maddened by the sight of such a city. Whatever
the case, he seemed to lose control of himself and ordered an all-out
assault on Alexandria's walls. The garrison – an enormous one,
swelled by new arrivals – had the simple task of shattering the Arabs
within range of their huge catapults. For such a shrewd general as
Amr, bringing his troops to such a vulnerable position was an
elementary blunder but one which he would not repeat. With the
Byzantines totally dominant at sea and with the city's population
well supplied with food, there was no way, short of treachery, for the
Muslims to capture Alexandria. So dominant were the city defences
that it is even doubtful whether the Arabs could get within bowshot
of the walls in any numbers without attracting the attention of
soldiers manning the massive stone-throwers. Only if the defenders
came out to fight in the open, as they had at Heliopolis, was it
possible for the Arabs to take the city. And, as the commander of
Alexandria was Theodore, the same man who had earlier made that
very mistake, it was too much to hope that he would do so again.

The city of Alexandria was the highpoint of Hellenistic civilization. However, while its soldiers and citizens were able to watch in
relative safety the frustrations of the Arab invaders outside, they
were impotent to protect those areas not defended by sea and city
wall. The Byzantines, by taking refuge within Alexandria itself, were
abandoning the rich suburbs beyond the walls, the villas and
splendid personal estates that had housed the wealthiest of their
citizens. The Arabs simply pillaged the environs of the city, gathering
so much treasure that it was almost unnecessary to break down the

city walls to look for more. Most of the fine buildings, both houses and churches, were demolished by the invaders so that the wood, iron and stone could be employed elsewhere. Barges collected the wood and iron to provide bridging and siege equipment in other parts of the country. Meanwhile, Alexandria remained invulnerable, a virtual concentration camp for the Hellenic population in Africa.

Eventually the fate of Alexandria was decided in Constantinople. The succession to the throne on the death of Heraclius in 641 had become so confusing – and so bloody – that little effective action could be expected on behalf of even so vital a strategic outpost. The disputes in the capital revolved – as they had since her marriage to the emperor in 613 – around the person of Martina, daughter of Heraclius's sister Maria. In 638 Heraclius had willed the throne jointly to his two sons Constantine, his only son by his first wife Fabia, and to Heraclonas, his son by his second wife Martina. Constantine, aged twenty-nine, was a mature man and a father; he was also a popular figure with the Constantinopolitan public. Heraclonas, on the other hand, was just fifteen and quite incapable of ruling alongside his stepbrother. Had it not been for the ambition of his mother, Heraclonas would probably have stepped aside in favour of Constantine. However, it was generally known that Constantine was suffering from tuberculosis and would not live long. Thus the problem arose as to who should succeed him, his ten-year-old son Constans or Heraclonas? The dying Heraclius had hoped that the throne would go to Heraclonas after Constantine and this is clearly what Martina expected. But her own unpopularity with the people of Constantinople was great. Although she had been a good wife to Heraclius, had borne him ten children and had travelled thousands of miles at his side on campaign, she could never overcome the accusations that she had committed incest by marrying her uncle and that this had led God to curse the marriage with misfortune and to heap down on the empire the disasters of the Muslim invasions. As a result, most people in the capital hoped to see the succession pass from the consumptive Constantine to his son Constans. Martina, however, was not going to give up her ambitions easily. She intended to fight for the rights of her son.

After Heraclius was buried Martina made his will public. In it he said that his wife must be honoured by the people as 'mother and empress'. This seemed to indicate that Martina should be given some role in the affairs of state even though her stepson, Constantine, had been accorded the rank of co-emperor since 613 when he was just a baby. It soon became obvious that relations between Constantine and Martina had broken down when the new emperor, clearly dying, sent an enormous sum of back-pay to the army to persuade the men to support his son Constans against Martina and Heraclonas.

Constantine died after a rule of just 103 days. The fact that he was coughing blood suggests that he died of tuberculosis and was not poisoned by his stepmother as the rumours suggested. Heraclonas now became emperor with Martina as virtual head of state. The day that everyone had feared since her marriage to Heraclius had arrived. The clergy reacted almost as a man. John of Nikiou spoke for them all when he said: 'It is not fitting that one derived from a reprobate seed should sit on the imperial throne: rather it is the sons of Constantine, who was the son of Eudokia, that should bear sway over the empire.'

Martina now instigated a purge of supporters of the dead Constantine. She also recalled Patriarch Cyrus of Alexandria, whom Heraclius had exiled, and sent him back to Egypt with instructions to come to terms with the Arabs and end the war there. By this stage Martina, and through her the wretched Heraclonas, were unpopular with everyone outside the palace walls. The Domestic of the East, Valentinos, immediately raised an army in revolt against Martina, but the empress was a 'real trooper', having accompanied Heraclius on so many campaigns, and responded by calling on the support of the army of Thrace, accusing Valentinos of wanting the throne for himself. However, the mind of the people was reflected in the riots that took place in the city and the Senate decided that Martina must go.

After ruling for just six months Martina and Heraclonas were deposed. To prevent any attempt by them to regain power they were subjected to brutal mutilation – tradition had it that nobody with a visible defect could succeed to the imperial throne. Heraclonas had his nose cut off and Martina's tongue was split, then both were sent into exile in Rhodes. Two of Martina's other sons, David and Marinus, lost their noses and her youngest was castrated. While it

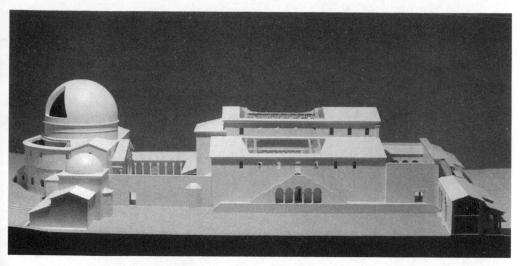

Constantine's Church of the Holy Sepulchre as dedicated in 335. After the discovery of the site of Christ's crucifixion and burial in 326 the Emperor Constantine commissioned the magnificent church, illustrated above, consisting of the Anastasis rotunda, beneath which an aedicule housed the rock tomb that was the actual Holy Sepulchre and a basilica, known as the Martyrion. This model, by the late H.R. Allen, gives us an impression of how the original church must have looked. The current church in Jerusalem dates from the crusader period in the twelfth century. Virtually nothing remains of Constantine's building, which was damaged by the Persians in 614 and demolished by the fanatical Fatimid caliph al-Hakim in 1009. *(Tower of David Museum, Jerusalem)*

City walls, Constantinople. The massive defences of Constantinople were built by the Emperor Theodosius in the fifth century, enabling the city and its huge population to survive numerous sieges by Persians, Avars, Arabs and Russians. Combined with a powerful navy and the chemical weapon known as Greek fire, the walls meant the Byzantines were safe within this bastion of Christianity until the crusaders of the Fourth Crusade, notably the Italians, captured the city in 1204, stripping it of many of its glorious works of art and transporting them to Italy, particularly in Venice. *(Warwick Ball)*

Mosaic from Hagia Sophia. A detail from the thirteenth-century Deesis in the south gallery of Hagia Sophia. This astonishingly lifelike portrayal of Christ is a triumph of the mosaicist's art. *(Turkish Tourist Office)*

Carthage. Capital of the Roman Exarchate of Africa, Carthage was one of the main sources of corn shipped each year to feed the population of Constantinople. In 608 it was in Carthage that the Exarch Heraclius the Elder began the revolt against the tyrant Phocas that was to bring his son Heraclius to the throne in Constantinople. *(Warwick Ball)*

Basilica of Bahira, Bostra. Legend and history combine in the story of the Christian monk Bahira and the future Prophet Mohammed. Some time in the 580s a camel train from the Hijaz led by the Meccan merchant Abu Talib stopped at the desert city of Bostra, a meeting place of five important roads and an important centre of Christianity. There lived a monk named Bahira, who identified Abu Talib's young nephew Mohammed as a future prophet, examining his back and finding the seal of prophecy between his shoulders. Then Bahira said to Abu Talib: 'Go back to your own land and keep him safe from the Jews. If they see him and get to know what I know about him they will try to harm him.' *(David Nicolle)*

Nineveh. The ruins of the ancient Assyrian capital lie on the east bank of the River Tigris. Here in 627 Heraclius faced the pursuing army of Sasanians under Rahzadh and fought the decisive battle that ended the last war of antiquity. (*Warwick Ball*)

The Great Mosque in Damascus. In 379 the Roman emperor Theodosius I built an early Christian church in Damascus on the foundations of a temple to Zeus. However, after the Arab conquest of Syria, Muawiya, son of the formidable Hind and her husband Abu Sofyan, established the Omayyad dynasty in 661, choosing Damascus as his new capital city. In 705, Theodosius's Christian church was rebuilt as the Great Mosque, one of the largest in the Islamic world. (David Nicolle)

One of the greatest Roman fortifications along the River Euphrates was the fortress of Zenobia or Halabiya.
After the collapse of the Palmyrene state it became one of the strongpoints in the Roman and Byzantine

defences against the Persians. Immensely powerful as its walls were, they were breached in 610 by the Sasanians under Shahrvaraz, opening the way for the Persian conquest of Syria in the next four years. *(Warwick Ball)*

The Dome of the Rock. In 661, Muawiya was proclaimed caliph in Jerusalem and his love of the city, 'the place where the people will gather and arise on the Day of Judgement', caused his descendant Abd al-Malik to build the Dome of the Rock there in 691. Aware of the visual impact of Constantine's Anastasis on the Western Hill, Abd al-Malik was determined to offer all Muslims something that was 'unique and a wonder to the world'. By choosing to build the first major Islamic building on the Temple Mount he was linking the new faith with older traditions, which saw the site as the centre of the world and the entrance to the Garden of Eden. The Dome of the Rock is unique in the Islamic world. It is not a mosque but a shrine and an assertion of Muslim identity. (A.F. Kersting)

was usual to carry out this gruesome mutilation on failed usurpers, it was unknown to act against an empress in this way. The splitting of Martina's tongue indicates a more personal hatred of the empress and may point to an aspect of her personality that was held in particular contempt. We know nothing about who ordered this punishment but a powerful figure was clearly acting on behalf of the new boy-emperor, Constans. It has been suggested that this may have been his mother Gregoria, daughter of Heraclius's cousin Nicetas.[112] Peace was restored by the succession of Constans, grandson of the great Heraclius and his beloved Fabia, though with the Arab threat ever present Constans was to know little peace.

On 8 November 641, the Patriarch Cyrus once again met Amr at Babylon to discuss the surrender of Alexandria. As he told the Arab leader, 'God has given this country to you: let there be no more enmity between you and the Romans.' The treaty signed that day sealed the Arab conquest of Egypt. The Byzantine garrison embarked from Alexandria by sea and returned to Constantinople. This epoch-making event, the end of Christian Egypt, had less effect on the Muslims than might have been expected. The messenger whom Amr sent to inform the caliph at Medina told him, 'Good news, O Commander of the Faithful. God has opened Alexandria to us.' He was rewarded for his news with some dates, while the muezzin called the faithful together for a service of thanksgiving.

Amr's soldiers had been astonished when they first viewed Alexandria from a distance. When they entered, their reaction revealed the essential simplicity – call it barbarism, perhaps – of these desert warriors at being confronted by this early vision of Paradise. In Butler's words:

Amazed as they were at the size and splendour of Alexandria, they were even more struck by its extraordinary brilliancy. 'Alexandria is a city containing much marble in pavements, buildings and columns,' says one writer. 'The city was all white and bright by night as well as by day,' says another: and again, 'By reason of the walls and pavements of white marble, the people used all to wear black or red garments: it was the glare of the marble which made the monks wear black. So too it was painful to go out by night: for the moonlight reflected from the white marble made the city so bright that a tailor could see to thread his needle without a lamp. No one entered the city without a covering over his eyes to veil him from the glare of the plaster and marble.' Yet a third Arab writer, of the tenth century, alleges that awnings of green silk were hung over the streets to relieve the dazzling glare of the marble.[113]

The loss of Egypt and Syria left the heartland of the Byzantine Empire open to Arab attack and the Muslims made it clear that Constantinople itself would be their next target. However, their relentless advance was halted temporarily by the civil war that rent the Muslim world, between the governor of Syria, Muawiya and the Caliph Ali. In 661, Ali was assassinated and Muawiya had himself crowned caliph in Jerusalem, establishing the Omayyad Caliphate. His new capital was the city of Damascus in Syria, which was far better placed to act as the headquarters of an empire than either Mecca or Medina had been. Within two years Muawiya had restarted the Muslim offensive, aiming to capture Constantinople and incorporate the remaining Byzantine lands within the Caliphate.

Arab naval forces, mainly from North Africa, secured many of the Greek islands, including Cyprus and Rhodes, from which they planned to launch their attack on the Byzantine capital. In 672 they sailed into the Hellespont and established a naval base at Cyzicus, just fifty miles from Constantinople. By 674 the Arabs were ready to launch their assault against the city, and that summer and for the next four summers, successive fleets left Cyzicus in hope but returned defeated. The Arab ships were loaded with heavy siege engines and catapults which they used to bombard the city's sea walls but each attack was repelled and during the final siege the Byzantines first used the secret weapon that was to give them command of the seas for centuries: Greek fire.[114] The Byzantines fitted pumps onto their warships from which they were able to spray the inflammable substance onto enemy ships. In the next centuries many fleets of potential conquerors, Arab and Russian notably, were destroyed in the harbour of Constantinople by burning.

The ingredients of Greek fire were a closely guarded secret in Byzantium. Although Muslims and western Franks eventually produced a similar weapon, this did not come until much later and it was not identical to the Byzantine invention. Many historians – and scientists – have tried to recreate it with varying degrees of success. The advantage that the Byzantines undoubtedly had was not simply the ability to produce the 'fire' itself but – crucially – the means of delivering it to the enemy.

Mere possession of a weapon brings no advantage without the capacity to use it to maximum advantage. Chinese fireworks and rockets were inferior in military terms to the way in which gunpowder was exploited in the western world. Historians J. Haldon and M. Byrne have reconstructed an apparatus based on evidence from the few available Byzantine sources. It consisted of a cauldron of the oily chemical used in Greek fire, which was heated from below and then had air forced into it from a pump. Under pressure the heated oil was projected from a nozzle and ignited as it emerged in a thin stream. The nozzle could be moved in any direction by a swivel device and the fire emerged 'like thunder from heaven'. One of the unusual characteristics of Greek fire, which made it a deadly weapon in sea warfare, was that it burned when in contact with water and could not be put out when water was thrown upon it. Originally the apparatus to deploy it was fitted in the bows of Greek warships but eventually it was found that mounting the devices along the vessels' sides was more deadly for enemy ships and safer for operators. Modern readers will identify the similarities of Greek fire to napalm.

A later Arab recipe for Greek fire had some unlikely ingredients: besides distillate of tar, resin, sandarac and powdered sulphur, it also contained dolphin fat and goat kidney fat. The medieval chronicler Joinville left us an eyewitness account of the effect of Greek fire when hurled from a siege catapult against a city's walls during the Fifth Crusade in 1250:

It came straight at you, as big as a vinegar barrel, with a tail of fire behind it as long as a long spear. It made such a noise as it came that it seemed like thunder from heaven; it looked like a dragon flying through the air. It gave so intense a light that in camp you could see as clearly as by daylight in the great mass of flame which illuminated everything. Three times that night they bombarded us with Greek fire, and four times they fired it from the revolving crossbow.[115]

Supposedly designed by a Syrian architect and mechanic of Greek extraction named Callinicus of Heliopolis, Greek fire was one of the most decisive inventions in history. It turned the tide of war and undoubtedly saved Byzantium – and consequently the whole of Europe – from Muslim conquest. At a time when there existed in western Europe no state with the military capability to halt the Arab advance this single weapon changed the direction of history, allowing the development of a Christian Europe and New World instead of a Muslim one.

The annihilation of the Arab navy by Greek fire in 678 was followed by the defeat of the land forces by an unexpected enemy. Since the fall of Syria in 638 large numbers of Christian freebooters had fled from the Arab advance and found a haven in the mountains between Syria and Cilicia. From here these 'Mardaites' raided Arab and Byzantine territory indiscriminately. However, the return of the defeated Arab army from Constantinople was too good a target to be missed and the Mardaites fell upon them as they passed. Having annihilated this army, the Mardaites began to raid into Palestine, even as far south as the Dead Sea. Most eventually resettled inside Byzantine territory and many served as marines in the Byzantine navy.

Muawiya was shocked by the outcome of four years of fighting against the Byzantines. He was still inspired by the previous successes of Islam and assumed that Constantinople would fall, just as all previous Christian targets had fallen to the followers of Mohammed. But it seemed to him that God had at last decreed an end, albeit temporary, to the triumphs of Islam. He sought a truce with the new Byzantine emperor, Constantine IV, great-grandson of Heraclius. In 679 the Arabs paid a tribute to the emperor of 216,000 gold pieces as well as 100 slaves. The Byzantines even regained Rhodes.

The Arab setback in front of Constantinople in 678 was decisive yet nobody could be certain that the successes of Islam would not return. In fact, in 717 the issue was to be re-enacted in front of the mighty walls of the 'Queen of Cities'. The *dramatis personae* were different but otherwise little had changed. The great first wave of Muslim conquests was over: all that remained was for the Arabs to accept it.

After the emperor Theodosius III had chosen to enter a monastery in 717, he was succeeded by one of Byzantium's best warrior-emperors, Leo III (717–41), known as 'the Isaurian'. Aware that the caliph was preparing another attack on his capital, Leo worked tirelessly to fill the granaries and arsenals of Constantinople, trusting to its powerful walls to repel the Arabs. Leo knew that a blockade by the Arab navy was far more likely to force the city to surrender than any land assault. He therefore looked to his navy to save Constantinople, both by employing Greek fire once again and by breaking through the Arab blockade.

The Arabs launched land and sea attacks on the walls of Constantinople but to no avail and eventually tried to blockade the city with an estimated fleet of 1,800 vessels of all kinds. However, the Byzantine fleet was able to emerge from the Golden Horn and catch the Muslim ships by surprise on several occasions, destroying many vessels with Greek fire. The entrance to the Golden Horn was guarded by an immense chain which could be raised and lowered to allow Christian ships to pass out into the Sea of Marmara but preventing Muslim vessels from penetrating into the Golden Horn. Morale in the Muslim navy fell to such a low ebb that Arab crews preferred flight to combat with the dreaded Christian fire-ships.

The onset of a harsh winter completed the work of the Byzantine navy. In their ill-prepared camps the Arab soldiers suffered in the appalling weather and their animals died in their thousands. It was even said by gloating Byzantine chroniclers that the Arabs had been forced to turn to cannibalism. When a Christian army of Bulgars led by their king, Tervel, probably bribed by Leo, attacked the main Arab army it is said that over 20,000 Muslims died in the rout. On 15 August 718 the Arabs abandoned their twelve-month siege, having suffered crippling losses in men and ships. Leo's successful defence of Constantinople marked a watershed in relations between Christians and Muslims. Since the time of Mohammed no Arab army had suffered so terrible a defeat. For the next 700 years Constantinople, 'Queen of Cities', marked the limit of Muslim conquests.

TEN

Ersatz Crusades

For much of the eighth and ninth centuries Constantinople was the bastion of eastern Christianity in a world increasingly dominated by Islam. During this period the Muslim Arabs enjoyed a golden age under the Abbasid Caliphate, during which they were the strongest power in the world, military, culturally and, above all, economically. The Christians of the Byzantine Empire were on the defensive militarily. Facing threats on all fronts, there was never any possibility that her emperors or soldiers would attempt to recover the provinces lost at the end of the reign of Heraclius. They were hard-pressed to maintain their Balkan territories against Bulgars and Rus, the Greek islands against Muslim pirates and the Anatolian heartland against the Abbasids. Survival was the Byzantine watchword. This created a fortress mentality in which the Christian empire and its chosen people were constantly at war with the representatives of Evil, whether pagan Slavs, western heretics or Muslim infidels. Under such circumstances the teachings of a gentle Nazarene rabbi and his mother, the young virgin Mary, were simply not the sort of militant Christianity that was needed if God's empire on Earth and his chosen people were to survive. Heroes from the Old Testament were in more demand than the 'Lamb of God', with the figure of David, saviour of his people, particularly popular among the chroniclers. The images of the warrior-saint, like George, Theodore the Recruit, Demetrius, Anastasius the Persian or Merkurius, became potent symbols of Byzantine iconography.

The concept of Byzantine holy war had foundered on the inherent ambiguity between warfare and Christianity. In 354 St Athanasius had given a pragmatic answer to the problem: 'It is not permissible to murder anyone, yet in war it is praiseworthy and lawful to slay the adversaries.'[116] It was the context that gave the justification – the pursuit of the 'greater good' and the 'lesser evil'. Academic opponents of the concept of Byzantine 'holy wars' have built their case around the early writings of Paulinus of Nola and Basil of Caesarea, the latter of whom, in his famous Thirteenth Canon, declared that those who killed in war should 'abstain from communion for three years, since their hands were unclean'.[117] Yet, this text was written in the fourth century at a time when the threats to the empire from external foes were limited. It is a moot point whether St Basil would have taken so strong a view had he lived in the early seventh century when the future of the empire and of Christianity itself hung in the balance.

Despite St Basil's canon, the symbol of the cross had become the most important insignia used by Byzantine armies even before Heraclius's Persian War.[118] James Howard-Johnson has demonstrated that one of the earliest manifestations of religious imagery as an incentive to military morale came during the attempt by Zoroastrian Persia to eradicate Christian worship in Armenia in 450–1. The Armenian clergy preached 'holy war' to the Christian soldiers who fought for their faith. During the war between the Romans and the Persians in 421 the same issue was at stake, with Rome intervening to protect Persian Christians from enforced conversion by Zoroastrianism.[119] Such military action became an example of a Byzantine 'just' war, where the Christian power was fighting to defend Christians. On another occasion 'the emperor despatched a bejewelled gold cross to the patriarch at Jerusalem as a token of imperial devotion to the Christian cause, while a new iconography on imperial coinage, showing the figure of Victory raising a cross aloft, betokened divine support for the Christian empire.[120]

After Constantine, Church and state were never so close that they were able to establish a theory of 'holy war', certainly not one of the kind that was part of Mohammed's jihad. There was an assumption that war carried out by a Christian state like Byzantium was intrinsically 'holy' because it was concerned with defending the faith, protecting the faithful and even extending the chosen religion of God's representative on Earth. The parallels between the role of Mohammed in the development of Islam and that of the Roman/

Byzantine emperor in the development of Christianity have received scant attention until recently. Nevertheless, as God's representative, the emperor's decisions, particularly in a military sense, cannot be understood in isolation from those of God himself. Enemies of the emperor, like the pagans who threatened Byzantium's Balkan territories or the Zoroastrian Persians, were consequently seen as enemies of the Christian God and were portrayed as evil, Satanic figures. Consequently, it became the responsibility of Christians everywhere to resist them. Ecclesiastical pronouncements based on St Basil's canon therefore represented a challenge to the earthly power of God's chosen representative and were redolent of early Christian attitudes to the military policies of pagan Rome. They were not in step with the realities of a Christian empire. It is not surprising that the threats to Christianity and the Christian empire in the early seventh century marked the point where theologians and military statesmen had to agree to exploit religious issues for the welfare of the state. Yet the transmogrification of the Virgin Mary from gentle Madonna to bloodthirsty Valkyrie is one of the more remarkable effects of the *modus vivendi* Heraclius and Sergius reached and it cast a veil of divine protection over Constantinople during the Avar siege of 626. Here there are closer links between the helmeted goddess Athene of Pagan times and the warlike Theotokos of Byzantium than with any figure drawn from Christian teachings.

From the ninth century onwards, the linking of Christianity with warfare was no longer apologetic, an acceptance of a necessary evil, but was increasingly assertive, even triumphalist. It is easy to mistake this for the kind of crusading zeal which appeared in the West following Pope Urban's appeal at Clermont in 1095 but I prefer to describe it as a kind of 'ersatz crusading'. It took its place in a recruit's training manual, alongside duty to the state, obedience to his officers, cleanliness in his personal life and diligence in weapons drill. Just as Sol Invictus had been removed from the shields of Constantine's legionaries and replaced by the chi-rho sign of the early Christians, so now the icon of the Virgin or of St Demetrius acted as a charm for the simple soldier hoping to shelter under its protection or good fortune. Talismanic, like a rabbit's foot or a lucky mascot, the holy relic or icon reflected less a Christian faith than a return to pre-Christian superstition.

The defenders of the Christian frontiers in Asia Minor during the eighth and ninth centuries had to adopt a more pragmatic and common-sense approach to the essential contradictions inherent in Christian warfare. Whereas the prominent theologians in the Orthodox Church might endlessly debate the minutiae of the faith, the men who protected the empire against the Turks, the Arabs and the Slavs could not afford such fine feelings. They knew that they were fighting to protect their faith and its earthly manifestation in the shape of the Byzantine Empire. The enemy forces meant harm to the empire and were thus challenging God's chosen land and people. They had to be resisted at the cost of their own lives and of those Christians whose task it was to guard the frontiers. As for the prominent families of military magnates in border regions who provided leadership in war, this defence of the empire against the enemies of the state was a distinct service offered by men at great risk to their lives. Aristocratic generals, like the Phocas brothers Nicephorus and Leo, felt that the Church in whose name these soldiers fought and died should recognize in their sacrifice a martyrdom that God would acknowledge and reward with salvation and eternal bliss. The Muslims had used this argument from the beginning of their conflict with the Christians and pagans, and there was no avoiding the fact that it had inspired the early Arab warriors in their unparalleled series of conquests.

The development of powerful military families, notably in Asia Minor, was a two-edged weapon for the Byzantine emperor in Constantinople. Certainly these clans produced excellent soldiers and some of the best generals available to any state at this time, but they also reflected a tendency towards decentralization and independent policy-making on the margins. Like successful generals in Roman times their loyalty to an emperor who was hundreds, perhaps thousands, of miles away in his capital, was sometimes suspect.

As we have seen, the surge of Arab conquests subsided within fifty years of its beginning in the seventh century, yet until the tenth century the Abbasid Caliphate enjoyed a military superiority over the Byzantines. However, during the tenth century the Byzantines entered the period of their greatest power. Under a series of brilliant generals like the Domestic John Kourkuas, and the Emperors

Nicephorus Phocas, John Tzimisces and Basil II, the Byzantines reconquered lands they had lost to the Muslims in the seventh century and, under John Tzimisces, instilled into their soldiers a religious zeal that resembled the crusading spirit generated by Heraclius in 622. The power balance tipped back in favour of the Byzantines and the Muslims stood in awe of the advance of the apparently invincible Christian armies. However, the fact that Jerusalem was neither recaptured nor even besieged during the reigns of John Tzimisces or his successor, Basil II, has persuaded me to term the 'holy wars' of this period 'ersatz crusades' rather than crusades of the western type. To the Byzantine generals of the tenth century, Jerusalem and the Christian holy places in Palestine were never more than rallying cries in contrast to the deep conviction felt for them by Heraclius or the western crusaders of the eleventh century.

The resurgence of Byzantine power still lay far in the future when, in the year 863, an event occurred that marked a watershed in relations between the Christian empire of Byzantium and the world of Islam. For some two centuries the Christian lands in Anatolia had been subjected to regular raids from the Muslim rulers of Melitene and Tarsus. The Byzantines were accustomed to making counter-raids into Arab territory because they were unable to meet the Muslims' armies in open battle. However, everything changed when the Emperor Michael III's brother-in-law, Petronas, assembled a large army consisting of four Tagmata, the forces from nine Themes and other frontier troops. The army achieved an unprecedented victory, annihilating the forces of the Emir of Melitene in a battle near the River Halys. The emir was killed along with most of his troops and this was followed, within weeks, by a second Byzantine victory over the ruler of Tarsus, who was also killed. The victorious Petronas returned to Constantinople with the heads of his enemies held high on lances and enjoyed a triumph, something hardly seen in the capital for centuries.

The religious element in this triumph cannot be overlooked as it marked the start of a process that was to see the conquests of the next century on the eastern front regarded as a specific kind of Byzantine 'crusade'. The invocations spoken during the ceremony for Petronas contained three references to the role of God in securing victory in the battle and a clear emphasis on the divine source of imperial authority. It was nothing that Heraclius – or indeed Constantine – would have found surprising. In fact, the notion of a 'Christian empire' had been built upon this very assumption. However, the wars of the seventh and eighth centuries in the empire had all been defensive. In 863, for the first time, the paraphernalia of holy war – relics, icons and holy crosses – were being employed in offensive campaigns concerned with conquest, although admittedly only the reconquest of lands that had once been Christian. Nevertheless, the message was clear enough for all to understand, both friends and foes. In Baghdad the shock of such a decisive defeat was tangible. Muslim fanatics called for volunteers to join a jihad against the Byzantine infidels.

It was during the reign of Romanus Lecapanus (920–44) that Byzantium made a fundamental shift in policy away from the Balkans to concentrate on its eastern lands. Reinforcing the Domestic John Kourkuas, and forming an alliance with the Armenian King Gagic, Romanus launched a major offensive against an unsuspecting Muslim world in 927. The religious significance of this great counter-attack was clearly indicated when Kourkuas took the Muslim city of Khelat and ordered the inhabitants to put a cross over their mosque and to destroy their minarets. In another city he had his men enter mosques and bang gongs at the Muslim hour of prayer. Childish as these antics may appear to modern readers, they demonstrated a new confidence and a new motivation among the Christian forces. For the first time in nearly 300 years, the Byzantines were able to carry their struggle against the Muslims into previously held Christian provinces.

Like Belisarius in the fifth century, John Kourkuas was so successful that he overshadowed the emperor he served and aroused jealousy among the Constantinople cliques who had the imperial ear. Every victory brought him the acclaim and love of the people, the terror of his Muslim enemies and the jealousy of the politicians at home.

When Melitene was captured in 934 only Christians were allowed to remain within its walls. Significantly, most of the population converted to Christianity, while the few remaining Muslims were transported to Muslim territory in safety. The fall of Melitene was a symbolic event. For the first time in three centuries a major city of Greek origin that had been lost during the Arab conquests of the seventh century had been regained for Christianity. Was it a sign of what lay ahead for triumphant Byzantine armies?

Sayf al-Dawlah, Abbasid ruler of Mosul and known as 'Sword of the Dynasty', was determined to prove the contrary. A young zealot, he led his men with the cry 'Victory or death for the Faith'. In warfare he was pitiless but in peacetime the young emir was a poet and a scholar. Like a figure from the *Arabian Nights*, Sayf al-Dawlah was a lover of fine things; he had the largest stables, the best equipped library and a harem of which other men could only dream. However, it was a tragedy for Islam that other Muslim leaders did not share his commitment to the struggle against the growing power of Byzantium. Sayf al-Dawlah invaded Greek territory and achieved some temporary successes before the armies of Kourkuas rolled down towards him.

Beginning in 942, Kourkuas carried out one of the most successful Byzantine campaigns since the days of Heraclius in Persia. Advancing towards Aleppo he captured Hamus, taking 10,000 prisoners. He then followed the Tigris river like invaders of old, captured Amida and Nisibis, and advanced on the old city of Edessa. The latter had been a devoutly Muslim city for three centuries but, of course, its Christian history had been much longer. It also housed one of the holiest relics of Christianity, a towel bearing a supposedly authentic portrait of Jesus Christ on which the Saviour was said to have wiped his face. In the tenth century the symbolic significance of this relic was almost as great as the inspiration the fragments of the True Cross had given to the warriors of Heraclius. John Kourkuas was prepared to stop at nothing to secure this relic and, rather than risk its loss in a siege, he offered terms to the Edessan people. In return for the relic he would spare the city, free his prisoners and make peace.

The Muslims of Edessa knew that their duty was to defend their city and so they sent an embassy to Baghdad to ask the Abbasid caliph how they should treat with Kourkuas. Meanwhile, the Byzantine army ravaged Mesopotamia, capturing more cities, including Dara. John Kourkuas had ringed the walls of Edessa with siege engines and the pumps that delivered the dreadful flame weapon known as Greek fire. The Edessans knew what to expect if they were ordered to resist the Byzantine general. Eventually, the answer they sought arrived from the caliph: the freeing of Muslim prisoners was of paramount importance. They were ordered to surrender the relic on the terms Kourkuas had agreed. This was the highest point reached by Greek arms for centuries, a triumph of the cross over the crescent. The Byzantines carried the relic back to Constantinople where it was regarded as of greater importance than any of the cities Kourkuas had regained. Kourkuas concluded his campaign by crossing the Euphrates river and taking Birijik and Germanicea.

It was then that the political infighting that blighted the empire, even in its best years, temporarily came to the rescue of Islam. The emperor had planned to honour Kourkuas for his great achievements by marrying the heir to the throne, his grandson Romanus, to the general's daughter Euphrosyne. But the emperor's relatives were unwilling to see Kourkuas elevated so high and while the emperor was ill, they secured the dismissal of the great general and his replacement by an incompetent member of the family called Pantherius. He suffered a disastrous defeat within weeks at the hands of Sayf al-Dawlah.

For the next ten years Sayf al-Dawlah was the sole champion of the Muslims, resisting the build-up of Byzantine military strength on his frontier. However, he could do nothing to hold back a group of brilliant Byzantine generals as able, perhaps, as those who, along with Belisarius, had been at the disposal of Justinian in the mid-sixth century. Pre-eminent in this group were the two men who were to be become emperors themselves – Nicephorus Phocas, dubbed 'The White Death' by the Muslims, and John Tzimisces, perhaps the most charismatic emperor since Heraclius. Before being elevated to the purple both achieved tremendous victories over the Muslims and regained previously held Christian territory for the empire.

During the 950s, the Domestic Nicephorus Phocas and the Strategos of Mesopotamia John Tzimisces took the reputation of the Byzantine Empire to its apogee. Never since the days of Constantine had the empire's neighbours, both in Europe and in Asia, been in such awe of its immense power and never since the days of Justinian had the cause of Christianity stood higher. The heroic Sayf al-Dawlah found himself outmatched at every turn by the brilliant and ruthless Byzantines. This was a period, of course, when Byzantium's strategy became so subtle and successful that her generals almost took it as an insult that they had to take the field against the enemy at all. Military treatises seemed to originate from minds of Machiavellian – or should one say 'byzantine'? – cunning. Intelligence was the watchword rather than brute strength or courage. This is what the western Frankish crusaders failed to understand when they first encountered the eastern Christians in the next century and thereafter. They found the Byzantines 'effete' and 'cowardly', while the Greeks in turn found the Franks 'bullish' and 'boastful'.

The policy of divide and rule was a typical Byzantine ploy. They would attempt to divide the enemy commander from his senior officers, either by bribery or trickery. Once confidence was lost, the battle was lost with it. Techniques included sending treacherous letters to the second-in-command on the enemy side but ensuring that they fell into the hands of the enemy commander. Bribes were also offered, for example to the officers of Sayf al-Dawlah. Nicephorus Phocas found some of the Abbasid leader's retinue who were willing to abduct him for the right price. In the event, the ploy failed but this hardly mattered as the infuriated 'Sword of the Dynasty' called off his proposed campaign and returned to Aleppo to punish the plotters. John Tzimisces, meanwhile, sacked Dara and annihilated an Abbasid army sent by the much-tried Sayf al-Dawlah, killing an immense number of Muslims. After receiving reinforcements John captured the city of Adata and crushed a second Abbasid army, this time keeping enough prisoners alive to make a show in Constantinople. Sayf al-Dawlah must have begun to realize that he was out of his depth. He had in fact taken on three of the greatest of all medieval commanders and was never disgraced.

By this time the Phocas family was challenging the authority of the emperor in Constantinople. At first, the Emperor Constantine Porphyrogenitus (913–20, 944–60) tried to use the successes of Nicephorus and Leo Phocas to boost his regime, virtually hijacking their triumphs as merely part of the overall triumph of the empire. In 956, for example, the emperor himself carried out the ritual trampling of Sayf al-Dawlah's cousin, who had been captured by the Phocases. However, over the next few years the balance of power between the emperor and his generals shifted in favour of the latter. In 960 Leo Phocas's triumph was very much his own – he paraded his booty and his captives through the Hippodrome.

The death of Constantine Porphyrogenitus in 960 brought the young Romanus II to the throne. While he was prepared to keep up the pressure on the Muslims, the Phocas brothers were content to serve him loyally. The Domestic of the East, Leo Phocas, inflicted a tremendous defeat on the Abbasids by ambushing Sayf al-Dawlah in a pass in the Taurus mountains. Few of the Arabs except their commander and his guards escaped from Leo's troops.

Nicephorus's great expedition to capture Crete from Arab pirates in 961 was the triumph of the age. He succeeded in regaining the island and earning his emperor the greatest loot ever to be paraded through the streets of Constantinople. The Abbasids were reeling from successive blows received from the Byzantine army. During 962, Nicephorus Phocas and John Tzimisces campaigned virtually unchallenged in Arab territory with the biggest Roman armies seen since ancient times. The holy relic believed to be the cloak of John the Baptist was prominently paraded in Nicephorus's triumphal procession through Constantinople.

The intense training to which Nicephorus subjected his soldiers, just as Heraclius had in 620–2, gave his army a distinct edge over the enemy. In addition to good training and high morale, Nicephorus also reintroduced the *cataphractarii*. These armoured knights, operating in a tight, triangular formation, provided Byzantine armies with a powerful new weapon that the Arabs found almost irresistible. The Arab poet al-Mutannabi recorded the amazement of his people when they first encountered the Byzantine cataphracts. He had never seen armoured horses before and wrote of 'horses which seemed to have no legs', while their riders had 'helmets and garments of iron like their swords'.[121] The cataphracts were used as shock troops – there were only about 600 of them in an army of perhaps 25,000 men. The *Blitzkrieg* effect of the heavy cavalry and its resistance to Muslim firepower won Nicephorus victory after victory.

When Nicephorus Phocas took Aleppo at the end of the 963 campaigning season it seemed that he and his young emperor were unstoppable. However, when the triumphant Byzantine generals returned to Cappadocia before Christmas they were shocked to find that Romanus II had died suddenly at just twenty-three years of age. The heir to the throne, Basil, was five and it was decided that his mother, Theophano, should become regent for him. But it was clear that the political uncertainty associated with a regency might just be enough to save the Muslims of the East from the hammer blows of the Byzantine generals. With the prospect of a regency and a minor on the throne, civil war broke out in Constantinople between supporters of the Grand Chamberlain Joseph Bringas on one side and on the other the empress, the eastern generals Nicephorus and Leo Phocas, and John Tzimisces. Bringas, determined to keep the Phocases and their eastern allies out of power, offered the throne to Marianus Argyrus, commander of the western army. Marianus occupied Constantinople with his troops but when Nicephorus Phocas arrived in the capital most of the western troops deserted to him and he won the throne through popular acclamation.

The main aim for Nicephorus was to legitimize his claim to the throne by marrying the widowed Theophano. He could then act as stepfather for the empress's two young sons and share the throne with the five-year-old prince Basil. However, he had reckoned without the Patriarch Polyceutes. Just as Polyceutes' famous predecessor in the seventh century, the Patriarch Sergius, had tried to prevent Heraclius marrying his niece Martina on the grounds of incest, so Polyceutes challenged Nicephorus's right to marry Theophano. The patriarch objected to the marriage because for both of the participants it was a second union. Moreover, according to Polyceutes, Nicephorus had stood as godfather to one of the young princes and it would therefore be incestuous for him to marry the child's mother. Nicephorus eventually got his own way, just as Heraclius had, but only at the expense of alienating the Church and most of the God-fearing people of Constantinople. In any case, the marriage of

Nicephorus and Theophano was never going to be a one made in heaven. If history contains a clearer example of 'Beauty and the Beast' then it would be truly surprising. Theophano was reputed to be the most beautiful woman in the Byzantine world, though she was as ambitious and avaricious as she was lovely. Nicephorus was ugly, dwarfish and terrifying. Yet Theophano saw Nicephorus as the current 'strong-man' and the individual most likely to be able to protect her and her two sons from ruthless opportunists. She sought safety in marriage to him and that was enough until someone else offered her something more.

Further problems flared up between the new emperor and the patriarch. Nicephorus had tried to reintroduce to Byzantine warfare the 'holy' element that had lain dormant since the time of Heraclius. Determined to win back for the empire the Christian lands of Syria, Palestine and Egypt, he approached the patriarch with the proposal that soldiers who died fighting the Muslims should be recognized as martyrs. This once again raised debate about the Thirteenth Canon of St Basil, which had formed the intellectual basis of Byzantine warfare since the fourth century. The decision by Polyceutes to refuse Nicephorus's request was not based on St Basil's canon alone, nor indeed on the traditions of the Orthodox Church in the previous 500 years. The clash between emperor and patriarch was part of an ongoing dispute over the new emperor's religious policies. Nicephorus clearly thought that too much imperial revenue was being paid to monasteries and that they were growing far too rich. He therefore passed a law forbidding further grants and also insisted that in future all church appointments should be made by the emperor. Had this policy originated in the mind of an irreligious emperor the nature of the dispute would have been clear. However, Nicephorus was himself a man of known piety and so the dispute with Polyceutes and the Orthodox Church was more subtle. The Church objected to the emperor's support for 'ascetic monasticism', which was strongly favoured by the eastern military families. Moreover, the Church of Constantinople objected to the close relations that the emperor and his eastern supporters were establishing with the Monophysites and Nestorian Christians who lived in the eastern lands recently recaptured from the Arabs. As a result of the emperor's support, many Monophysite monasteries and bishoprics were established in the area of Syria and Mesopotamia won during Nicephorus's campaigns.

The dominant military figures in the empire, the emperor himself and the new Domestic of the East, John Tzimisces, represented a new way forward for the Byzantine world. Both were great soldiers, experienced middle-aged men, spectacular in their daring. Yet, each combined these characteristics with a serious religious impulse. While Tzimisces devoted his spare time to the inmates of the Nosocomium leper hospital, Nicephorus was a great admirer, disciple even, of the monk Athanasius who lived in the monastery on Mount Athos. On his return from his Cretan expedition Nicephorus gave his share of the immense loot to Athanasius to pay for the building of the Grand Lavra, where he hoped to spend his declining years with the monk, tasting 'the joys of the Eucharist'.

The relentless Nicephorus renewed the dismemberment of the crumbling Abbasid Caliphate in 965 by capturing Tarsus. The Abbasid leader Sayf al-Dawlah succumbed to a stroke at the age of fifty-one and was buried with a brick made of earth taken from all his conquests placed under his head. It was lucky it was buried deep for the grim Nicephorus meant to take back all Christian lands.

Once installed in power Nicephorus began to favour his own family and its network of supporters in terms of land allocation in the newly won territories. Yet, even though Nicephorus had won the acclaim of the people through his great victories over the Arabs, he could not win popularity. In addition to his obvious physical ugliness, the emperor had a stern, unlovable nature which made him deficient in public relations. The reign of Nicephorus Phocas, brilliant though it was in military terms, was viewed in Constantinople as little less than the rule of a military dictator and a grim religious fanatic. The emperor's unpopularity was symbolized by the high walls that he had built around his palace, reminiscent of a fortress rather than an administrative centre or even a luxurious home.

Nicephorus's operation of a virtual spoils system to benefit his own supporters in the East was bound to win him many enemies, not least among those who were overlooked in the distribution. Civilians, particularly government bureaucrats, resented the way in which Nicephorus had turned the empire into a military state. The wars that were fought seemed only to be an opportunity for generals to win renown, for soldiers to gain loot and for the main military families to enlarge their estates in the reconquered territories. And as a result of the conflict the empire risked bankruptcy. Nicephorus was often accused of favouring the military profession as a whole and his soldiers in particular. New taxes were raised to support the numerous campaigns and a devaluation of the currency was cunningly employed as an invisible levy. Even the emperor's brother, Leo, was accused of illegal speculation in the city's grain market.

The so-called 'crusades' of the tenth century are properly examples of propaganda in warfare and its exploitation in the interests of troop morale. Heraclius's appeal had been to the whole Byzantine people, rather than simply to the soldiers he commanded. Whereas the political and the Church establishment in Constantinople did not regard the eastern campaigns of Nicephorus Phocas as crusades, the same people in the seventh century had no doubt that Heraclius was fighting to regain the True Cross and the Holy Sepulchre in Jerusalem, and to preserve the Christian empire of God's chosen people. In a way, when Polyceutes rejected Nicephorus's demand that his soldiers become martyrs he was protecting the concept of martyrdom from being cheapened by overuse and becoming part of the reward system of ambitious and greedy generals.

For Nicephorus Phocas, religion was a powerful part of military efficiency. In his *Praecepta Militaria* he included the following passage:

As the enemy draws near, the entire contingent of the host, every last one of them, must say the invincible prayer proper to Christians, 'Lord Jesus Christ, our God, have mercy on us, Amen', and in this way let them begin their advance against the enemy, calmly proceeding in formation at the prescribed pace without making the slightest commotion or sound. Have the signal given to them either by trumpet or another instrument for them to repeat the same prayer at the signal's end, 'Lord Jesus Christ, our God, have mercy on us', and, 'Come to the aid of us Christians, making us worthy to rise up and fight to the death for our faith and our brethren by fortifying and strengthening our souls, our hearts, and our whole body, the mighty Lord of battles, incomparable in power, through the intercession of the Mother of God who bore Thee, and of all the saints, Amen.'[122]

The austere tone of the emperor's instructions are clear in this extract:

Once the plan is made, the commander of the army should assemble all the *strategoi*, officers, and all the host under their command and counsel and enjoin them to purify themselves and fast for three days before the battle, maintaining a dry fast and eating once a day towards evening. Each and every one of them should expel from his soul any spite, grudges, or grievances toward one another. Similarly, let each one make a promise of repentance to God for his other sins, not to be caught in the same sins by returning to those ways, but to live a repentant life pleasing to God. When these rituals have been properly completed, the priests must perform bloodless sacrifice the day before the battle, and upon completion of the Liturgy the army must partake of the Holy and undefiled Mysteries. And so then, confidently and courageously with conviction and faith in God, they are to go forth against the foe.[123]

To the political and religious establishment at the heart of the empire, Nicephorus Phocas seemed to be the most dangerous emperor for a long time. He was an obvious threat to the *status quo* and his plans for the future of the empire threatened many vested interests. To depose such a powerful soldier, however, required another powerful soldier. If the emperor's wife, Theophano, would join a conspiracy then the matter might be resolved. If, on the other hand, she stayed loyal to her husband and the protector of her two young sons, then the emperor was secure. Ultimately, it was through Theophano that the conspiracy was made to work.

As nephew to Nicephorus Phocas, John Tzimisces, whose mother was the emperor's sister, had originally been part of the Phocas family group. However, he was also closely linked to the Kourkuai and the Skleroi, two families who had suffered at the hands of the Phocas family. Moreover, jealousy of his brilliant nephew had caused the emperor to remove him from his command as Domestic of the Scholae. On the grounds of ambition and revenge John Tzimisces had good reason to hate the emperor and to wish to overthrow him. However, there existed an even stronger motive – lust.

We cannot know how close the relationship was between Theophano and the dwarfish and ugly Nicephorus. She was a young, beautiful woman, apparently helpless in a world of powerful courtiers and generals who might threaten her two young sons. The emperor was an elderly, monkish figure, more concerned with war or religion than the pursuit of earthly delights. One might presume that Nicephorus married Theophano to secure the throne. Yet there is just the possibility, according to some chroniclers, that he had been smitten by her youth and beauty. Whatever the case, Theophano was not content to live for long with this old monk. She had soon taken John Tzimisces as her lover, partly no doubt because of his glamour but partly also because he was probably the only man who could rid her of her husband.

Nicephorus must have been aware of the potential danger from Tzimisces because before 969 he had exiled him to the Asiatic shore, forbidding him to set foot in the capital. This, presumably, convinced Tzimisces of the need to act quickly before Nicephorus eliminated him. He did not find it difficult to secure allies: three senior officers shared his resentment towards Nicephorus – Michael Bourtzes, Leo Balantes and Isaac Brachamius. Bourtzes and Brachamius were the real heroes in the capture of Antioch in 969 but had been overlooked by the emperor and went unrewarded for their efforts. Now they were linking their futures to Tzimisces as the 'coming man'.

John Tzimisces passes across the skies of Byzantine history like a brilliant shaft of sunlight. However, his assassination of Nicephorus Phocas is one of the blackest deeds in Byzantine history. Theophano, still only twenty-eight, had shifted her hopes to the handsome Domestic of the East. Beauty had found beauty at last but first they had to dispose of the beast. The killing took place on 10 December 969 on a bitterly cold night with snow intermittently blowing across the waters of the Bosphorus. Perhaps the clinical planning of the murder, speaking as it does of such human cruelty, leaves one feeling even colder than the weather. Some of the conspirators had arrived at the palace during the late afternoon; disguised as women they passed the emperor's huge but slow-thinking guards on their way to meet the empress. Theophano hurried to intercept them in person and dispersed her visitors to a number of different rooms where they could wait without being discovered. The main conspirator, John Tzimisces himself, was still on the Asian shore, apparently observing the emperor's order that he did not cross the Bosphorus. When one of the emperor's chaplains took a warning to Michael, the chief eunuch, that an attempt was going to be made on the emperor's life a complete search of the palace took place without revealing anything. Theophano, of course, had already bribed Michael not to enter the rooms where her 'women friends' were resting.

As darkness fell and the temperature dropped even further, there was a blizzard blowing across the capital. Would Tzimisces dare to cross the Bosphorus in such weather? Nobody who knew the man could have had any doubt. As he set out from the Asian shore his small boat was tossed by the icy waves and Tzimisces and his three companions huddled under their cloaks for shelter. A journey that should not have taken an hour took three. Just before midnight the four knights arrived at the prearranged spot, whistling a signal to one of the 'women' who waited above and who lowered a rope from a window in Theophano's apartments. Twisting and turning at the end of the rope the four men, with Tzimisces coming last, climbed up the high wall and clambered into the open window. They were met by a eunuch who had been paid to lead the conspirators to the emperor's bedchamber. Throwing aside their cloaks, Tzimisces and his three companions were revealed in full mail and with sheathed swords at their belts. Suddenly all was action. While the eunuch led them through the dark corridors, the assassins followed, finding it hard not to break into a run so keen were they to complete their task. As they entered the emperor's room they found to their astonishment that his bed was empty. Had the plot been revealed? Was the dreaded Nicephorus waiting for them with his giant guards? The four warriors must have been close to panic until the eunuch, alone in keeping his head, pointed to the figure sleeping in the corner of the room on the ground.

At the sound of the four knights Nicephorus woke and struggled to his feet but was struck a terrible blow across the shoulder by Leo Balantes. Balantes' sword then slid and cut deeply into his face. Screaming and roaring simultaneously Nicephorus begged the help of the Theotokos – Mary, Mother of God. While Tzimisces sat cross-legged on the emperor's bed like some judge at a trial, the three others dragged Nicephorus and threw him down in front of Tzimisces in a pool of blood. The killers, all senior officers in the imperial army, had bitter scores to settle with the emperor. They kicked the figure writhing on the ground and ripped out his hair and beard. Next Tzimisces leaped from the bed and joined in, smashing the emperor's jaw. Nicephorus Phocas's face was beaten to a pulp, his teeth knocked out. Only when they had silenced him did each in turn run him through with their swords.

Now was the moment of greatest danger for John Tzimisces. As word spread around the palace the guards, giant Vikings and Russians armed with battle-axes, came running to the royal bedchamber. Too late! The body had gone! Tzimisces and his followers had decapitated the emperor and were running through the streets towards the Bucoleon Harbour, carrying Nicephorus's head on a pike and shouting, 'John, Emperor of the Romans!' Chaos ensued as crowds assembled in the snowy streets; some, no doubt paid to do so, were calling out the name of John Tzimisces, while others were answering with the names of Theophano's sons, Basil and Constantine, who were the true emperors by blood. There must have been one more moment of drama, unrecorded but inevitable as so often in the history of Rome and Constantinople. Royal guardsmen, praetorians or Varangians, came with swords and axes in hand into full view of the killers they were pursuing. It was their task to protect the emperor and to strike down any would-be assassins. John Tzimisces turned to face his pursuers, holding the head of the dead emperor on the pike so that there could be no doubt. Sword arms relaxed, the axes fell to men's sides. The guards saw that their job was over. In front of them stood the new emperor. The more quick-witted of them must have raised the cry for John Tzimisces and fallen in behind his supporters. The empire always needed an emperor and emperors always needed guards.

Like Heraclius before him, John Tzimisces had no claim to the throne other than the fact that he had overthrown an unpopular

tyrant. Like his famous predecessor, Tzimisces was Armenian by
birth and had the good looks that the crowds loved. The chronicles
record him as blond-haired and blue-eyed, though his complexion
was darker than that of Heraclius. He was short but very strong and
remarkably agile. He had risen to the top in the army through sheer
ability. He was a remarkably athletic soldier and could outface and
outfight much larger men.

When the news reached the Patriarch Polyceutes, he was presumably not displeased. He had never liked Nicephorus and now
had an opportunity to reassert his power. When he met Tzimisces he
told him that before he would crown him emperor there would have
to be concessions. Tzimisces was surprisingly cooperative, particularly as the first condition was that he sacrifice the beautiful
Theophano by having her committed to a nunnery. Theophano did
not go quietly and used her vitriolic tongue against JohnTzimisces. It
must have seemed worse to her lover than facing Russian or Saracen
warriors in battle.

John Tzimisces was a more rounded human being than the grim
monk he had murdered. The example of leadership that he brought
to the Byzantine army cannot be overstated. More a glamorous
'dasher' of the Prince Rupert type than a *Coeur de Lion*, Tzimisces
was loved by chroniclers and soldiers alike. For the former he
provided colour in that greyest of professions, while for the latter he
shared the risks with his men and knew how to enjoy the good times
when they came. Leo the Deacon has left us a very detailed picture
of this *beau sabreur*:

> He had a fair complexion with a ruddy aspect, blond hair, and a
> cheerful demeanour. His eyes were manly and bright. He had a
> small, well-proportioned nose. His cheeks were tawny and evenly
> proportioned, square set, while his jaw was nicely tapered and
> full. He was short in stature, although very broad chested, and he
> was also broad across the back. He possessed the strength of a
> giant and was well coordinated, a man who stood unrivalled in
> might. A heroic spirit reigned within him, fearless and unshak-
> able, a spirit of excessive daring displayed in such a short frame.
> He was not afraid to attack a whole body of the enemy by him-
> self, killing many of them before returning with great dash to his

own formation without suffering a scratch. In agility, in games with balls [polo], jousting and shooting the bow, he towered over all men of his generation. The story goes that setting four horses side by side, he could vault over them from one side to the other, and land on the ground light as a bird. Loosing an arrow, he was so much on the mark that he could send an arrow through a finger ring. He used to place a leather ball at the bottom of a glass bowl and then, spurring his horse to a great speed, he struck the ball and made it leap up and fly through the air; the glass bowl he left undisturbed lying in its place. He was very generous and the most munificent of all men.[124]

This remarkable man was one of the most extraordinary of all the emperors of Byzantium. In warfare his influence over his own army was that of a hero in a heroic age. His battles with the Russians had a Homeric or biblical quality with his well-trained Christian Davids taking on huge troll-like Viking and Rus Goliaths in single combat.

In peace he combined humility and generosity with an extravagant love of life that made him the most attractive of imperial personalities. His favourite charity was the Nosocomium, the leper hospital at Chrysopolis, where he was a regular visitor, encouraging the inmates and even washing the sores of the afflicted. Leo the Deacon, however, reports that in his private life he loved wine, women and song. Constantine Manasses describes Tzimisces as 'a new paradise, from which flowed the four rivers of justice, wisdom, prudence and courage . . . Had he not stained his hands with the murder of Nicephorus, he would have shone in the firmament like some incomparable star.'

The accession of John Tzimisces did not mean the end of rule by the eastern military families. Admittedly, members of the powerful Phocas clan were removed from positions of power – in fact, Leo and Nicephorus's son of the same name were blinded in 971 after they tried to oust Tzimisces. However, the Skleroi and the Kourkuai were back in favour and John Tzimisces' 'holy wars' followed a similar pattern to those of his predecessor.

In 972 John decided to remove once and for all the shadow that loomed over the empire from the north. Svyatoslav, Prince of Kiev and his horde of pagan Russians had been summoned – unwisely – by Nicephorus who had bought their services with Byzantine gold and had thought they would be content to pillage the lands of the Bulgarians once they had annihilated those particular enemies of Byzantium. It was just one of Nicephorus's diplomatic errors for, great general though he had been, he was no man of peace. Svyatoslav, encouraged by the sight of so much Greek gold, decided that his next target would be Constantinople itself. It was this threat that Tzimisces was determined to eradicate.

His preparations for the campaign against the pagan Russians bore the hallmarks of a Byzantine 'holy war'. Tzimisces planned a combined operation, utilizing the Byzantine riverine fleet to cooperate with the land army along the Danube. Before leaving the capital the emperor, whose sincerity we have no reason to doubt, prayed at the chapel built by one of his predecessors, Romanus Lecapanus, near the Chalke Gate. Although he had already enlarged this building and planned for it to become his final resting place there was something intensely personal and private in this act of devotion by the most flamboyant of emperors. However, ceremonial now replaced private devotion as he moved on to Hagia Sophia which, in its 400 years, had been the site of many triumphs and tragedies but had still never seen enemy or invader below its vast dome. Tzimisces arrived on foot, carrying aloft in his right hand a wooden cross in which was set a fragment of the True Cross. In the great church he prayed for victory. He then passed on to Blachernae, where he invoked the aid of the Theotokos, as all Byzantine emperors had done since the time of Heraclius. It was not a great distance now for him to move to the seafront where the fleet was laid out in the Golden Horn. He signalled and the ships weighed anchor and began their journey. After watching for a while he mounted his horse and led his guards westwards to rendezvous with his army at Adrianople. The first crusade of John Tzimisces was in motion.

Glimpsing the emperor on the battlefield one might almost have been forgiven for thinking that the Romans – or Byzantines – had returned to the worship of Sol Invictus. John Tzimisces was a simply dazzling figure, dressed in golden armour from head to foot and surrounded by a 'solar system' of brilliantly equipped officers.

Nobody, least of all a pagan enemy, could doubt for one moment that this Byzantine emperor was the chosen one of a very powerful god. The campaign against the Russians revealed that the Byzantine troops of the tenth century were far from the 'effete' warriors that the western crusaders branded them in the eleventh. Golden as their emperor was on the surface, there was steel beneath and in a series of dreadful, sanguinary encounters, during which he did his share of fighting, John Tzimisces inflicted crushing defeats on the Russians. At one stage in the desperate battle outside Dristra, St Theodore Statilates, one of the warrior saints of Byzantium, was clearly seen in the heart of the battle, mounted on a magnificent white horse. Once the Russians were defeated the emperor entered Dristra and renamed it Theodoropolis to commemorate the actions of the warrior saint in the battle. To modern readers this may seem like pure theatre but in the context of the age of faith it was a further confirmation that the Byzantines were the chosen people and that God would not let them fall under the swords of a pagan foe.

For three years the Balkan front had occupied Nicephorus Phocas and his successor John Tzimisces which meant that the eastern front had not seen the best of the Byzantine generals. In July 973, with Tzimisces occupied elsewhere, the Fatimids had destroyed a Byzantine army at Amida. The Byzantine capture of Aleppo in 963 by Nicephorus Phocas had been taken by most Muslims to mean that the Abbasid Caliphate was no longer able to hold the frontier against the resurgent power of the Christian empire. This setback had been exploited by the Fatimids of North Africa as the justification for their capture of Muslim Egypt and their proposed occupation of Syria. No sooner had the Fatimids completed their conquest of Egypt than a Berber general, Jafar ibn Falah was sent northwards into Palestine and Syria to secure Muslim possessions. At once he captured Ramla and Damascus, before moving further north to take Tripoli, which then became the Fatimid capital of Syria. Only when the Berbers attempted to take Antioch were they repelled by the Byzantine garrison.

John Tzimisces decided to remove the Fatimid threat to Antioch and to drive the Muslims out of Syria. In alliance with King Ashot III of Armenia, from whom he received a contingent of 10,000 soldiers, he proclaimed a 'crusade' against the Fatimids and assembled a powerful army. Not since the Persian crusade of Heraclius in 622–8 had a Byzantine emperor conducted such a famous campaign as that carried out by John Tzimisces in 975. Yet, unlike Heraclius's desperate, life or death campaigns, the crusade of John Tzimisces was almost ceremonial, more processional than military. From Antioch Tzimisces advanced deeper into Syria, receiving the surrender of Emesa, Baalbeck and Damascus, where the inhabitants met the invader with flowers rather than stones and boiling oil. Tripoli successfully resisted him but Muslim control of Syria and Lebanon had been seriously weakened. However, glory, as the wisest conquerors know, is a fragile thing. A fall from a horse, a stray arrow or an assassin's blade can alter the balance between triumph and disaster. We can never be certain what killed John Tzimisces. When a man of middle years and rude health dies suddenly one suspects foul play. But when that man is a soldier, returning from a campaign in a Middle Eastern climate there can be other explanations. Most of the chroniclers who record the events of this period believe the emperor was poisoned on the orders of the Parakoimomenos Basil, who believed Tzimisces was going to act against him for corrupt land speculation. To a modern eye, however, the manner of his death, drawn out rather than sudden, indicates a death from a disease typical of hard campaigning, such as typhus or dysentery.

Without realizing it the Byzantines conducted the 'crusade' of 975 in the middle of a Muslim civil war of bewildering complexity. In May 975 news reached Fatmid-controlled Damascus that the 'King of the Romans' was coming up the Orontes valley with an enormous army. A question must have been in every Muslim mind: was he coming to relieve Antioch and protect Byzantine Syria, or was he coming to threaten Tripoli, Damascus and even Palestine? Muslim indecision arose from skilful manoeuvring by Tzimisces, who first feinted towards Tripoli, which caused the Fatimid commander, who feared being cut off inland, to abandon Damascus and head for the coast. The Byzantines then moved instead into the Orontes valley, capturing Baalbeck. A Muslim army tried to block Tzimisces' approach to Damascus but he brushed it aside before threatening the city. In true Byzantine fashion Tzimisces used psychology as his main weapon during the campaign, avoiding pitched battles but relying on the threat of his powerful army to force the Muslims to surrender. As he told those who sought terms with him, 'Our goal in taking money is that it be said we took possession of the city. Therefore we take its gifts.'[125]

The Damascene population realized that it had no option but to treat with the Byzantines. The commander of the Turkish garrison, Alptkin, rode out in his most splendid attire, accompanied by the most senior citizens, and offered fealty to Tzimisces, who claimed just Alptkin's horse and spear. In return the Byzantines loaded the Turks with gifts of their own. Tzimisces then appointed Alptkin his own commander in Damascus. This ceremonial process was apparently repeated in several Syrian cities and by it Tzimisces avoided unnecessary bloodshed and destruction.

After the 'conquest' of Damascus all existing Byzantine and Arab sources report that the Byzantine army marched directly west to the coast. All, that is, except one – and that one has the authority of being written by the emperor himself. The letter was preserved in Armenian royal archives in the original Greek but during the twelfth century it was incorporated into the history of Matthew of Edessa. It contains the following account of what took place after the Byzantine army left Damascus:

We went to the Sea of Galilee, where our Lord Jesus Christ had performed a miracle with 153 fish. We were intent on laying siege to the town of Tiberias also, but the townspeople came in submission to Our Imperial Majesty and brought us many gifts like the Damascenes had done and also tribute in the amount of 30,000 dahekans, not counting many other valuable presents. They requested that one of our commanders be put over them and gave us an affirmation of loyalty as had the Damascenes, promising to be subject to us perpetually and to give us tribute ceaselessly. On that basis we left them free of enslavement and did not devastate the town or the region; moreover, we did not plunder them because the region was the native land of the holy apostles. We felt the same way about Nazareth where the Theotokos, the holy Virgin Mary, heard the good tidings from the angel. We also went to Mount Tabor and climbed up to that place where Christ our God was transfigured. While we remained in that place, people came to us from Ramla and Jerusalem to beseech Our Imperial Majesty, looking for compassion from us. They asked that a commander be appointed over them and became tributary to us, swearing to serve us; all of these things which they asked we indeed did. We also were intent on delivering the holy sepulchre of Christ our God from bondage of the Moslems. We established military commanders in all the areas which had submitted and become tributary to Our Imperial Majesty; these were Baisan called Decapolis, Genesareth and Acre also called Ptolemais, and by a written statement they undertook to give tribute ceaselessly from year to year and to serve us. We went up to Caesarea which is on the coast of the great Mediterranean sea, and they also submitted and came under our rule. If the abominable Africans had not fled to the coastal fortresses where they had taken refuge because they feared us, by the assistance of God we would have gone to the holy city of Jerusalem and would have stood in prayer at the holy places of God. When we heard that the coastal inhabitants had fled, then we brought to submission the upper part of the country, subjecting it to the rule of the Romans and establishing a commander there. We brought under our control many towns, besieging and assaulting those which did not submit; having captured them we went by the coastal route which leads directly to the famous, renowned and heavily fortified town of Berytus, which today is called Beirut.[126]

Historians have found this letter highly suspect. The route taken by the Byzantine army is illogical – marching north from Caesarea to Beirut then turning around and marching south again to capture Sidon. Furthermore, there simply was not enough time to have done all that was supposedly done. The historian Paul Walker has suggested several reasons for these apparent inaccuracies. One is simply that during the letter's translation in the twelfth century from Greek to Armenian mistakes were made. This is unconvincing. However, Walker's other suggestions have the ring of truth. The exaggerations and fantasies in Tzimisces' letter were either included by the Byzantines to boost the reputation of the emperor or, more likely, to smooth relations with Christian Armenia, which had recently been disturbed.[127]

So parts of John Tzimisces' account of the 975 'crusade', notably the description of the army's movements in Palestine, never took place. The campaign in Syria was clearly a great success but the emperor's letter was exaggerated at a later date to make it sound more impressive in view of the success of the western crusaders. Had Tzimisces really rampaged around Palestine virtually unchallenged, threatening Jerusalem and even the Egyptian frontier, then he would have achieved the very opposite of what he intended. He would have united the disparate warring Muslim factions in a holy war aimed at driving the Christians out of the centre of Islam. What he did achieve, however, was the creation of a buffer between Christendom and Fatimid Islam. He had also made it impossible for the Fatimids to threaten the Byzantine position in Syria, centred on Antioch. This was a strategic achievement rather than a spiritual one. Whatever use was made of the 'crusading spirit' of the soldiers, or the holy relics and icons that were carried into battle, or the numerous priests that accompanied the army, John Tzimisces' aim was not to recapture the Holy Sepulchre in Jerusalem or regain the Holy Land; it was to demonstrate the resurgence of Byzantine power in a region that had not seen Christian troops for centuries. He thus demonstrated to the Christian Armenians the spiritual leadership that the Byzantines still offered to the Christian world.

Ironically, the application of the title 'crusade' to Tzimisces' campaign of 975 might have been a product of Arab propaganda. The Fatimids justified their conquest of Egypt and Palestine with the argument that Islam needed a stronger force to combat the threat from the Christian empire in the north. While they viewed the campaigns of Nicephorus Phocas and John Tzimisces as 'Christian assaults on Islam' they were able to present themselves as the legitimate defenders of Islam.

Yet the conclusion of the campaign, with the dying emperor attending a church service in Hagia Sophia to present the main 'booty' acquired – a pair of Christ's sandals and the hair of John the Baptist – indicates the religious significance of the event for both Tzimisces and his people. The dying emperor gave all his worldly goods to the poor and made a last confession, calling on the Mother of God, symbol of the city's protection, to look after him. At the last his mind must have turned to the dreadful deed which had brought him to the throne. Yet it was the same deed that had given the empire some of the greatest successes in its history. Truly this dying man left the final judgement to God.

The 'crusade' by Tzimisces in 975 has been used by scholars and others to argue the case for the existence of distinctly Byzantine holy wars prior to the arrival of the western crusaders a century later. I feel, however, that the 975 campaign is even more an 'ersatz crusade' than those conducted by Nicephorus Phocas. Whatever the feelings of the emperor himself – and we know him to be a very devout man – his aim in 975 was not essentially religious. The letter to the King Ashot of Armenia, from which the evidence for a crusade is mainly taken, is an example of political propaganda. Intending to improve relations with a neighbouring Christian state and to win military support for future campaigns against a common enemy, Tzimisces' advisers saw that the religious theme was the safest one to exploit and one that could be exaggerated to the point where faith replaced reality. Thus much of the letter's content relating to Tzimisces' crusade is not simply fantasy – or lies – but a kind of visionary appreciation of what was possible if Christian allies fought together in the Holy Land against enemies of the faith.

ELEVEN

The Dreadful Day

The accession of the sons of Theophano as co-emperors symbolized the problems of an empire that veered between extremes, as if involved in an eternal struggle between good and evil. On one side was the eighteen-year-old Basil, third in a trio of brilliant generals on the throne of Byzantium; on the other was the sixteen-year-old Constantine, as pointless a wastrel as ever wore the imperial purple. Ironically, however, it was the very success of Basil that was to undermine the empire in the East and prepare the way for the western crusades.

The balance of power in the frontier zone between Byzantium and the Muslim world had changed, partly due to developments within the Christian empire itself and partly through the splintering of the Abbasid Caliphate. In 900 most Muslims still regarded the Abbasid caliphs of Baghdad as the leaders of Islam but by 1000 that position had collapsed in the face of invaders from two directions: from the East came the Turks and from the south the Shiite Fatimids, who had moved along the North African coast and eventually, in 969, conquered Egypt and then moved northwards towards Baghdad. The civil wars that divided Islam during the tenth century weakened Muslim defences and opened the way for a resurgent Byzantine army to reconquer provinces that had not been in Christian hands since the seventh century. In view of this, one might raise the question why, given weakened Muslim resistance, did the Byzantines under their remarkable generals of the mid-tenth century not make more effort to reconquer the provinces of Syria and Palestine. Perhaps the answer lies in the field of grand strategy, in the struggles between 'Easterners' and 'Westerners' in the Byzantine state.

Just as the Abbasid Caliphate splintered and disintegrated during this period so the Byzantine Empire was riven by internal disputes of religious, political and military kinds. The struggle to hold the periphery of the empire against Muslim invaders over the centuries had developed a frontier mentality among the population of the eastern lands of the empire. This frontier mentality affected all aspects of life so that attitudes differed markedly between the frontier families and the more sophisticated courtiers who surrounded the emperor in the capital.

A second problem in the eastern lands was the continuing religious schism between Orthodoxy and Monophysitism. This had been one of the factors that had undermined the integrity of the empire in the first place and had weakened Heraclius's resistance to the initial upsurge of Islam in the 630s. After 950 large areas of northern Mesopotamia were recovered for the empire but the Christian inhabitants immediately resented their religious domination by Orthodox Constantinople. As a result of this schism the Orthodox authorities in the capital were uneasy about any apparent identification of the frontier families with the Monophysite Christians of the reconquered territories.

The great eastern military families, like the Phocases, the Argeroi, the Skleroi, the Kourkuai and the Doukai, built vast estates in the eastern lands and played an increasing role in imperial politics as a result of their ability to raise armies. In Cappadocia the Phocases had become rulers of a state within a state by the ninth century. During the reign of Romanus Lecapanus the process by which the military magnates bought up the land of peasants and small landowners was facilitated by extremely harsh conditions during the winter of 927–8 and a subsequent famine. The booty and treasure won by the successful generals enabled them to increase their landholdings in the frontier areas and the newly conquered lands. Under Romanus the family and friends of the great general John Kourkuas were the main beneficiaries of Kourkuas's numerous victories over the Muslims.

This problem of 'over-mighty subjects' was as real in the Byzantine Empire during this period as it was in western Europe during the Middle Ages. The centralism of the state was threatened by pressures from provincial magnates, determined to increase their own local authority and, ultimately, gain their independence. Whereas their ancestors had fought defensive wars as appointees of the state to preserve the land they now owned, the decline of the Abbasid Caliphate meant that their frontier lands became springboards for Christian assaults on the Muslim lands. These campaigns would be holy wars fought by Christians to regain Christian lands from the hands of the Muslims. The generals who conducted these eastern campaigns, fought in the name of God, were more than simply the servants of a state ruled by a faceless figure in the capital; they were Christian soldiers in the tradition of the warrior-saints, or even of emperors like Heraclius or Constantine himself.

The disadvantages brought about by these magnates had to be set against the advantages they offered in military terms. The Thematic armies of the empire were most powerful in the East, where they were controlled by the military families. The heads of these families looked forward to an enlarged Christian empire based on foreign conquest, in which liberated Christians in Syria, Persia and other former imperial territories would return to their 'Roman' allegiance. The power of Islam would be overcome by a resurgent Christianity. The expansion of Fatimid power in the mid-tenth century resembled the original Arab explosion of the 630s. It is hardly coincidental that this new threat from Islam produced a corresponding religious response from successive emperors, Nicephorus Phocas and John Tzimisces.

However, this was not the future envisaged by the Greek, Orthodox Empire centred on Constantinople. In the person of the Emperor Basil II the magnates faced their greatest threat. In his struggle with the military families during the civil wars of 976–89 Basil benefited from the fact that the assassination of Nicephorus Phocas by John Tzimisces had divided the eastern families into two hostile groups. In this internecine struggle the only certain casualty was the empire itself.

Basil made it his first priority to reverse the trend of the military families towards independence from the central government. Clearly he must not weaken them too much for they represented the main military strength of the empire and provided the best generals. A contemporary commentator, Michael Psellus, observed that Basil 'surrounded himself with a body of picked men, who were not outstanding in intelligence, nor remarkable in their family, nor very much educated in letters, and to these he entrusted imperial missives, and confided secret matters'.[128] Unfortunately, what suited him did not necessarily suit his successors or benefit the empire as a whole.

Under Basil the great military families lost power to new ones like the Comnenoi. Moreover, Basil's policy against the military families reduced Byzantine military potential on the frontiers with Islam. As a result, in 995 Fatimid armies were able to threaten the city of Aleppo, keystone of Byzantine policy in the East, after defeating the Byzantine army in the area. The Aleppans appealed to Basil to come to their aid, pointing out that if they fell to the Fatimids Antioch would soon follow. Although busy campaigning in Bulgaria, Basil recognized the danger. His reaction was an example of what might have been possible for Byzantine arms had this great warrior-emperor not confined himself to destroying the Bulgarians in the Balkans. He mounted an entire army of 40,000 men on horses and mules and moved them and their equipment over 600 miles across Anatolia in just sixteen days. Arriving outside Aleppo with some 17,000 of the fastest riders, Basil caught the Fatimid commander Manjutekin completely by surprise. The Fatimids, astonished by the appearance of the emperor with such a powerful force when no Byzantines had been expected, fled to Damascus. Basil contented himself with a demonstration of his power, sacked Emesa, regarrisoned Antioch and returned to Constantinople. Having saved the Byzantine position in the East, Basil was eager to return to his campaign in Bulgaria. However, before he went, he issued an edict which so damaged the Christian position with the Muslims on the frontier that he might as well have stayed in Bulgaria and let Aleppo fall to the Fatimids.

During his journey through Anatolia, pell-mell though it had been, he had seen at firsthand the vast estates of the military families that had been built on what he regarded as imperial territory. The magnates, fatally, welcomed him to their splendid estates as he passed through and he was able to see how they lived like princes.

As a result, once he returned to Constantinople, he decided to assert his authority in the clearest manner. In 996 Basil issued a 'New Constitution by which are Condemned those Rich Men who Amass their Wealth at the Expense of the Poor'. In this document he accused many wealthy Anatolian lords of acquiring land illegally. Significantly, he singled out the Phocas family 'who, from father to son over more than a century, have succeeded in retaining estates to which they have no legal title'.[129] All territory acquired within the previous sixty years was immediately returned to its previous owners without compensation. Some of the empire's richest men were arrested and imprisoned while the Phocas family, the military backbone of the empire for the previous fifty years, was reduced to beggary. At a stroke Basil won his battle with the military families and, with the same stroke, destroyed the military strength of the eastern empire. Peasants, who had formed the backbone of Byzantine armies for decades, now had their lands returned to them and took up farming once again on their own estates.

Basil's reforms and conquests, while impressive, hung uncompleted in mid-air because he had no son to succeed him. What was needed was a successor who could fill the military void that now existed on the eastern front. With no Phocas general to keep at bay the Seljuk Turks, the new threat from the East, the empire needed a new Basil at the centre. Instead, when he died in 1025, he was followed by his wastrel brother and co-emperor Constantine VIII, and then by his niece Zoë. The fifty years that followed the death of Basil II saw the weakest government in the empire's history.

The Christian holy places may have been the ostensible target of the period of 'ersatz crusades' but the emperor in Constantinople was still helpless to protect pilgrims on their way to Jerusalem within a volatile and constantly changing Muslim world. Even at the height of Byzantine power the Christian world faced the most destructive threat Islam had ever posed to the Christian holy places. The death of the Fatimid Caliph al-Aziz in 996 and the accession of his son al-Hakim unleashed on Palestine a personality that seemed to symbolize the problems of the deeply troubled area. Religious conflict was in the very blood of the austere young man who now came to the throne of Egypt.

With a Christian mother and a Shiite Muslim father he seemed to symbolize hope for an era of better relations between the two religions within the Fatimid lands. At first al-Hakim even played the part of the moderate, concluding a truce in 1001 with the Emperor Basil that put an end to the eastern campaigns of the Christians who had threatened to shake Muslim control of Palestine. Instead, it appeared – at least temporarily – that there might be an era of friendship between the erstwhile enemies. What precisely pushed al-Hakim over the edge and into hostility is unknown. Perhaps the burden of being caliph proved too much for an essentially unbalanced personality. In any event, in 1003 he began a campaign of persecution against the Christians within his lands. First, St Mark's Church at Fustat, in Egypt, was destroyed on the grounds that its erection had violated Islamic law. It was immediately replaced by a mosque, which was extended over Christian and Jewish cemeteries as if deliberately to foster a religious backlash. Once started on the road to persecution al-Hakim began confiscating Christian property, desecrating churches and holy shrines, and – most provocative of all – ordering the construction of small mosques on the very roofs of Christian churches. Even his own people began to suspect that al-Hakim was going mad. Never in the 400 years that the Muslims had held Egypt and Palestine had any of their rulers carried out such religious persecution. It violated much of what Muslims held dear and seemed to have no foundation in the teachings of the Prophet.

In order to understand why al-Hakim behaved in this extraordinary way it is necessary to examine more than just his confused personality. With the approach of the year 1000, many Christians believed that the Second Coming would occur and that the Day of Judgement was near. This created a kind of triumphalism that disrupted relations between Christians and their Muslim neighbours. One story says that al-Hakim was infuriated by the confident rejoicing of a large crowd of Coptic Christians whom he observed preparing to set off for Jerusalem at Easter. To his eyes their behaviour resembled the actions of Muslim hajjis travelling to Mecca. When he discussed this with his religious advisers they told him that the Christians of Jerusalem were immensely rich and drew their wealth from all the noble pilgrims from the West and the

Byzantine world. Moreover, al-Hakim learned, the Christian priests worked magic within their churches at Easter, drawing fire from the darkness without any apparent earthly help. This 'Holy Fire', the Shiite priests told al-Hakim, was such an impressive trick that in spite of every effort to find out how it was done, no Muslim could match it. As a result, the simpler souls, of whatever faith, were filled with amazement. Al-Hakim, already uneasy at the confidence of the Christians at the new millennium, responded with fear and envy.

In 1009 al-Hakim ordered the destruction and eradication of the Anastasis and Martyrion that Constantine had built at the Holy Sepulchre nearly seven centuries before. By this single gesture he hoped to settle not only the religious ambiguities of the Fatimid lands but also the emotional confusion within himself. The Christian historian Yahya ibn Sa'id recorded what happened next:

Al-Hakim likewise sent to Syria, to Yarukh, governor of Ramla, written orders to destroy the Holy Resurrection, to get rid of the Christian emblems and to destroy completely the Christian relics. Yarukh sent to Jerusalem his son, Yusuf, and Husayn ibn Zahir, the Inspector of Currency. They confiscated all the furnishings that were in the church, after which they razed it completely, except those parts that were impossible to destroy or would have been too difficult to carry away. The Cranion [Golgotha] was destroyed, as well as the Church of Saint Constantine, and everything that was found in the precinct. The complete destruction of the relics was accomplished. Ibn Zahir bent every effort to demolish the holy sepulchre and to remove its every trace; he broke up the greater part of it and removed it. In the neighbourhood of the holy sepulchre there was a convent of women called Dayr al-Sari, which he likewise destroyed.[130]

Thousands of Christian churches in Fatimid lands were destroyed and many Christians faced religious persecution as severe as any since Roman times. Although the Emperor Basil II allowed Syrian Christians to emigrate into imperial territory, his response was not what one might have expected from God's chosen one on earth and the defender of His chosen people. It is highly likely that both

Nicephorus Phocas and John Tzimisces would have regarded al-Hakim's actions as a *casus belli* and declared a holy war against the Fatimids. Instead, Basil, who was totally preoccupied with his war against Bulgaria, merely renewed the ten-year truce he had signed with the Fatimids in 1001. Basil apparently decided that no issue of decisive Byzantine interest was at stake, a very revealing attitude in contrast to the holy wars or 'crusades' of his two predecessors.

Al-Hakim next turned his attention against his own co-religionists, declaring himself divine in 1016 and forbidding pilgrimages to Mecca and the honouring of the month of Ramadan. The caliph, hated now by his own people, began to favour Christians and to restore property taken from them during the persecution. It was only a matter of time before the Muslims overthrew the madman who had substituted his own name for that of Allah in mosque services. Eventually al-Hakim disappeared, probably murdered by his sister Sitt al-Mulk. In 1023, she asked Nicephorus, Patriarch of Jerusalem, to go to the capital of Christendom, which is how she regarded Constantinople, and consult the emperor with a view to rebuilding the Christian holy places. Before he could do so, however, the area around Jerusalem was invaded by Bedouin tribesmen, who took advantage of the chaos in the Fatimid administration to wreak havoc in the countryside.

It was not until 1030 that peace returned to Palestine under stronger Fatimid control. With money donated by the Byzantines, notably Constantine IX, Monomarchus (1042–55), the new Anastasis church was built, though no attempt was made to replace Constantine's basilica, the Martyrion. Through their financial support for the rebuilding programme in Jerusalem the Byzantines established what has been regarded as a Christian enclave separate from the Muslim city and an area which they regarded as a Byzantine protectorate. The existence of Christian authority within the holy city encouraged pilgrimages, notably in the second half of the eleventh century.

Pilgrimages to Jerusalem had a long tradition in European life, from the earliest recorded examples in the fourth century right up to the millennialism of those who thought the world would end in the year

1000 or in 1033, the thousandth anniversary of the death of Christ. Encouraging this growth were developments in the nature of pilgrimage itself. During the eleventh century monks at the great monastery of Cluny in central France began to develop the idea of penitential pilgrimage as a form of canonical punishment. Individuals travelled to the Holy Land in groups for greater safety, while collective penance was undertaken by companies in large-scale pilgrimages. It was but a small step before the pilgrims began to take up arms for their protection on the journey and became, under the direction of the supreme Church authority, crusaders. What really divided the armed pilgrims or crusaders from previous participants in holy war was the issuing of indulgences, by which the crusaders enjoyed 'special privileges' that could only be granted by the pope. While the crusader was away, his family, assets and lands were all protected and for his military service to the Church he received 'remission of his sins', or martyrdom and entry to Paradise should he die.

In 1064 a large pilgrimage, led by Bishop Arnold of Bamburg, known as the 'Great Western Pilgrimage', left Germany. Travelling in this large band of pilgrims were many wealthy merchants and noblemen who sought safety in numbers. In fact, the size and splendour of the pilgrimage had precisely the opposite effect: as they approached the holy city they were set upon by bands of Bedouin who killed many of the pilgrims in anticipation of the gold they were thought to be carrying. It is reported that the members of this pilgrim army actually fought off the Bedouin attacks for several hours, even though they were not supposed to be armed. Clearly the dividing line between pilgrim and crusader was becoming blurred.

Who was to protect the growing numbers of pilgrims visiting the Holy Land? Not, apparently, the Byzantine emperor. Since the death of Basil II in 1025 stringent cutbacks in military expenditure and the collapse of the system of local defence meant that the Byzantines had to hire mercenaries to defend their own lands. There was no money left over to police pilgrim routes in the same way. As a result, the pilgrims suffered at the hands of the desert tribes as well as the local Muslims.

From 1025 until the accession of Romanus Diogenes in 1068 the empire was governed by rulers who were more administrators than warriors. The once-feared Byzantine army was becoming impotent as the contemporary chronicler, John Scylitzes, described:

Here one could see a dreadful sight: those celebrated Roman regiments who had brought both East and West under their sway consisting now of only a handful of men – and men, moreover, bowed down with poverty and ill-health no longer even fully armed. Instead of swords and other weapons they held, as the Bible has it, only pikes and scythes. And this was not even in time of peace. Yet because it was so long since any emperor had fought there they lacked warhorses and equipment of every kind. And since they were considered weak and cowardly and of no serious use, they had received no subsistence money, nor their customary allowance to buy grain. Their very standards rang dully when struck, and looked dirty as if blackened by smoke; and there were few to care for them. All this caused great sadness in the hearts of those who saw them, when they thought upon the condition from which the Roman armies had come, and that to which they had fallen.[131]

Much stronger government was imperative and when, in 1068, the feeble Constantine X Ducas died, his widow Eudokia chose as her husband the able soldier, Romanus Diogenes. Romanus came from Cappadocia and was from a famous military family. In his mid-thirties in 1068, the same age as Heraclius was when he came to the throne, he was regarded less as emperor than as guardian of the Empress Eudokia and of her son Michael VII, who was physically and mentally backward. Romanus made the reform of the Byzantine army his main priority, but he faced strong opposition to his policies from the Ducas family, who saw him as a usurper and, in the case of Caesar John Ducas, the dead emperor's brother, were eager to to overthrow him. A more ruthless man than Romanus would have eliminated them. Instead he merely exiled John Ducas rather than risk civil war with the family by taking more direct action.

In one of history's ironies it was to be the same steppe nomads who had come to the aid of Heraclius during his epic campaign against the Sasanids in the 620s who were to shatter the Byzantine Empire 450 years later. In the early eleventh century Seljuk Turks from the region of Transoxania began raiding and plundering Armenia, which bordered the Byzantine heartland of Anatolia. Recent converts to Islam, the Seljuks captured Baghdad in 1055 and proclaimed themselves protectors of the decrepit Abbasid Caliphate. The fanatical Turkish Sunnite Muslims were less concerned with attacking the Christian Byzantines than with fighting the Shiites of Fatimid Egypt, whom they regarded as Islamic heretics. The Fatimids were then at the height of their power and exercised control over much of the Middle East, as far north as Aleppo in Syria. For the next two centuries the Islamic world was to be split by the Sunnite–Shiite struggle.

It is important to realize that the Seljuk newcomers were not intrinsically anti-Byzantine. The Byzantine Empire was so ancient and so fundamental to their world picture that they viewed it as little less than a monolithic paradise for nomadic raiders, to be nibbled at but never to be challenged in its integrity. The Turkish leaders looked south rather than westwards, saving their most profound energies for the religious struggle against the Fatimids. However, Armenia, which acted as a buffer between the Byzantines and the Seljuks, had been pushed into prominence by the absurd policies of the emperors who succeeded Basil II after 1025. Persecution of the Monophysite Armenians by the religious authorities in Constantinople mirrored the problems experienced by Heraclius in Syria in the seventh century, while the disbandment of the local militia in Armenia meant that the defence of the region against invaders imposed an even greater burden on the Byzantine regular army. Such idiotic policies did not pass unnoticed among the Seljuks. Essentially a nomadic steppe people, accustomed to raiding rather than settling, the Turks could not resist increasing their attacks on the now largely undefended Armenian border lands.

Romanus faced the perennial problem of Byzantine emperors: a lack of native manpower for the army. With Normans threatening Byzantine possessions in Italy and Turks and steppe nomads threatening imperial lands in the east and north-east, it seemed the height of folly for the empire to fill the ranks of its army with mercenary Normans and Pechenegs (who were Turkish-speaking nomads from the steppelands between the Ural mountains and the Volga river in southern Russia), but it employed them in their thousands. Were such mercenaries reliable and how would they behave if they were called upon to face their own people?

The new emperor was aware of this fundamental flaw in Byzantine military thinking. He decided to try to impose himself on the Seljuks with a decisive victory and for this he resolved to raise the biggest army that money could buy. This was poor strategy: the Turks would have been more impressed had the Byzantines strengthened their frontier defences so that they could resist Seljuk raids. The immensely mobile Turks could only be crushed by the weight of an enemy if they allowed themselves to be brought to battle and fixed by difficult terrain, as they were to be by the western Franks at Dorylaeum in 1097. They had little to fear from a juggernaut of the kind Romanus Diogenes was preparing to use against them.

In early March 1071 Romanus left Constantinople to rendezvous with the polyglot force he had ordered to assemble near Sebastea. Medieval chroniclers generally overestimate numbers and the figure of 100,000 combatant troops may seem a wild exaggeration. However, huge though this figure is, we do know that Romanus had placed great emphasis on the size of the army rather than its efficiency.

Through the streets of the capital, crowded with cheering on-lookers on that brisk March day, Romanus rode surrounded by the imperial cavalry of the Tagmata, regiments of cataphracts in all their regalia, who comprised the armoured fist of the Byzantine army. Following these knights on their mailed horses were European mercenaries – clean-shaven Normans with conical helms and kite-shaped shields, and rough red-bearded Rus, clad in mail coats with fur cloaks and striped baggy trousers. And in pride of place rode the Varangian Guard, the emperor's personal bodyguard, made up of axe-wielding Vikings and English housecarls.

For the superstitious there were ill omens, such as the grey dove that landed on the emperor's hand and seemed to presage disaster. Perhaps it did. Near Dorylaeum the emperor's accommodation caught fire, destroying some of his carriages and personal equipment, as well as killing his finest horses, which ran through the camp screaming and burning like torches. Near Coloneia the Byzantines came upon the scene of Manuel Comnenus's defeat the previous year, and the troops became sullen and gloomy as they rode past the sun-bleached bones of old comrades lining their path for miles.

At the fortress of Sebastea, Romanus met the main Byzantine field army, which contained many Asiatic mercenaries of tribes and people from throughout the Near East. Full-bearded Pechenegs in fur caps brushed shoulders with pigtailed Khazars, their faces hideously scarred from birth, while blond-haired Alans in brightly coloured jackets and trousers, mixed with Cumans in thick sheepskin jerkins and heavily armoured Georgian and Armenian knights. It was a colourful and warlike assembly, but it served only to emphasize how little unity there was in the Byzantine army by that date. Only a century before, the warrior emperors had honed the Anatolian peasantry into an elite infantry force that was more than a match for the empire's enemies. Now, the reliance on ill-disciplined mercenaries meant that the Byzantine military manuals that had once been every general's second Bible were no longer effective. Only the guards regiments and the Varangians were entirely reliable in the heat of battle. And if Romanus could not rely on his troops, he had even less reason to trust his generals. As a usurper he could never be certain of their loyalty or their friendship, and he was always in danger of assassination or desertion in battle by an ambitious rival. Romanus certainly had rivals and bitter enemies, notably from the Ducas family. Incredibly, he had already decided to give command of the reserve regiments to Andonicus Ducas, son of the very man he had exiled, John Ducas. It was a foolish mistake which was to cost him his crown and the empire its future.

The Seljuk sultan, Alp Arslan, was not interested in a serious conflict with the Byzantines and had he known what Romanus was planning he would have tried to negotiate a truce. However, when he received news that an immense Christian force was operating in Armenia, cutting him off from his homeland, he had no option but to make a hasty withdrawal from Syria and race back to confront the Byzantine horde.

The subsequent battle at Manzikert, the most famous and also the most disastrous in the entire history of the Byzantine Empire, was tragic because it was unnecessary. It was fought by a state that had fallen so far from its highpoint less than fifty years before that it was still living on its reputation and by an emperor who, as a usurper, felt he had something to prove. Having emptied his treasury to raise an apparently powerful army, Romanus knew he would have to use it. If he returned without a victory his throne and his life might well be forfeit.

The battle began with Romanus charging the Seljuks with his heavy cavalry, trying to use his armoured knights to smash the Turkish centre. Making supplications to Allah the Almighty the Seljuks rode straight towards the Byzantines, firing their arrows, but at the last moment swinging away and riding out of range, using their favourite tactic of the feigned retreat. The air was filled with a cacophony. In the front rank of each Seljuk regiment rode men clanging timbrels, rattles, gongs and cymbals with all their might, while others blew loudly on trumpets. These were the men whose duty it was to terrify the enemy with noise and to inflame the passions of their own warriors.

As the Turks raced back and forth across the open plain, drawing ever closer to the distant foothills, Romanus became desperate to come to close-quarters with them. He knew there was a likelihood of ambushes yet he could think of no alternative but to press on. The Turks kept up a barrage of arrows on the Byzantines from long range to which Romanus could only respond with his Pecheneg and Cuman mercenaries – as fast and as mobile as the Seljuks, but incapable of delivering a telling blow. Hour followed hour as the Byzantines pressed on with their advance, periodically halting to fight off the swarms of Seljuk horse-archers, until they reached the now abandoned Seljuk camp. With dusk falling Romanus decided that he had come far enough for one day. He had left his camp undefended and was afraid that the enemy might capture his baggage train. He therefore called a general halt and ordered his commanders to reverse the imperial standards as the sign for an orderly withdrawal. But on a battle-front stretching perhaps five or six miles and in the heat of fighting, parade-ground manoeuvres were almost impossible to interpret.

Watching from the hills, at the edge of the plain, Alp Arslan could hardly believe his eyes. The huge Byzantine army was beginning to break up in confusion. He sent for his horse and rode out at the head of his reserve cavalry. The Seljuks circled around Romanus's division in the centre, cutting it off from the wings. The emperor was trapped and fighting for his life. In this moment of crisis Romanus sent riders to Andronicus Ducas ordering him to lead the reserve to his aid, but Ducas took no notice and continued retreating, unmolested by the Turks. Seeing that the emperor was in difficulties he had set up the cry that Romanus was dead and ordered his men to withdraw to the camp. He had chosen his moment supremely well: the Ducas clan was avenged – but at what cost to the people and nation?

With both Byzantine wings in full retreat pursued by thousands of triumphant Muslim warriors, Alp Arslan concentrated his attacks on the cream of the imperial army, which was trapped and fighting desperately around the emperor. Pouring volleys of arrows into the fast-diminishing circle of defenders, the Seljuks soon identified Romanus himself, surrounded by a ring of Varangian Guards in their scarlet cloaks and swinging their deadly axes. Some of them were replaying the tragic scene of five years before when they had fought around Harold Godwinson's banner of the Fighting Man at Hastings. Romanus himself fought furiously until his horse was killed by an arrow and fell, pinning him to the ground. A Mameluke warrior dragged him clear, taking a living Byzantine emperor prisoner for the first time in the history of the empire.

Alp Arslan treated the captive emperor with more kindness than his own people were to show him. When news of the disaster reached Constantinople the exiled John Ducas returned to the capital and seized power, deposing Romanus in favour of the young Michael VII. Shortly afterwards, Romanus was released and allowed to return home, but the traitor Andronicus Ducas led an army against him and, in spite of giving him a guarantee of safety, seized the ex-emperor and blinded him so horribly that he died from his wounds.

It seemed that the empire had a death wish. Within a century of its apogee under the warrior-emperors of the tenth century it had sunk to its nadir under squabbling and self-seeking nonentities. Only a political or military genius could save the day as Heraclius had done in 610. However, military geniuses were in short supply and the Byzantines had to make do with the Byzantine ruler *par excellence*, Alexius Comnenus, part soldier, part priest, part diplomat but wholly politician.

In the aftermath of the 'Dreadful Day', as the battle of Manzikert became known to contemporaries, the assumption was that the Byzantine Empire could not survive without immediate help. This proved to be wrong. The Seljuks had no plan to conquer the empire and the Byzantines were soon to discover that they faced more danger from the Normans in Italy than they did from the Turks in Asia Minor. Nevertheless, the survival of the empire was the most important issue in the eyes of the Byzantine rulers and when they made their appeals to the West for help their intention was to recruit enough mercenary soldiers to guarantee this aim. As the people of the 'Christian empire', the Byzantines saw their own survival as a religious as well as a military issue. Constantinople was, to their mind, the centre of Christianity, not Jerusalem, which had been in Muslim hands for more than 400 years. Yet, it was out of their appeals to the West that the Crusades grew, the great movement to free the holy city of Jerusalem. And rather than strengthening the Byzantines with western troops the Crusaders began to see the Greek Christians as part of the problem rather than the solution.

TWELVE

The First Crusade

The unexpected splintering of Seljuk authority in the 1090s offered the new emperor, Alexius Comnenus, an opportunity to reconquer Asia Minor but only if he were able to enlarge his army by recruiting more foreign mercenaries. Already the Byzantine army had been reduced by the loss of its usual recruiting areas in Anatolia and things would have to get worse before they could get better. The western troops that Alexius had been able to hire allowed him to guard the territory that he still had but not to mount any campaigns of conquest. For this he would need a large influx of western military strength. Alexius hoped to win allies in the West, both political and ecclesiastical, who could help him solve his military deficiencies and when, in 1089, he met Count Robert of Flanders, who was undertaking a pilgrimage, he immediately raised the subject of recruiting soldiers. Count Robert seemed happy to help and sent a small contingent of Flemish knights to Constantinople where their military qualities were much admired by the emperor. This encouraged Alexius to widen his approach by asking the new pope, Urban II, to see if he could spread the word throughout western Christendom.

Hopeful of mending the doctrinal rift with Constantinople which had occurred in 1054, the pope entertained some of Alexius's envoys at the Council of Piacenza in March 1095. Whoever these envoys were, they were very persuasive talkers and convinced their listeners that the Greek Empire's future was on a knife's edge. Without help from a western army the eastern Christians were doomed. They never actually mentioned Jerusalem or the Holy Sepulchre because their need was for mercenaries to help Alexius regain the Anatolian territories lost after the battle of Manzikert. In fact, contrary to the claims of Pope Urban, pilgrims to Jerusalem were not suffering mole-station at that time and the Holy Sepulchre was safer in the 1090s than it had been a century before. However, the Byzantine emissaries overplayed their hand and, ironically, helped Pope Urban to advance his own hobby-horse: Church unity under the primacy of Rome.

Once Alexius's emissaries had spoken at Piacenza there was no stopping Pope Urban. It was undeniable that since the time of Constantine in the fourth century the emperors at Constantinople had been the defenders of Christendom. However, Alexius's appeal to the West was a clear indication that he was no longer able to carry out this function and therefore the West must take on the mantle, with the pope standing in for the emperor as the spiritual head. Urban left Italy and began spreading his ideas as he passed through southern France, an area that had already played a part in the Spanish Reconquista and would therefore be receptive to the idea of holy war.

Urban summoned a Church council to attend him at Clermont, in Burgundy, and decided to leave the matter of help for Byzantium to a public meeting on the last day of the council, 27 November, when he would make a speech. So many prominent figures, both clerical and temporal, were invited that it was decided to hold the meeting in a field on the edge of the town. Alexius had asked for mercenary troops but what he got was beyond his expectations or his wishes; it was almost an invasion of the sort Rome had faced in the fourth and fifth centuries. It was a crusade: not the sort of 'ersatz' crusade in which the Byzantines had themselves indulged in the previous cen-tury, but a real crusade of potential Christian martyrs. This was not holy war as the Byzantines understood it; it was something very different. In the first place, whereas the Byzantines regarded all wars as holy, they also saw war itself as evil, if occasionally necessary, and not something to be undertaken lightly. However, the concept of the 'crusade' as it developed in western Europe was very much linked to the notions of the 'just war'. Holy war or crusading was seen as positively pleasing to God and those who fought in holy wars were fighting in a blessed cause which merited God's special favour. For this they could expect to have their sins forgiven and their penance commuted by papal proclamation.[132]

At Clermont the pope's throne was set up on a platform so that he could look out over his entire congregation. Urban must have struggled to project his voice but there is no doubt that he was heard by ears straining not to miss a word or even a nuance. What followed was one of the most famous and most important speeches in history. Certainly the arguments of Alexius's delegates formed a part of Urban's great appeal. Yet where the Byzantines had been most concerned with the fate of Constantinople and the need to regain their lands lost to the Seljuk Turks since Manzikert, the pope soon began to follow his own agenda. He apparently started by painting a vivid picture of the oppression of the eastern Church at the hands of the infidel Turks and stressed the widespread destruction of churches and monasteries. He also pointed out that the great city of Antioch, the city of St Peter, had been taken by the Turks and that its holy places were at the mercy of the infidel. Then Jerusalem became the subject of his speech. He told his listeners that Christian pilgrims on their way to the holy places were frequently robbed or even murdered by the Muslims. It was time, he told them, for the Christians of the West to go to the defence of their co-religionists in the Holy Land:

O what a disgrace if a race so despised as the Turks, so base and full of demons, should overcome a people faithful to the All-powerful God, and resplendent with the name of Christ! O what reproaches will be charged against you by the Lord Himself if you do not help our fellow Christians! Let those who delight in making private wars against the Faithful turn their wrath against infidels, who should have been driven back before now. Let robbers become soldiers of Christ. Let them fight barbarians, not brothers. Let those who will fight and kill for any low wage now labour instead for an eternal reward. Let those dejected in mind and body offer themselves to the glory of heaven. And if any who goes should lose his life, by land or sea, or in fighting the pagans, his sins shall be remitted. This I will grant by the power invested in me by God.[133]

Then he issued the incentive which had not been heard in the Christian world since the days of Heraclius and which had formed part of the psychological armour of Muslim armies since the time of Mohammed. Pope Urban told them that those who took the cross and marched to Jerusalem 'from devotion only, not from advantage

of honour or gain' and who died in the service of their faith were
absolved from their sins and died as Christian martyrs:

> If it befall you to die this side of Jerusalem, be sure that Christ
> shall number you in His army. God pays with the same shilling,
> whether at the first or at the eleventh hour. To kill Christians is a
> matter of horror; but it is not wicked to flourish your sword
> against Saracens. That is righteous warfare, and it is charity to
> risk your life for your brothers. Do not trouble about the concerns
> of tomorrow. Those who fear God want nothing, nor those who
> cherish Him in truth. Moreover, the possessions of the enemy will
> be yours, since their treasures will be the spoil for your victorious
> arms. Or if your blood gushes out, and you die, you will have
> gained everlasting glory. For such a commander as Christ you
> ought to fight. Short is the way, little the labour, which will repay
> you with the crown that does not fade. Accordingly, I say to every
> one of you: gird yourselves, and be valiant sons. For it is better to
> die in battle than to behold the sorrows of your race and the
> distress of the Holy Places.[134]

Although we have four separate accounts of what the pope said
we do not have the precise text. Nevertheless, this extract conveys
the spirit of the occasion:

> Enter upon the road to the Holy Sepulchre, wrest that land from
> the wicked race and make it subject to yourselves. Jerusalem is the
> navel of the world; the land is fruitful above others, like another
> paradise of delights. The Redeemer of the human race has made it
> illustrious by His advent, has beautified it by His presence, has
> consecrated it by His suffering, has redeemed it by His death, and
> has glorified it by His burial. Now this royal city is held in
> subjection by those who do not know God. Therefore, she cries
> out to be liberated and implores you to come to her aid. She calls
> to you, in particular, because God has given you, above all
> nations, great glory in arms.[135]

The response was immense, beyond anyone's imaginings.
Hundreds of the pope's listeners led by Bishop Adhemar of Le Puy

immediately jostled around Urban's throne to take the cross there and then. It is almost impossible for modern readers to appreciate the importance of the religious sites in Jerusalem, notably the Holy Sepulchre, for the medieval mind. It was the supreme penitential shrine in Christendom, the place a pilgrim visited not only to be cured physically, as at Lourdes, but to be cured spiritually too. The journey to Jerusalem and the suffering it engendered was in itself the penance an individual pilgrim paid God for his sins.

The idea of the crusade spread like wildfire and soon, not just in France but in western parts of Germany and in Anglo-Norman lands, thousands of potential crusaders were responding to the pope's appeal. However, in Constantinople, the Byzantine emperor was shocked at the outcome of Urban's speech. The crusade might very well be a western concept but it was in his lands that it was going to take place. The nature of the crusaders, ranging from penitential peasants to land-hungry nobles, was not at all what Alexius needed. He knew that the former could be of no military use and would just be a drain on resources until they met martyrdom at the hands of the Turks. The latter, on the other hand, would be as much of a threat to the Byzantines as the Turks themselves, using their military skills to win lands for themselves that had previously belonged to the Byzantine Empire. With the Byzantines playing hosts to these ragtag Christian armies, Alexius could see nothing but trouble and expense for his people and himself. To make matters worse, one of the crusading armies was being led by Bohemond of Taranto, one of the bitterest of all the enemies of Byzantium and somebody who would happily usurp Alexius's throne if he got the chance. Yet Alexius would have to welcome him as a friend and ally.

Alexius realized the danger posed by the logistical needs of thousands of soldiers and began to stockpile food supplies along their expected route. He also recruited thousands of extra Pecheneg mercenaries to supervise the marchers and try to prevent them ravaging the countryside through which they travelled. He realized that the peasant armies, which were the first to leave western Europe and travelled without disciplined leadership, could legitimately be seen as little less than a swarm of locusts passing through the lands of unsuspecting Christian villagers. Their aims might be laudable but their methods would hardly be so and violence was almost certain.

Towards the end of March 1096 crowds of poor crusaders began to leave northern France on their way to the East led by Peter the Hermit, a fanatical French monk who expected God to show him the way, and a knight known as Walter Sans-Avoir, 'the Penniless'. First they moved through Germany, picking up large numbers of crusaders, including two monks named Gottschalk and Volkmar, and a very dubious nobleman known as Count Emich of Leiningen, who seemed to have his own agenda and claimed to have a cross miraculously branded on his back. Contrary to some historical accounts, this crusade did have a military element, counting many of the poorer footsoldiers and occasional renegade knights among its number. Even some respectable German lords, like Walter of Tegk and Hugh of Tubingen, joined the crusade, along with bands of soldiers, some disciplined others little more than groups of criminals and outlaws. One group of simple peasants who travelled with these desperadoes were said to be following a goose that had been inspired by God and others had a nanny goat pointing the way. But with no overall military leadership and without a strong cadre of junior officers the military potential of this crusade was negligible, though the capacity of so many violent men to work harm on friend and foe alike was much more considerable.

Peter the Hermit left Cologne in April 1096 but many Germans decided to follow him later in the companies assembled by the monk Gottschalk and Count Emich. Unfortunately, some of the German crusaders had no intention of following the cross to Jerusalem but were planning to exploit the opportunity to attack the Jews of the Rhineland cities. French Jews had written to those in Germany warning them of the danger of Peter's crusaders but unwisely they assumed that the rowdier elements would be kept under control by their leaders. With Count Emich as one of the leaders this was never going to happen. In fact, Emich used religious arguments to justify some of the pogroms that followed. As he claimed, why did he need to go all the way to Jerusalem to kill the Muslims who had seized the holy places of Christianity when the people who had killed Christ were living as their neighbours?

At Worms, Emich's crusaders killed 500 Jews, even though they were protected by of the local bishop and the crusaders had to violate the laws of sanctuary to do so. The Jews of Mainz sent Emich a seven pound weight of pure gold to pass by their city but it was not enough. They had begged the protection of the archbishop himself but Emich's followers burned the archbishop's palace and killed up to a thousand Jews. The crusaders next moved on to Cologne, but warned by the news from Mainz the Jews scattered into the countryside or were sheltered by Christian families.

The pogroms spread to Hungary, where the German crusaders who had followed Volkmar began massacring Jews, but the Hungarians would not allow the atrocities and used force to resist what they saw as a barbarian invasion. After a series of small battles the German crusaders were annihilated. Count Emich's crusaders were not so easily defeated and it took a number of pitched battles with the Hungarians to turn them back at the border. Eventually, many of the German crusaders were killed but Count Emich and some of the worst of his followers were able to return to Germany unharmed. The collapse of these disreputable expeditions cast a cloud over the whole crusading movement. For some observers it seemed to indicate God's disapproval of the whole enterprise.

The well-meaning Peter the Hermit was the leader of the first crusading force to approach the Byzantine frontiers. It is said that 40,000 French and German pilgrims followed Peter, including women, children and the sick or lame who hoped to be healed in Jerusalem. Few knights or professional soldiers travelled with this force and, as Alexius realized, it would take a miracle for Peter's followers to avoid annihilation by the first Muslim army they encountered. In fact, Peter's followers had had their own adventures on the way and had began to suffer severe losses even before they left Christian lands. The ragtag army had reached Hungary where a dispute with local villagers – apparently about a pair of wooden clogs – escalated and finally resulted in the crusaders overrunning the town of Semlin and killing as many as 4,000 of the local inhabitants, as well as capturing the citadel overlooking the Sava river. They then crossed the river and burned the city of Belgrade, after pillaging it as if it were the home of infidels. Peter the Hermit had given no orders for the atrocity and Alexius's worst fears were being realized. When the crusaders attempted to storm the city of Nish, the local Byzantine commander sent in his mounted troops and put them to the sword, killing hundreds, perhaps thousands. He had no real option and after the 'battle' it was decided to allow the survivors to continue with their crusade, hopefully without further incident.

Peter the Hermit's army arrived at Constantinople on 1 August 1096 and, probably to their surprise, received a hearty welcome from Alexius and his people. As an experienced commander Alexius could see that this so-called army had no chance against the Turks. He should probably have advised them more strongly to await the arrival of the soldiers who were coming along behind them. On the other hand, he had already witnessed the dangers posed by this unruly mob and wanted to see the back of them. While they were camped on the outskirts of his capital, and allowed into Constantinople only in small, manageable groups, Alexius worked hard to assemble the ships necessary to transport them across the Bosphorus to the Asian shore. Even so, they still continued to loot villages, raping and robbing everywhere they went. It was with a profound sigh of relief that, on 6 August, he managed to get the whole of Peter's party across to the Asian shore to continue with their journey. As far as Alexius was concerned, Peter the Hermit's crusade was exactly what he had feared when he first heard of Pope Urban II's appeal. However, there was worse to come.

The Byzantines were neither surprised nor disappointed to hear that most of Peter's crusaders were wiped out by the Turks within weeks of entering Anatolia. The disaster put an end, for the moment, to the idea that God would steer the faithful a safe route to a land 'full of milk and honey'. In the meantime, Alexius began to prepare for the arrival of the other crusading armies that he knew had left France and Germany. Peter's rabble may have been a nuisance but they had in no way threatened the survival of the Byzantine state. Alexius had recognized the zeal of the crusading fanatics and had understood that these people were, in the main, driven by profound religious impulses. The emperor's daughter, Anna, described his feelings on the imminent arrival of the Franks:

Alexius had no time to relax before he heard a rumour of the approach of innumerable Frankish armies. He feared their arrival since he knew their uncontrollable passion, their unstable and erratic character, and all the other peculiar traits of the Celtic temperament, with their inevitable consequences: how greedy they were for money, which led them to break agreements for the slightest whim and without scruple.[136]

The lords who would presently arrive in Constantinople were very different to the crusaders who had preceded them and posed greater problems for the Byzantines. They could not simply be shipped to the Asian shore and left to their own devices. They were coming as potential conquerors, Alexius believed, and were travelling under the respectable cloak of religion. He had experienced the ferocious acquisitiveness of the Normans and decided to extract from each of the lords who came on the crusade an oath of loyalty to him, so that if they reconquered Byzantine territory from the Turks it was on the condition that it should be returned to the Byzantines. Alexius saw this as no more than such lords had done for their feudal lords in Europe. In fact, he started well by successfully extracting an oath from the first to arrive, Hugh of Vermandois, brother of King Philip I of France, who came by sea. However, the next two proved thoroughly intractable.

Viewed as two of the greatest of all crusaders, Godfrey of Bouillon and his brother Baldwin of Boulogne were not at all happy about swearing an oath to Alexius. Their intentions were clear. Baldwin, who arrived with his wife and family, clearly wanted to find himself a kingdom at the expense of the Turks and, if necessary, even of the Byzantine Christians. The forces that accompanied the brothers comprised some of the cream of western chivalry, numbering many famous knights from northern France, Flanders and the Low Countries. These men posed a real threat to the Byzantines and Alexius felt it absolutely necessary to tie Godfrey and Baldwin to him by an oath. He therefore decided to use Hugh of Vermandois as a go-between. Hugh arrived at the brothers' camp and invited them to a meeting with the emperor at which they would swear allegiance to him. Godfrey, as Duke of Lorraine, refused, saying that he had sworn fealty to the king of Germany for his lands.

In order to exert pressure on the new arrivals Alexius began reducing food supplies to their camp but when Baldwin began raiding villages in the vicinity of the capital Alexius could see that his bluff had been called. The two brothers now increased their pressure on the emperor by drawing up their troops along the land walls of the city. The fact that they had chosen to begin the operation on the Thursday before Good Friday in Holy Week had almost as much effect on the Byzantines as the military threat they seemed to pose. Godfrey and Baldwin had heard from survivors of Peter the Hermit's crusade that their disaster had been the result of Byzantine treachery and so they were prepared to fight their hosts if necessary. Alexius, hearing that Bohemond's Normans were not far away, decided he must act quickly to get control of the situation. He therefore called out his own troops and manned the city walls, ordering his archers to fire over the heads of the crusaders. At first the crusaders withdrew but after reorganizing themselves they turned and began to assault the walls. Alexius had no option now but to send in his best regiments and a battle took place before the city walls. A number of lives were lost before the crusaders at last retreated. Alexius's strong response eventually won the day and Godfrey and Baldwin agreed to swear an oath to return to the empire any former Byzantine lands that they subsequently conquered. Nevertheless, the boorish behaviour of the crusaders contrasted sharply with that of the Byzantines, who loaded these troublesome westerners with gifts and helped them on their way.

The crusaders were overawed by the splendour of the Byzantine court but would not admit it. For the last 300 or 400 years Byzantine emperors had been using psychological weapons as often as military ones to overcome the numerous barbarian tribes who surrounded the empire's frontiers. When emissaries from all parts of the world were presented to the emperor they were subjected to a process which was designed to amaze and baffle them, and which had apparently been created by the Emperor Theophilus in the ninth century. In the emperor's throne room artificial trees housed mechanical birds which sang while the emissaries were brought in by eunuchs. They were led up towards the bronze and golden throne, in front of which apparently live lions beat their tails and roared. They were then instructed by the eunuchs to carry out the *proskynesis*, throwing themselves forward three times in front of the throne, before lifting their heads and gasping in amazement.

The throne, which had originally been set on a simple raised platform, had somehow risen up to the height of the ceiling and the seated emperor was now bathed in lighting which made his clothes dazzle like those of a god.

But the westerners refused to show that they were impressed. One incident illustrates the cultural divide that existed between the two parts of Christendom. During the oath-swearing ceremony one of Baldwin's knights, having taken the vow to Alexius, promptly sat down on the emperor's throne. When Baldwin remonstrated with the man he replied that it was boorish of the emperor to sit while so many valiant captains were forced to stand. Alexius had the comment translated and then spoke to the knight, possibly a man named Rainauld de Toul. Rainauld boasted that he was invincible in single combat, whereupon the emperor wisely observed that before he met the Turks he had better develop some different tactics.

The next day Alexius arranged the shipment of Godfrey and Baldwin's troops to the Asian shore. The emperor acted just in time for within days the Norman contingent of Bohemond of Taranto arrived. If there was going to be real trouble, Alexius concluded, this was the occasion. Bohemond was the eldest son of Robert Guiscard, one of Alexius's most formidable enemies during the previous decade, who, before his untimely death in 1085, had come close to taking the throne of Byzantium itself. As Anna Comnena records, Bohemond was one of the most impressive of all the crusaders, towering over virtually everyone and pre-eminent in every fight. His commitment to the crusade might be questioned by modern historians but when he took the cross at Amalfi it was with a show of sincerity that persuaded many others to follow suit. In Steven Runciman's words: 'In front of his assembled army Bohemond took off his rich, scarlet cloak and tore it into pieces to make crosses for his captains.'[137]

With Bohemond's army travelled not only his dynamic nephew Tancred, but also six direct descendants of the almost legendary Norman hero, Tancred de Hauteville, who had established Norman rule in southern Italy. Bohemond and his close relations were heading east to find themselves land, which is exactly what Alexius feared. Nevertheless, the further from Constantinople Bohemond travelled, the better the emperor would be pleased. At their first

meeting Bohemond showed himself willing to swear an oath to
Alexius but he also made an extraordinary and cunning suggestion.
Bohemond asked Alexius to appoint him Grand Domestic of the
East, a military command held in the previous century by such
famous generals as Nicephorus Phocas and John Tzimisces. In
refusing, Alexius had to think no further than the fact that both
these men had become emperor and that Bohemond was certainly
no more to be trusted than those great heroes. Bohemond, in fact,
was quite unlike the uncouth northern knights who had only
recently passed through Constantinople. He spoke Greek fluently
and was a skilful diplomat as well as a famous warrior. As Grand
Domestic, of course, he would have had both a Byzantine rank and
command of an army. For Alexius to grant this to the enemy of his
house would have been supreme folly. Nevertheless, Bohemond
behaved impeccably, hoping no doubt to win the support of Alexius
and possibly gain overall leadership of the crusade. Alexius must
have been relieved when he was able to transport Bohemond and his
party to the Asian shore.

The next crusader to arrive at Constantinople was a most distinguished one, with a great deal of experience of fighting the Muslims
in Spain. He was the immensely rich Raymond of St Gilles, Count of
Toulouse. As the very first crusader to take the cross at Clermont
and one who had made it clear that he did not intend to return
home from the Holy Land he held more prestige than any of the
others. Escorted as he was by a substantial army, possibly 10,000
strong, and Bishop Adhemar of Le Puy, the pope's representative
and spiritual head of the crusade, he had a strong claim to command
of the entire expedition.

Surprisingly, Raymond and Adhemar as chief representatives of
the 'official' party showed a lax attitude towards discipline in their
army. Their soldiers were as badly behaved as the followers of
Godfrey and Baldwin had been and soon Alexius was faced with the
problem of enforcing discipline. In fact, the matter was taken out of
his hands by his Pecheneg mercenaries. These fierce tribesmen
preyed on crusaders who strayed from the allotted roads and one
extraordinary incident almost cost the life of the bishop himself – he
was badly injured by a Pecheneg attack, as were some of his
clergymen. Even Count Raymond himself suffered an assault near

Odessa. On the other hand, the patience of the Pechenegs must have been sorely tried by the unruly Franks, who plundered and burned the city of Roussa, in Thrace.

Alexius, hearing of the progress of this powerful and dangerous army through his territory, sent messengers asking Count Raymond to come ahead of his army to Constantinople. This was a mistake. In the absence of Raymond, his army became even more ill-behaved, so much so that local Byzantine commanders were forced to call up reinforcements and fight a pitched battle against the crusaders, killing some and seizing their camp. Count Raymond was in the capital with Alexius when this news reached him. It merely confirmed him in his determination not to swear an oath to the emperor. He had heard of Bohemond's attempt to gain a military rank in the Byzantine army and believed that if he swore an oath to Alexius this would enable Bohemond to gain total command of the crusade. He therefore suggested that he would follow Alexius if he, as emperor, took command of the crusade. Alexius, however, had no intention of leaving Constantinople and heading this risky operation to Jerusalem while anyone might usurp his throne in his absence. For two weeks an impasse existed between the emperor and Count Raymond. Alarmed at the possibility that the crusade's most powerful contingent might withdraw, other leaders, including the bishop, pleaded with Raymond to reach a compromise. Eventually, the count agreed to take an oath 'to respect the life and honour of the emperor' and to do nothing to his detriment. It was as vague as Raymond wanted it and Alexius wisely accepted it.

The last crusader force to arrive was one of the most impressive, comprising an army of English, Norman and Breton knights commanded by Robert of Normandy, eldest son of William the Conqueror. With him travelled Count Stephen of Blois, Count Robert of Flanders and the famous survivor from the battle of Hastings, Bishop Odo of Bayeux. This party included some of the most civilized of the western crusaders who greatly appreciated the luxury of Constantinople and the gifts with which Alexius plied them. Stephen of Blois was so impressed that he wrote home to his wife Adela, daughter of William the Conqueror, to tell her that compared to Alexius and his lords William had been 'almost nothing'.[138] (In view of the fact that William had been dead for ten years Stephen was presumably confident in saying something he would not have dared to speak to the Conqueror's face.) This group of crusaders brought no problems for the Byzantines, swore their oaths without difficulty, and spent much of their time acting like tourists in Constantinople. Suitably wined and dined they were shipped over to the Asian shore to join their fellows and the united Christian force then advanced, still through Byzantine territory, towards their first target, Nicea.

The cultural clash between East and West cast long shadows. Each had been offended by the other and just as some of the Franks would have been happier to travel no further than Constantinople in pursuit of their aims, there were some Byzantines who would not have been unhappy to learn of Turkish success against their erstwhile guests.

Once out of the emperor's reach few of the westerners, with the exception of Count Raymond of Toulouse, kept their word. Instead they won kingdoms for themselves from territory that had been Byzantine, although not since the time of Heraclius and perhaps that was just too long ago.

The main Byzantine gain from the crusade was Nicea, which was besieged and captured by combined Byzantine and Frankish forces in June 1097. Nicea brought with it strategic control of Western Anatolia and so Alexius was able to reflect on a major gain for the price of a few good dinners and some trifling gifts that were more valued by the recipients than by the Byzantines themselves. However, relations between Alexius and the crusaders was strained by the way in which the Byzantines tricked their allies. To prevent an essentially Christian city suffering a sack the Byzantines secretly negotiated for the Turks to surrender Nicea. Robbed of a city to pillage, the crusaders blamed the Byzantines and accused them of treachery. Alexius responded by trying to compensate them with more gifts. Every crusader, rich or poor, received a gift of fine food, while the lords were given piles of treasure. Stephen of Blois was impressed with Alexius's generosity and did not join his colleagues in condemning the emperor for his treachery at Nicea.

The Frankish crusaders were also horrified at the elegant way in which the emperor received the aristocratic prisoners taken in Nicea.

Centuries of warfare between Christians and Muslims in the East
had shown both sides the futility of mistreating prisoners and so
senior officers were allowed to ransom themselves while the sultana,
wife of the Emir Chaka, was taken to Constantinople to live in royal
state until her husband could arrange to collect her and her children.
She was eventually released to him without any ransom.

Added to the acquisition of Nicea was the major effect on the
Seljuk Turks of Bohemond's decisive victory at Dorylaeum on 1 July
1097. The damage to Seljuk military potential in the region was
so great that the Byzantines had no reason to fear them again.
However, that was the extent of Byzantine profit, for as the
crusaders pressed on, one of the men who had sworn fealty to
Alexius, Baldwin of Boulogne, left the main body of the army and
captured the former Byzantine city of Edessa, on the middle
Euphrates, where he carved out a state with himself as count. His
stay in Edessa was a short one because within two years he was
forced to travel south to Jerusalem to replace his brother, Godfrey of
Bouillon, as ruler of the kingdom and to become its first anointed
king, his brother having refused to take such a title and being
known instead as the Advocate of the Holy Sepulchre. Bohemond,
ironically, was the only one of the crusaders who acknowledged
Alexius as his liege lord; he did so when he captured Antioch and
declared himself prince of the city.

Fortune favoured the First Crusade in that, divided as its leaders
were, its Muslim enemies were even more so. Moreover, the Saracens
– a term one increasingly needs to use for the mixed forces of
Syrians, Turks, Iraqis, Kurds and Egyptians that made up the armies
of Islam – found themselves up against the heaviest cavalry they had
faced since the brief period when the Byzantines, under Nicephorus
Phocas, reintroduced the cataphracts as a shock force. The western
Franks, in the tradition of the Parthian and Sasanian *clibonarii* and
cataphractarii, were simply irresistible in the charge and prompted a
tactical rethink on the part of the Muslim military establishment. At
Dorylaeum in 1097 the crusader rearguard completely changed the
outcome of the battle by a devastating charge when the Seljuks were
convinced that victory was theirs.

Ultimately the difference between the 'ersatz crusaders' of Byzantium and the 'true believers' from the West was demonstrated, as

indeed it should have been, by the final challenge of the entire enterprise: the capture of Jerusalem.

Alexius clearly identified the Frankish leaders, notably men like Bohemond and Tancred, or the brothers Godfrey and Baldwin, as little different from the military families that grew up on the Anatolian frontier in the previous century, who the Emperor Basil II had crushed to such unfortunate effect for the empire. Indeed, Alexius was one of the more recent parvenus himself. He presumed that they were coming east to find land for themselves, even kingdoms in some cases.

When the western lords were in Constantinople they expected Alexius to take the leadership of the crusade, particularly as he had demanded that they should swear fealty and homage to him. However, he refused, claiming that his capital was in too much danger from hostile neighbours for him to be able to leave it. There was some truth in this but almost certainly he doubted that the crusaders could achieve their aim of taking and keeping Jerusalem. Their astonishing triumph at Antioch, won apparently with God's help against overwhelming odds, seems to have caused him to reconsider. After the capture of the city the dispute between Bohemond and Raymond of Toulouse prompted the latter to renew the offer of the leadership of the crusade to Alexius. This time he agreed but the rest of the crusaders were not prepared to wait for the Byzantines to arrive in force and continued towards the holy city without imperial help. Alexius was playing a political game but to his astonishment he found that most of the westerners, with the exception perhaps of Bohemond, were taking the spiritual side of the crusade very seriously.

By the early summer of 1099 when the westerners reached Jerusalem it was too late for Alexius to assume the leadership of the crusade which should by seniority and tradition have been his right and duty, and so, by default, Latin Christendom was to take possession of the Holy Land.

By 1099 Jerusalem had seen much blood and suffering. It had undergone many sieges and had changed hands many times. Destroyed by the Romans in 70 and by the Persians in 614, it had passed to Muslim control in 638 with hardly a struggle. Now, on 15 July 1099, it was about to return to Christian hands in a bloody massacre that would set the pattern for centuries of holy war. The

Frankish leaders had never had to besiege such powerful fortifications in Europe and found it impossible to secure enough wood in the environs of the city to build siege engines. For four weeks the crusaders conducted their siege, becoming more desperate all the time. It was only the fortuitous arrival at the port of Jaffa of six Genoese and English ships under the command of the Embriaco brothers that changed the situation. Some of the Italian ships were dismantled; the wood, masts and ropes enabled the carpenters to construct two siege towers called belfreys, which could be wheeled towards the walls of Jerusalem. It was one of these machines that enabled the vital breakthrough to take place.

At noon, the hour Christians traditionally associate with the crucifixion of Jesus Christ, the movable siege tower of Godfrey of Bouillon was in position at the eastern end of the northern walls of Jerusalem. At this point, east of the Gate of Flowers, the walls were some fifty feet high, but the tower overlooked them by some seven to ten feet. In the upper section of the tower were Duke Godfrey himself, his brother Eustace of Boulogne and a company of knights; while in the middle section were Ludolph and Engelbert of Tournai. Amidst the noise of war – the crashing of great boulders on the timber of the tower, the crackling sounds of burning thatch, the curious whirring and hissing noises as pots of Greek fire flew through the air like shooting stars emitting fiery tails – the grim crusaders had little time for reflection. As they crouched low to the floor the siege tower was moved towards the walls of Jerusalem. The goal of their journey and all their suffering was now just feet away; and yet these last few steps would be the hardest of any they had taken since they left France two years before. Crouching, and occasionally crossing themselves or wiping the sweat from their eyes in the burning heat, the Frankish knights could sometimes make out the faces of the Muslims on the walls, faces contorted by fear and hatred, just as theirs must have seemed to their enemies. They were hardened soldiers, bred to their trade, veterans of a dozen such sieges and many battles in the field, and yet this was different. They had fought for their faith at Dorylaeum and Antioch, but it had not been like this. The Muslims who manned these walls seemed less than human, mere servants of Antichrist who were fighting now to prevent true believers from inheriting the city of God. Here in Jerusalem there was to be salvation for all, forgiveness for sins, cures for physical and mental ills, and – in the Church of the Holy Sepulchre – a tangible link with their Saviour Jesus Christ. In the heart of the crusaders there was a hatred more bitter than any they had known before.

The Muslim defenders made a final effort to halt the inexorable progress of Godfrey's tower. Ropes were thrown over the wooden leviathan and efforts made to topple the whole structure while rocks and pots of naptha crashed onto its walls of hide. But the crusaders managed to keep the tower intact by scything through the ropes which threatened it, and by using vinegar to extinguish the flames of a combustible log swung out against it by the defenders. In the smoke and confusion the Franks began to detect a slackening resistance. At once, Ludolph and Engelbert pushed out wooden planks from the middle section of the tower to the top of the walls and clambered onto the battlements, soon followed by Duke Godfrey and his knights. With a shout of triumph from the waiting troops below, a dozen ladders were placed against the walls and chosen soldiers now scaled them to join the Lorrainers on the battlements. There was hand-to-hand fighting now in which little skill was displayed. Men wrestled with each other, sometimes toppling together from the battlements, sometimes gouging at each other's eyes or tearing at throats. The press was too close for sword strokes, and handles were used like hammers. But the longer Duke Godfrey and his men held the wall, the longer it gave the Lorrainers and Normans to use their ladders, while across the perilous bridge of planks first tens and then hundreds of warriors flooded onto the walls. Soon, by sheer weight of numbers, the Muslims were pressed back and then turned to flee. At last Godfrey of Bouillon raised his banner above the walls as a signal that the city had been entered.

What followed was a terrible massacre born of frustration, of hope denied for too long and of fanaticism and hysteria that revealed the limitations of man as a reasoning creature. Significantly, during his recent visit to the Middle East, Pope John Paul II has seen fit to apologize for the crusades. No single event in the history of Christian–Islamic relations needed the apology of a descendant of Pope Urban II as much as this climax to the First Crusade in 1099.

In the Muslim holy places of the al-Aqsa Mosque and the Dome of the Rock, the bodies lay so thickly that they formed a mound of flesh. Moreover, the Christians had hacked their victims horribly, slashing open their stomachs in the search for the gold coins that it was rumoured the Muslims had swallowed to avoid losing them to the invaders. The result was blood literally ankle deep in some areas of the city where drainage was impossible. Yet the massacre was regarded by many of the crusaders as a sign of the triumph of Christianity.

Soon, however, the more practical among the crusaders realized that such killing was bound to spread disease unless the corpses were buried or burned. The immense task of disposing of the bodies proved too much for the few soldiers who were willing to stay in the city. Five months after the massacre Fulcher of Chartres, arriving in Jerusalem for the first time, commented: 'Oh, what a stench there was around the walls of the city, both within and without, from the rotting bodies of Saracens slain by ourselves.'[139] Just three days after the massacre, the crusaders tried to hold a street market in Jerusalem, amidst the carnage and in midsummer heat. It was no surprise when disease broke out in the holy city which was now little more than a charnel house. The heavenly city was now more like a medieval version of hell.

By a supreme irony, the crusaders had travelled to the Holy Land as penitents, asking to be forgiven their sins by God and in return, and in His name, they had committed a dreadful massacre. It was as if the western knights believed that fighting in the name of God removed from them any sense of individual guilt for their actions. Truly Christ had taken upon himself the sins of the world and had lifted from them any consequential responsibility. Many of the crusaders who intended to return home threw aside their weapons and their armour once the last Muslims were dead, and paraded to the River Jordan carrying palm fronds like penitential pilgrims. Either their temporary madness was past or it was just beginning. When all the palm leaves and corpses were cleared away from the streets of Jerusalem, and when all the promises to the Byzantine emperor were forgotten, those crusaders who stayed numbered just 300 knights and 2,000 infantry.

With Godfrey of Lorraine refusing the crown of Jerusalem and accepting instead the title Advocate of the Holy Sepulchre, the temporal government of the kingdom of Jerusalem was settled.

As the Orthodox Patriarch of Jerusalem had only recently been expelled by the Fatimid Arabs, the spiritual control of the holy city passed into the hands of the first Latin Patriarch, the pope's legate Daimbert, Archbishop of Pisa. He immediately banished all non-Latin Christians from Jerusalem: Greeks, Jacobites, Nestorians, Georgians and Armenians. The First Crusade was over and the schism in the Christian world was now deeper than it had ever been. The emperor in Constantinople was no longer the defender of Christians and Christendom, of the Holy Sepulchre and the True Cross, he was a potential enemy of the Latin Christians who now ruled the Holy Land. And instead of looking to him for protection as the descendant of Constantine, the first Christian emperor, the Franks of Outremer, as the conquered lands in Syria and the Levant would now be called, would instead look to the kings of France and England, to the emperor in Germany and, most of all, to the bishop of Rome.

APPENDIX ONE

Single Combat in Byzantine Warfare

Before the start of Persian and Byzantine battles it was customary for champions to ride out from the two sides to issue challenges. The Sasanians raised the cry of 'Mard u Mard' (Man to Man) which was a signal for these chivalric displays. The motive was perhaps twofold: morale might be raised by the success of the champions, while the more headstrong fighters who were disinclined to obey orders from their commanders would get their fill of fighting before more tactical manoeuvres took place. Byzantine chronicles contain accounts of many such challenges or duels, while the rock carvings in Persia show how important such actions were to Sasanian knights. Successes in such duels were attributed to the emperors Heraclius and John Tzimisces, and the Domestic Bardas Skleros achieved a well-documented victory over a Pecheneg champion, during which he almost cut his enemy in half.[140] The willingness of the Byzantine commanders to engage in single combat may not be as foolhardy as it appears. Byzantine armour was generally heavier and more resilient than that worn by their enemies, with the possible exception of the Persians. The iron maces carried by most of the *cataphractarii* (and commanders were always equipped as cataphracts) could crush the weaker helmets and armour of their opponents and yet resist the counter-strokes of the enemy. At Nineveh, for example, we are told that Heraclius suffered a number of blows but only minor wounds, while his horse was saved from serious injury by its armoured coat. In a battle against the Hamandrid Muslims John Tzimisces was isolated by the enemy and attacked by a mass of Arab spearmen. He suffered many blows but survived because of the quality of his armour. As one Arab writer recorded, spear points were no more harmful to him than feathers.

Heraclius, Mohammed and the Origin of Jihad

The extent to which Heraclius's use of the propaganda of holy war in 622 influenced Mohammed's development of the jihad has divided experts on the rise of Islam. Etan Kohlberg and Ella Landau-Tasseron believe that early Islamic chronology is so unreliable that any direct connection between Christian and Muslim thinking on martyrdom would be impossible to prove. They point out that holy war was practised as early as ancient Babylon and therefore Heraclius's use of it was by no means novel in the Near East. David Nicolle feels that martyrdom in warfare was by no means particular to Christianity but was instead more characteristic of Judaism, Zoroastrianism and even of some strains of militant Buddhism, which originated in Tibet and Afghanistan. Any of these sources might have influenced Mohammed's thinking in the seventh century as readily as Heraclius's Orthodox Christianity. Reuven Firestone demonstrates that martyrdom and the concept of winning Paradise through death in battle were not features of pre-Islamic Arabia but that Christianity from Monophysite areas, notably Egypt or Ethiopia, Judaism from Palestine and Zoroastrianism from Persia penetrated Arabia and may have had an effect on the development of Mohammed's ideas. Professor Firestone thinks it unlikely that Mohammed employed the 'martyrdom' argument prior to the battle of Badr because no large-scale offensive operations against tribes hostile to Mohammed took place before 624 and the battle of Badr itself only developed out of what had originally been intended as a raid. Patricia Crone points out that the ideas for jihad as expressed in the Koran are merely based on recollections recorded 200 years after the death of Mohammed, so that we cannot be certain about what similarities existed between Byzantine and Islamic holy war in the 620s. She doubts that much influence could have taken place as Heraclius's Persian crusade was based on a sudden and spontaneous doctrine that was more expedient than deeply philosophic. Dr Crone prefers the view that martyrdom in warfare was a very old doctrine in the Near East that resurfaced in Islam. Timothy Barnes, on the other hand, believes that martyrdom was a Christian concept from the second century, developing between the years 130 and 150. Gerald Hawting suggests it is possible that the Muslim jihad developed after the earliest Arab conquests but was then used in the earliest versions of the Koran as if it had been part of Mohammed's original teaching. Fred Donner questions the concept of an 'Arab world' as such and believes that at the time of Heraclius and Mohammed many of the inhabitants of the area known as Arabia were Christians, Jews or Zoroastrians who knew existing theories of holy war prevalent in the societies of Byzantium, Palestine and Persia. Thus so-called Christian Arabs of the period 570–620 would have been as aware as Greeks or Syrians of the part that martyrdom played in Christian holy warfare. Professor Donner, however, feels it would be difficult to evaluate the extent to which such Christian 'Arabs' could have influenced 'Arabs' living within the Hijaz, as Mohammed did.

Chronology

Zoroastrian Fire Temple. Battle of Badr – Mohammed first uses jihad against Arab pagans

625   Byzantines win three victories over Persians

626   Avar siege of Constantinople

627   Heraclius's third campaign against Persians in alliance with Turks Decisive Battle of Nineveh. Byzantines capture Dastagerd

628   Death of Khusro II. Kavad becomes king of Persia. End of war followed by Heraclius's triumphal entry into Constantinople

630   Heraclius returns True Cross to Jerusalem. Heraclius tries to repair split in Christian Church between Orthodoxy and Monophysitism. Mohammed enters Mecca – cleansing of Kaaba

632   Death of Mohammed

634   Muslim invasion of Palestine. Battle of Ajnadin: defeat of Theodore

635   Muslim occupation of much of Syria

636   Decisive Muslim victory over Byzantines at battle of Yamuk

638   Muslims capture Jerusalem. Onset of Heraclius's final illness

639   Arabs invade Egypt

640   Siege of Babylon. Arabs defeat Byzantines at Heliopolis

641   Death of Heraclius. Constantine III becomes emperor. Fall of Alexandria. Muslim conquest of Egypt

678   Defeat of Arabs at Constantinople by Greek fire

717–18   Arab siege of Constantinople defeated by Leo the Isaurian

863   Emir of Melitene defeated by Byzantines under Petronas

942   John Kourkuas's campaigns against Abbasids

963   Nicephorus Phocas becomes emperor

969   Overthrow and murder of Nicephorus Phocas by John Tzimisces. Shiite Fatimids conquer Egypt

972   John Tzimisces defeats Russians under Svyatoslav

975   'Crusade' by John Tzimisces into Syria and Palestine

976   Death of John Tzimisces. Basil II becomes emperor

1009   Caliph al-Hakim destroys Christian Holy Sepulchre

1054   Final split between Latin and Greek Christianity

1068   Romanus Diogenes becomes emperor

1071   Battle of Manzikert. Death of Romanus Diogenes

1081   Alexius Comnenus becomes emperor

1096   Council of Clermont. Start of western First Crusade

1097   Battle of Dorylaeum. Seljuks defeated

1099   Fall of Jerusalem. Godfrey of Bouillon becomes Advocate of the Holy Sepulchre. Kingdom of Jerusalem created

MAPS

AELIA CAPITOLINA 135–326

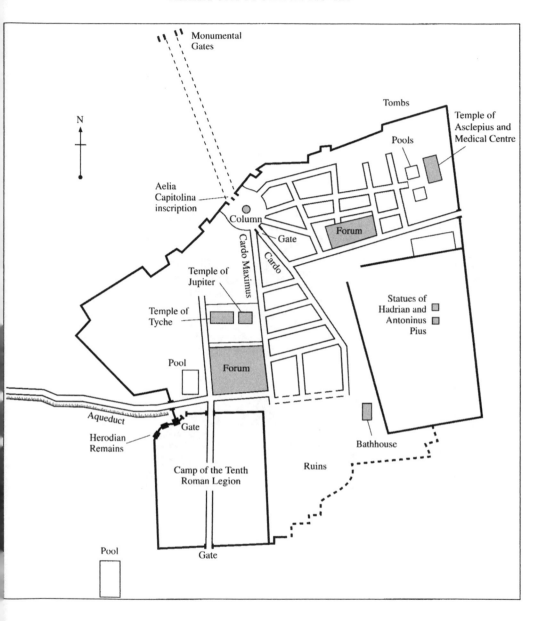

Monumental Gates

Tombs

Temple of Asclepius and Medical Centre

Pools

N

Aelia Capitolina inscription

Column

Gate

Forum

Cardo Maximus

Cardo

Temple of Jupiter

Temple of Tyche

Statues of Hadrian and Antoninus Pius

Pool

Forum

Aqueduct

Gate

Herodian Remains

Bathhouse

Camp of the Tenth Roman Legion

Ruins

Pool

Gate

CONSTANTINE'S CHURCH OF THE HOLY SEPULCHRE
reconstruction of fourth-century plan

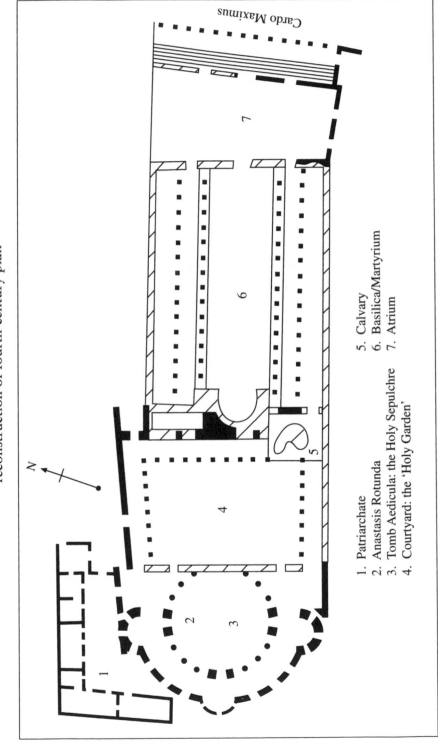

Cardo Maximus

1. Patriarchate
2. Anastasis Rotunda
3. Tomb Aedicula: the Holy Sepulchre
4. Courtyard: the 'Holy Garden'
5. Calvary
6. Basilica/Martyrium
7. Atrium

CONSTANTINOPLE IN THE SEVENTH CENTURY

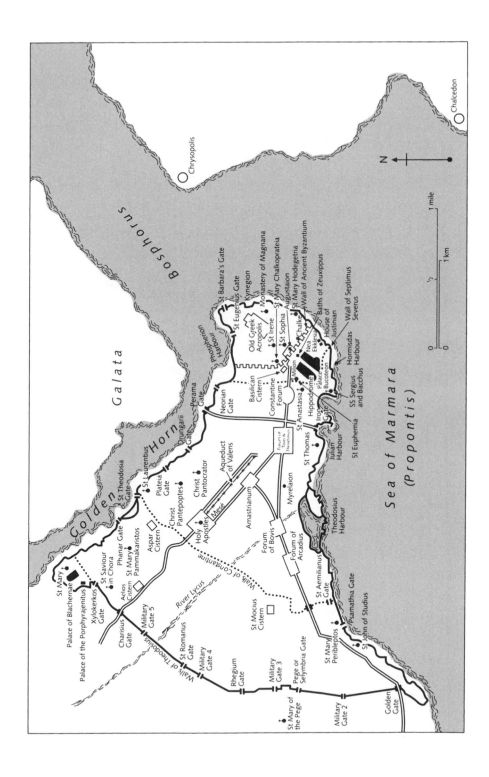

BYZANTINE JERUSALEM 326–638

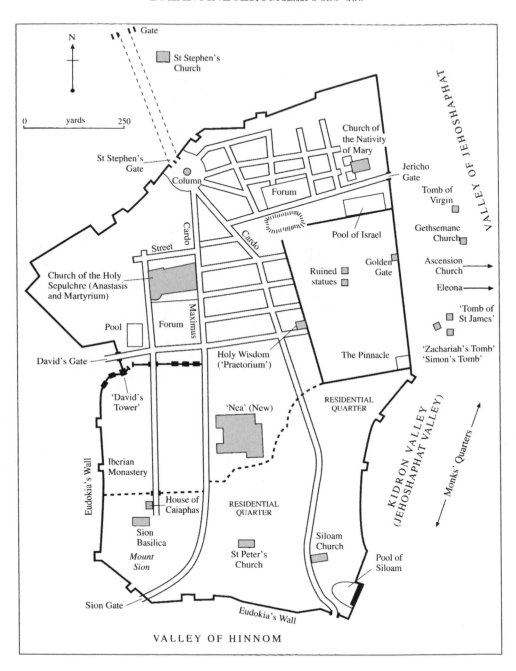

N

0   yards   250

Gate

St Stephen's
Church

St Stephen's
Gate

Column

Cardo

Street

Cardo

Forum

Church of
the Nativity
of Mary

Jericho
Gate

Tomb of
Virgin

Gethsemane
Church

Pool of Israel

Church of the Holy
Sepulchre (Anastasis
and Martyrium)

Maximus

Ruined
statues

Golden
Gate

Ascension
Church

Eleona

Pool

Forum

Holy Wisdom
('Praetorium')

The Pinnacle

'Tomb of
St James'

'Zachariah's Tomb'
'Simon's Tomb'

David's Gate

'David's
Tower'

'Nea' (New)

RESIDENTIAL
QUARTER

Eudokia's Wall

Iberian
Monastery

House of
Caiaphas

RESIDENTIAL
QUARTER

Sion
Basilica

Mount
Sion

St Peter's
Church

Siloam
Church

Pool of
Siloam

Sion Gate

Eudokia's Wall

VALLEY OF HINNOM

VALLEY OF JEHOSHAPHAT

KIDRON VALLEY
(JEHOSHAPHAT VALLEY)

Monks' Quarters

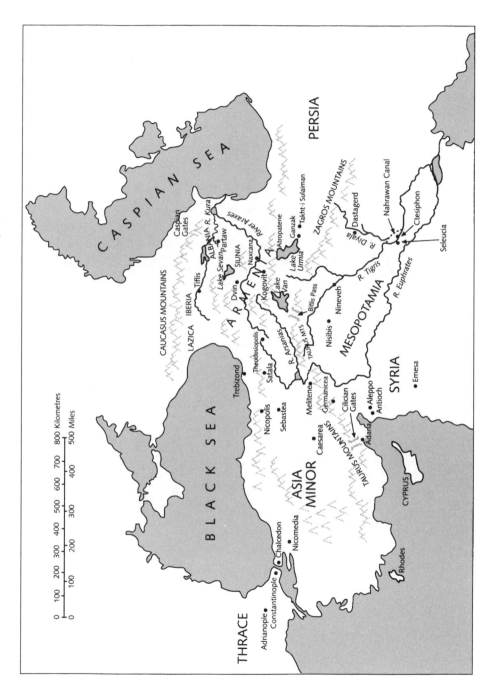

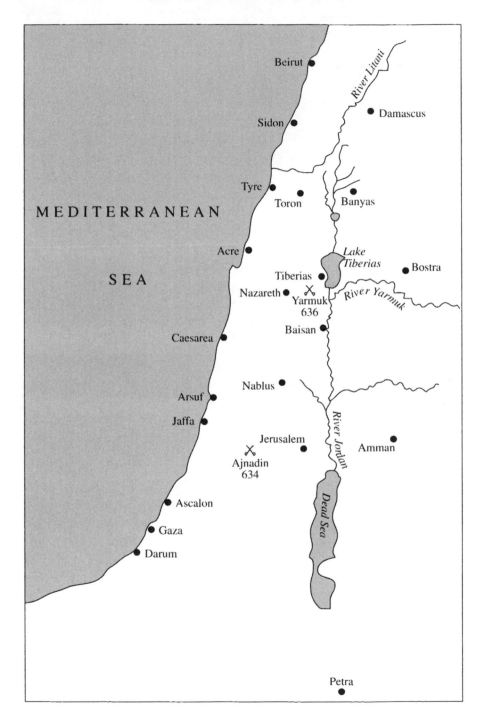

MEDITERRANEAN

SEA

Beirut

River Litani

Damascus

Sidon

Tyre

Toron

Banyas

Acre

Lake
Tiberias

Bostra

Tiberias

Nazareth

Yarmuk
636

River Yarmuk

Baisan

Caesarea

Nablus

Arsuf

Jaffa

Jerusalem

River Jordan

Amman

Ajnadin
634

Ascalon

Gaza

Dead Sea

Darum

Petra

ARAB CONQUEST OF EGYPT, 639–41: THE NILE DELTA

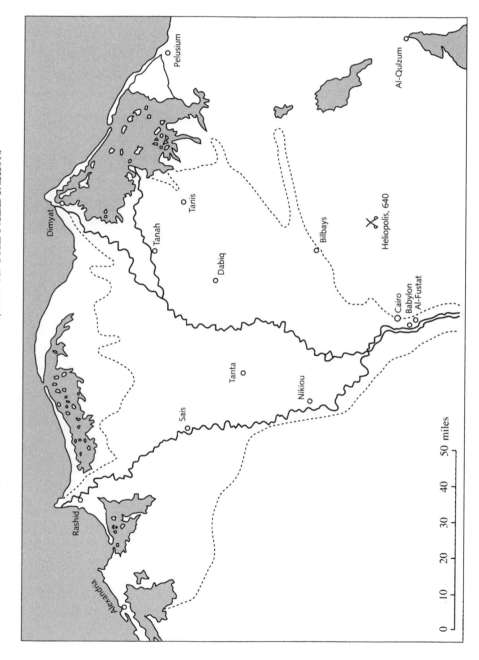

Notes

Publication details for sources quoted appear in the bibliography unless stated here.

1. T.M. Kolbaba, 'Fighting for Christianity: Holy War in the Byzantine Empire', pp. 210–11.
2. Ibid., pp. 210–11.
3. See M. Whitby, 'Deus Nobiscum: Christianity, Warfare and Morale in Late Antiquity' in M. Austin, J. Harries and C. Smith eds, *Modus Operandi: Essays in Honour of Geoffrey Rickman.*
4. Mary Whitby, 'A New Image for a New Age: George of Pisidia on the Emperor Heraclius' in E. Dabrowa ed., *The Roman and Byzantine Army in the East.*
5. J. Opsopaus, 'The Art of Haruspicy, which is the Etruscan discipline', passim.
6. Minucius Felix, 'Octavius', viii 3–xii 6, in N. Lewis and M. Reinhold eds, *Roman Civilization*, vol. 2, pp. 553–5.
7. T.D. Barnes, *Constantine and Eusebius*, p. 19.
8. Ibid., p. 21.
9. R. Lane Fox, *Pagans and Christians*, chapter 9; I. Lissner, *Power and Folly*, p. 336.
10. Barnes, *Constantine and Eusebius*, p. 29.
11. Lactantius, *On the Death of the Persecutors*, 33, 1–5.
12. Eusebius, *Life of Constantine*, I, 28.
13. Lissner, *Power and Folly*, p. 358.
14. J. Romer, *Testament*, p. 211.
15. R. Krautheimer, 'The Constantinian Basilica', p. 130.
16. A.H.M. Jones, *The Later Roman Empire*, p. 83.
17. Barnes, *Constantine and Eusebius*, p. 222.
18. J. Arnott Hamilton, *Byzantine Architecture and Decoration*, p. 23.
19. K. Armstrong, *Jerusalem*, pp. 180–2.
20. J. Wilkinson, 'Jerusalem under Rome and Byzantium' in K.J. Asali ed., *Jerusalem in History*, p. 88.
21. Ibid., p. 90.
22. M. Biddle, *The Tomb of Christ*, p. 57.
23. Eusebius, *Life of Constantine*, III, 26–8.
24. Biddle, *The Tomb of Christ*, p. 66.
25. Eusebius, *Life of Constantine*, III, 36.
26. See R. Ousterhout, 'The Church of the Holy Sepulchre'.
27. Ibid.
28. *Itinerary from Bordeaux to Jerusalem*, transl. A. Stewart, *Palestine Pilgrims' Text Society*, vol. 1, pp. 593–4
29. Egeria, 'Pilgrimage', p. 67.
30. Ibid. pp. 57–8.
31. Arnott Hamilton, *Byzantine Architecture*, p. 18.

32. S.P. Brock, 'Christians in the Sasanian Empire: A Case of Divided Loyalties', p. 7.
33. Ibid., p. 8.
34. Ibid., pp. 8–9.
35. See central thesis of D. Keys, *Catastrophe*.
36. For Maurice's wars against Persia see M. Whitby, *The Emperor Maurice and his Historian*, pp. 276–304.
37. See A. Cameron, *Circus Factions: Blues and Greens at Rome and Byzantium*.
38. J.J. Norwich, *Byzantium: The Early Centuries*, p. 278.
39. Ibid., p. 279.
40. For the collapse of Phocas's reign I am indebted to A.N. Stratos, *Byzantium in the Seventh Century*, vol. 1.
41. For these operations see A.J. Butler, *The Arab Conquest of Egypt*, pp. 1–41.
42. M. McCormick, *Eternal Victory*, p. 70.
43. *Nicephorus, Patriarch of Constantinople: A Short History*, transl. and ed. C. Mango, hereafter Nicephorus, *A Short History*, p. 2.
44. Ibid., p. 3.
45. C. Mango and R. Scott, *The Chronicle of Theophanes Confessor*, hereafter Theophanes, p. 430 and Nicephorus, *A Short History*, p. 11.
46. Nicephorus, *A Short History*, p. 11
47. See ibid., p. 179. I have discussed this at length with J. Howard-Johnson and Mary Whitby who favour a later date.
48. F.J. Conybeare, 'Atiochus Strategos's Account of the Sack of Jerusalem in AD 614'.
49. Ibid.
50. Stratos, *Byzantium in the Seventh Century*, I, p. 109.
51. Ibid., p. 116
52. Nicephorus, *A Short History*, p. 8
53. J. Howard-Johnston, 'The Official History of Heraclius's Persian Campaigns', p. 85.
54. Theophanes, p. 436.
55. Ibid, p. 439.
56. J. Haldon, *Warfare, State and Society in the Byzantine World*, p. 21.
57. Theophanes, p. 435.
58. Nicephorus, *A Short History*, p. 10.
59. A. Cameron, 'The Virgin's Robe: An Episode in the History of Early Seventh-Century Constantinople'.
60. J. Howard-Johnston ed., *The Armenian History attributed to Sebeos*, hereafter Sebeos, 38, 123.
61. Ibid., 38, 124.
62. M. Whitby, 'The Persian King at War', pp. 231–43.
63. Ibid., p. 230.
64. Ibid., p. 238.
65. Theophanes, p. 445.
66. G. Regan, *Lionhearts*, p. 210.
67. Whitby, 'Persian King at War', p. 253.
68. Cf Procopius's description of the Gothic king Totila before the battle of Taginae, *History of the Wars*, I, transl. H.B. Dewing, Cambridge, 1914.
69. A. Cameron, 'Images of Authority: Elites and Icons in Late Sixth-Century Byzantium', p. 20.
70. Ibid., p. 20.
71. Ibid., p. 34.
72. Ibid., pp. 5–6.
73. J. Howard-Johnson, 'Heraclius's Persian Campaigns and the Revival of the East Roman Empire, 622–630', p. 41.
74. Ibid., p. 24.
75. Theophanes, p. 449.
76. Ibid., p. 449.
77. Ibid., p. 449.
78. Ibid., p. 450.
79. Ibid., pp. 450–1.
80. Ibid., p. 451.

81. *Chronicon Paschale*, M. Whitby and M. Whitby eds, pp. 182–3.
82. See Stratos, *Byzantium in the Seventh Century*, I, pp. 240–5.
83. Ibid., I, p. 245.
84. Cameron, 'Images of Authority', p. 17.
85. The Second Nocturn of Matins of the Feast of the Exaltation of the Holy Cross contains the following miracle: 'For Heraclius, clad as he was in gold and jewels, was forced to halt at the gate which led to Mount Calvary. The more he tried to go on, the more he seemed to be held back. Heraclius and those with him were dumbfounded at this; but Zacharias, bishop of Jerusalem, said: "Consider, O emperor, how poorly you are imitating the poverty and humility of Jesus Christ when you carry his cross in your triumphal robes." Then Heraclius, taking off his ceremonial robes and his shoes and putting on a poor man's garment, easily went the rest of the way and placed the Cross on the same spot on Calvary from which it had been taken by the Persians. And so the Feast of the Exaltation of the Holy Cross took on still more lustre because of the memory of this event when Heraclius replaced the Cross where it had first been set up by the Saviour.'
    Two points need clarification here. First, Zacharias died in captivity in Persia and never lived to see this great day, and second, by this stage only a fragment of the True Cross remained and this was kept in an ornamental box. It was the box containing the relic that Heraclius returned to Jerusalem.
86. Soudia, *Lexicon*, I, 499, quoted in Stratos, *Byzantium in the Seventh Century*, vol. I, p. 259.
87. W. Muir, *The Life of Mohammed*

from Original Sources, p. 130.
88. B. Walker, *Foundations of Islam*, pp. 324–7.
89. Ibid., p. 342
90. Ibid., pp. 342-3.
91. *Chronicon Paschale*, p. 180.
92. Walker, *Foundations of Islam*, p. 132.
93. M. Rodinson, *Mohammed*, p. 277.
94. Walker, *Foundations of Islam*, p. 136.
95. Ibid., p. 137.
96. D. Nicolle, *The Battle of Yarmuk 636*, p. 19.
97. See ibid for the most up-to-date account of the battle.
98. Ibid., p. 85.
99. Ibid., p. 85.
100. Nicephorus, *A Short History*, p. 25
101 Ibid., p.25
102. P. Hitti, *A History of the Arabs*, p. 161.
103. Butler, *Arab Conquest of Egypt*, p. 202.
104. Ibid., p. 182.
105. Ibid., pp. 224–5.
106. Ibid., p. 228, n. 1.
107. Ibid., p. 258.
108. Ibid., p. 270.
109. Ibid., p. 270.
110. Ibid., pp. 291–2.
111. Ibid., pp. 291–2.
112. L. Garland, *Byzantine Empresses*, p. 70.
113. Butler, *Arab Conquest of Egypt*, pp. 368–9.
114. See J. Haldon and M. Byrne, 'A Possible Solution to the Problem of Greek Fire', in D. Kagay andL. Andrew Villalon, eds, *The Circle of War in the Middle Ages*, pp. 91–100.
115. Joinville, *Life of St Louis*, transl. Margaret Shaw, London, Penguin, 1963, p. 75.
116. Quoted in A.F.C. Webster, 'Varieties of Christian Military Saints: from Martyrs under Caesar to Warrior Princes', p. 5.

117. Ibid., p. 6.
118. Haldon, *Warfare, State and Society in the Byzantine World*, p. 20.
119. Sebeos, p. xxv.
120. Haldon, *Warfare, State and Society in the Byzantine World*, p. 18.
121. Quoted in E. McGeer, *Sowing the Dragon's Teeth*, p. 214.
122. *Praecepta Militaria of Nicephorus Phocas*, IV, 110–20, quoted in McGeer, *Sowing the Dragon's Teeth*.
123. Ibid., VI, 33–45.
124. Leo the Deacon, 96.16–97.22, quoted in McGeer, *Sowing the Dragon's Teeth*, pp. 219–21.
125. Quote in P. Walker, 'The 'Crusade' of John Tzimisces in the Light of New Arab Evidence', p. 318.
126. 'The Chronicle of Matthew of Edessa', quoted in Walker, 'The 'Crusade' of John Tzimisces'.
127. Walker, 'The 'Crusade' of John Tzimisces'.
128. Quoted in M. Whittow, *Making of Orthodox Byzantium, 600–1025*, p. 375.
129. Quoted in J.J. Norwich, *Byzantium: The Apogee*, p. 251.
130. Quoted in F.E. Peters, *Jerusalem*, p. 260.
131. Quoted in Norwich, *Byzantium: The Apogee*, p. 338.
132. J. Brundage, *Medieval Canon Law and the Crusader*, p. 29.
133. Quoted in M. Foss, *People of the First Crusade*, London, O'Mara, 1997, p. 38.
134. Quoted in ibid., pp. 42–3.
135. Quoted in ibid., p. 39.
136. Anna Comnena, *The Alexiad*, ed. B. Radice, Book 10, V.
137. S. Runciman, *A History of the Crusades*, I, p. 153.
138. Ibid., p. 154.
139. Fulcher of Chartres, *A History of the Expedition to Jerusalem, 1095–1127*, transl. F.R. Ryan, ed. H.S. Fink (New York, 1973), I, p. 33.

Bibliography

Armstrong, K., *Jerusalem*, New York, Random House, 1996

Arnott Hamilton, J., *Byzantine Architecture and Decoration*, London, Batsford, 1956

Asali, K.J., ed., *Jerusalem in History*, London, Scorpion, 1989

Ball, W., *Rome In the East*, London, Routledge, 2000

Barnes, T.D., *Constantine and Eusebius*, London, Harvard University Press, 1981

Baynes, N.H., 'The Military Operations of the Emperor Heraclius', *United Services Magazine* 47, 1913, pp. 401–12, 532–41, 665–79

Biddle, M., *The Tomb of Christ*, Stroud, Sutton, 1999

Bivar, A.D.H., 'Cavalry Equipment and Tactics in the Euphrates Frontier', *Dumbarton Oaks Papers* 26, 1972, pp. 271–91

Bowman, A.K., *Egypt After the Pharaohs, 332BC–AD642*, London, British Museum Press, 1986

Brock, S., 'Christians in the Sasanian Empire: A Case of Divided Loyalties', *Studies in Church History* 18, 1982, pp. 1–19

Brundage, J.A., *Medieval Canon Law and the Crusader*, Madison, University of Wisconsin, 1969

Bury, J.B., *A History of the Later Roman Empire*, London, Macmillan, 1889

Butler, A. *The Arab Conquest of Egypt*, Oxford, Oxford University Press, 1978

Cameron, Alan, *Circus Factions: Blues and Greens in Rome and Byzantium*, Oxford, Oxford University Press, 1976

Cameron, Averil, 'The Virgin's Robe: An Episode in the History of Early Seventh-Century Constantinople' in *Continuity and Change in Sixth-Century Byzantium*, London, Variorum, 1981

——, (1979) 'Images of Authority: Elites and Icons in Late Sixth-Century Byzantium', *Past and Present* 84, pp. 3–35

Christiansen, A., *L'Iran sous les Sassanides*, Copenhagen, 1944, repr. Osnabruck, O. Zeller, 1971

Chronicon Paschale, M. Whitby and M. Whitby eds, Liverpool, Liverpool University Press, 1989

Comnena, Anna, *The Alexiad*, transl. E.R.A. Sewter, B. Radice ed., London, Penguin, 1969

Contamine, P., *War in the Middle Ages*, transl. M.Jones, London, Blackwell, 1984

Conybeare F.J., 'Atiochus Strategos's Account of the Sack of Jerusalem in AD 614', *English Historical Review* 25, 1910, pp. 502–5

Cornuelle, C. *An Overview of the Sasanian Persian Military*, London, Slingshot, 1997

Dalrymple W., *From the Holy Mountain*, London, HarperCollins, 1997

Donner F.M., *The Early Islamic Conquests*, New Jersey, Princeton University Press, 1981

Egeria, 'Pilgrimage' in J. Wilkinson, *Egeria's Travels to the Holy Land*, Warminster, Aris and Phillips, 1981

Erbstosser, M., *The Crusades*, London, David & Charles, 1978

Eusebius, *History of the Church*, G. Williamson ed., London, Penguin, 1989

——, *Life of Constantine*, transl. A.C. McGiffert, vol. 2, Oxford, 1890–1900

Flusin, B., *Saint Anastase le Perse et l'Histoire de la Palestine au debut du Septieme Siecle*, vols 1 and 2, Paris, Editions C.R.N.S. 1992

Fregosi, P., *Jihad in the West*, New York, Prometheus, 1998

Frye, R.N., *The Heritage of Persia*, London, Weidenfeld, 1962

Gabrieli, F., *Arab Historians of the Crusades*, London, Routledge, 1969

Garland, L., *Byzantine Empresses*, London, Routledge, 1999

Gilles, P., *The Antiquities of Constantinople*, New York, Italica Press, 1988

Glubb, J.B., *The Course of Empire*,London, Hodder & Stoughton, 1965

——, *The Great Arab Conquests*, London, Hodder & Stoughton, 1963

Grant, M., *History of Rome*, London, Weidenfeld & Nicolson, 1978

Haas, C., *Alexandria in Late Antiquity: Topography and Social Conflict*, Baltimore, John Hopkins University Press, 1997

Haldon, J.F., *Byzantium in the Seventh Century*, Cambridge, Cambridge University Press, 1990

——, *Warfare, State and Society in the Byzantine World*, London, University College London, 1999

Heath, I., *Byzantine Armies, 886–1118*, London, Osprey, 1979

——, *Armies of the Dark Ages 600–1066*, London, Wargames Research Group, 1979

——, *Byzantine Armies, 1118–1462*, London, Osprey, 1995

Herrin, J., *The Formation of Christianity*, New Jersey, Princeton University Press, 1987

Herrmann G., *The Iranian Revival*, London, Phaidon, 1977

Hitti, P., *A History of the Arabs*, London, Macmillan, 1955

Howard-Johnston, J., ed., 'The Official History of Heraclius's Persian Campaigns' in E. Dabrowa ed., *The Roman and Byzantine Army in the East*, Krakow, University of Krakow, 1994, pp.57-87

——, 'The Siege of Constantinople in 626' in C. Mango and G. Dagron, *Constantinople and its Hinterland*, London, Variorum, 1995

——, 'The Two Great Powers in Late Antiquity: a Comparison' in A. Cameron ed., *The Byzantine and Early Islamic Near East*, New Jersey, Princeton University Press, 1994, pp.157–226

——, 'Heraclius' Persian Campaigns and the Revival of the East Roman Empire, 622–630', in *War in History* 6, 1999

——, *The Armenian History attributed to Sebeos*, Liverpool, Liverpool University Press, 1999

Isaac, B., 'The Army in the Late Roman East: the Persian Wars and the Defence of the Byzantine Provinces' in A. Cameron ed., *The Byzantine and Early Islamic Near East*, New Jersey, Princeton University Press,1995, pp. 125-56

Jenkins, R., *Byzantium: the Imperial Centuries*, London, Weidenfeld, 1966

Jones, A.H.M., *Constantine and the Conversion of Europe*, London, Hodder & Stoughton, 1948

——, *The Later Roman Empire*, Oxford, Blackwell, 1964

Kaegi, W., *Byzantine Military Unrest 471–843*, Amsterdam, Hakkert, 1981

——, *Byzantium and the Early Islamic Conquests*, Cambridge, Cambridge University Press, 1992

——, 'The Battle of Nineveh', *Abstracts of the 1993 Conference of the Byzantine Society*, New Jersey, Princeton University Press, 1993

Kagay, D. and Andrew Villalon, L., eds, *The Circle of War in the Middle Ages*, London, Boydell, 1999

Keys, D., *Catastrophe*, London, Century, 1999

Kolbaba, T., 'Fighting for Christianity: Holy War in the Byzantine Empire', *Byzantion 68*, 1998, pp. 194–221

Krautheimer, R., *Early Christian and Byzantine Architecture*, London, Penguin, 1965

——, 'The Constantinian Basilica', *Dumbarton Oak Papers 21*, 1967, pp. 117–40

Lactantius, *On the Death of the Persecutors*, transl. W. Fletcher, Edinburgh, Anti-Nicene Library, 1871

Landau-Tasseron, E., 'Features of the Pre-Conquest Muslim Armies in the Time of Muhammad' in A. Cameron ed., *The Byzantine and Early Islamic Near East*, New Jersey, Princeton University Press, 1995, pp. 229–336

Lane Fox, R., *Pagans and Christians*, London, Viking, 1986

Lewis, N., and Reinhold, M., eds., *Roman Civilization*, New York, Columbia, 1990

Lissner, I., *Power and Folly*, London, Jonathan Cape, 1958

Maalouf, A., *The Crusades Through Arab Eyes*, London, Al-Saqi, 1984

Mango, C., and Scott, R., *The Chronicle of Theophanes Confessor*, Oxford, Oxford University Press, 1997

Maurice, *Strategikon*, G.T. Dennis ed., Philadelphia, University of Pennsylvania press, 1984

McCormick, M., *Eternal Victory*, Cambridge, Cambridge University Press, 1986

McGeer, E., *Sowing the Dragon's Teeth*, Dumbarton Oaks, 1995

Muir, W., *The Life of Mohammed from Original Sources*, revised edn, Edinburgh, John Grant, 1912

Nikephoros, Patriarch of Constantinople: A Short History, trans. and ed. C. Mango, Dumbarton Oaks, 1990

Nicolle, D., *Armies of Islam 7th–11th Centuries*, London, Osprey, 1982

——, *The Age of Charlemagne*, London, Osprey, 1984

——, *The Normans*, London, Osprey, 1987

——, *El Cid and the Reconquista 1050-1492*, London, Osprey, 1988

——, *The Crusades*, London, Osprey, 1988

——, *Attila and the Nomad Hordes*, London, Osprey, 1990

——, *Rome's Enemies: The Desert Frontier*, London, Osprey, 1991

——, *Romano-Byzantine Armies, 4th–9th Centuries*, London, Osprey, 1992

——, *Armies of the Muslim Conquests*, London, Osprey, 1993

——, *The Battle of Yarmuk 636*, London, Osprey, 1994

——, *Sasanian Armies, Montvert*, London, 1996

——, *Armies of the Caliphate 862-1098*, London, Osprey, 1998

Norwich, J.J., *Byzantium: The Early Centuries*, London, Viking, 1988

——, *Byzantium: The Apogee*, London, Viking, 1991

——, *Byzantium: Decline and Fall*, London, Viking, 1995

O'Donnell, J., 'The Demise of Paganism', *Traditio 35*, 1979, pp. 45–88

Oikonomides, N., 'A Chronological Note on the first Persian Campaign of Heraclius (622)', *Byzantine and Modern Greek Studies I*, 1975, pp. 1–9

Opsopaus, J., 'The Art of Haruspicy, which is the Etruscan Discipline', *Harvest*, vol. II (1991), no. 4, pp. 224–4, no.s, pp. 11–14, no. 6, pp. 13–15, 2001

Ostrogorsky, G., *History of the Byzantine State*, London, Blackwell, 1980

Ousterhout, R., 'Rebuilding the Temple: Constantine Monomachus and the Holy Sepulchre', *Journal of the Society of Architectural Historians XLVIII*, 1989, pp. 66–78

——, 'The Temple, the Sepulchre and the Martyrion of the Saviour', *Gesta XXIX/1*, 1990, pp. 44–53

——, 'The Church of the Holy Sepulchre', *Biblical Archaeology Review 26*, no.6, 2000, pp. 21–35

Peters, F.E., *Jerusalem*, New Jersey, Princeton University Press, 1985

Phillips, J., *The First Crusade*, Manchester, Manchester University Press, 1997
Regan, G., *Lionhearts*, London, Constable, 1998
Rodinson, M., *Mohammed*, transl. Anne Carter, London, Penguin, 1976
Romer, J., *Testament*, London, Michael O'Mara, 1988
Runciman, S., *Byzantine Style and Civilization*, London, Penguin, 1975
——, *The Emperor Romanus Lecapenus*, Cambridge, Cambridge University Press, 1929
——, *A History of the Crusades*, Cambridge, Cambridge University Press, 1951
Saunders, J., *A History of Medieval Islam*, London, Routledge, 1990
Schafer, P., *Judeophobia: Attitudes towards the Jews in the Ancient World*, Cambridge, Mass, Harvard University Press, 1997
Severin, T., *Crusader*, London, Hutchinson, 1989
Spain Alexander, S., 'Heraclius: Byzantine Imperial Ideology and the David Plates', *Speculum* LIII, 1977, pp. 217–37
Stark, Freya, *The Valleys of the Assassins*, London, Murray, 1937
——, *Rome on the Euphrates*, London, Murray, 1966
Stratos, A.N., *Byzantium in the Seventh Century*, vol. 1, Amsterdam, 1968
Talbot Rice, T., *Everyday Life in Byzantium*, London, Batsford, 1967
Toynbee, A., *Constantine Porphyrogenitus and His World*, Oxford, Oxford University Press, 1973
Treadgold, W., *Byzantium and Its Army, 284–1081*, California, Stanford University Press, 1995
——, *A History of the Byzantine State and Society*, California, Stanford University Press, 1997
——, *Warfare, State and Society in the Byzantine World, 565–1204*, London, UCL, 1999
Vasiliev, A.A., *History of the Byzantine Empire*, Madison, Wisconsin University Press, 1980
Walker, B., *Foundations of Islam*, London, Peter Owen, 1998
Walker, P., 'The 'Crusade' of John Tzimisces in the Light of New Arabic Evidence', *Byzantion* 47, 1977, pp. 301–27
Webster, A.F.C., 'Varieties of Christian Military Saints: from Martyrs under Caesar to Warrior Princes', *St Vladimir's Theological Quarterly* 24, 1980, pp. 3–35
Whitby, M., *The Emperor Maurice and his Historian*, Oxford, Oxford University Press, 1988
——, 'Deus Nobiscum: Christianity, Warfare and Morale in Late Antiquity, in M. Austin, J. Harries and C. Smith eds, *Modus Operandi: Essays in Honour of Geoffrey Rickman*, London, 1998, pp. 191–208
——, 'The Persian King at War' in E. Dabrowa ed., *The Roman and Byzantine Army in the East*, Krakow, 1994, pp. 227–59
——, 'Recruitment in Roman Armies from Justinian to Heraclius', in A. Cameron ed., *The Byzantine and Early Islamic Near East* New Jersey, Princeton University Press, 1995, pp. 61–124
Whitby, Mary, 'A New Image for a New Age: George of Pisidia on the Emperor Heraclius' in E. Dabrowa ed.,*The Roman and Byzantine Army in the East*, Krakow, 1994
Whittow, M, *The Making of Orthodox Byzantium 600–1025*, London, Macmillan, 1996
Wilcox, P., *Rome's Enemies: Parthians and Sasanid Persians*, London, Osprey, 1986
Yar-Shater, E., *The History of al-Tabari*, New York, SUNY, 1999

Index